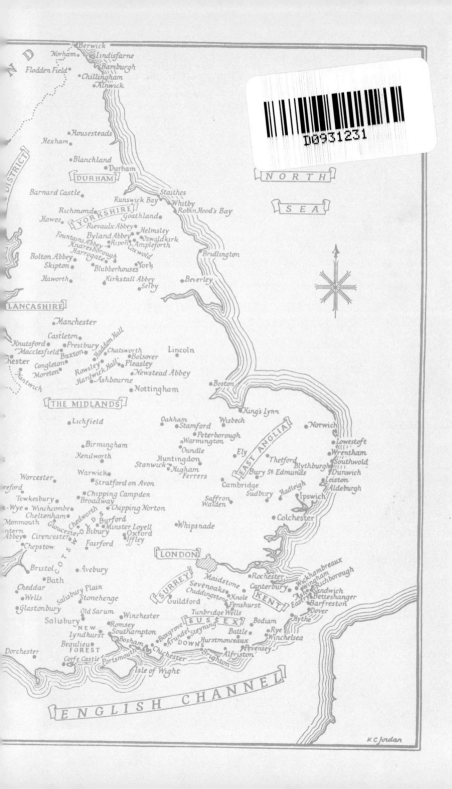

HERE'S ENGLAND
A Highly Informal Guide

Illustrations by Osbert Lancaster

HERE'S ENGLAND

A Highly Informal Guide

Ruth McKenney
&
Richard Bransten

THIRD EDITION

HARPER & ROW, PUBLISHERS
New York, Evanston, and London

3 7 5 6 1.

LIBRARY OF CONGRESS CATALOG CARD NUMBER: 75-123949

This book is dedicated, with respect and admiration, to the modern Marco Polo—the tolerant, curious, determined, durable, and ever-gallant American Tourist.

Contents

Illustrations

Preface

Here's England has enjoyed an odd and happy history. The original edition was published in 1950. People seemed to like it. It presented a new way of suggesting what to see, and why. But by 1955 readers were telling us that the delightful country inn recommended for Kent or the Cotswolds had turned into a gas station, if not worse.

Some of our correspondents of the period, carried away by an ingenious detective novel, thought we ought to know that King Richard III did not murder the little Princes in the Tower. It was mere Tudor propaganda, that canard. We stood our ground (with the *Cambridge Modern History of England*). Tudor propaganda, indeed! Bah! Humbug! The Tudors never heard of such a thing. They did not worry about their image, or bribe actor-scribblers to cast aspersions on Yorkists. The Tudors sincerely believed in their divine right to rule England. On the whole, Englishmen agreed with them. The Stuarts, now, could have used a Shakespeare.

But a country inn decaying into a gas station—that was serious. So, in 1955, *Here's England* was revised. This time, we left out restaurants, country inns, timetables, fashions, and everything else which seemed so immutable in 1955, but which, experience has taught us, could prove so mistaken, or quaint, by 1965.

The Revised Edition of *Here's England* was popular all through the sixties. As the decade drew to a close, however, correspondents reported that office buildings had destroyed the spacious view of St. Paul's from the ruins, or that some drowsy market town in Sussex was now imbedded in council houses and light manufacturing.

It seemed time for a third edition of *Here's England*. After some months of work, as I came to the last pages of this volume, I reflected that much has changed in England, over the past twenty years, but much more has not. Blanchland and Hadrian's Wall and the wild white cattle of Chillingham Castle—they are all still there, untouched by time.

Carbon monoxide poisoning wafts about London's streets, as it does in any city of the Western World. The ruins have been rebuilt, not to the glory of man, but to the satisfaction of the real-estate brokers.

On the other hand, many of Wren's city churches have been finely restored, a romantic story by itself. The Temple is charming, these days, the rubble buried under beautiful lawns. Hampton Court is lovelier than the first time I saw it. The Queen's ravens still strut about the lawn by the Tower. The interior of St. Paul's is even more magnificent than two decades ago. It has been "washed."

So it is all still there, waiting for you—England!

This Third Edition of *Here's England* was made possible by the spirited assistance of Professor and Mrs. Robert Lekachman, two friends who share the view that England is WONDERFUL.

Finally, my daughter, Eileen Bransten, who appears in the original edition, aged six, edited the manuscript of this Third Edition.

Preface to the First Edition

THIS is a book about England; a valentine, in fact, for the most beautiful, wonderful, exciting country in Europe. I admit the valentine, in advance. *Here's England* is no mealy-mouthed, judicious guidebook; my husband and I are not in the least neutral. We love England; but love has not totally dewed over our approach. Richard and I are American tourists: we belong to the great Solidarity of the Green Passport, long may it wave. England can be tremendous, terrific, ravishing, delightful—but you have to know how.

That is the theory and (we hope) the practice of *Here's England*. There is a mistaken notion abroad in American Express Company circles that just because we speak the language (or some approximation of same) and are brought up on Dickens, Keats, and Shakespeare, England is therefore easy. On the contrary, England is complicated, much more obscure and difficult than Brazil or Abyssinia. You do not have to know about the Wars of the Roses for Abyssinia, but unless you can get a grip on Margaret of Anjou and what happened to Henry VI (nothing good), England will slide out from under you. Alas, a standard sight in the English summertime is the harried American tourist, dismally trotting about the Tower of London or old St. Bartholomew's, afraid to ask what is *Per-*

pendicular, when was the Dissolution, and what happened for the eight hundred odd years after 1066?

Maybe these seem like minor points, back home in New York City, Mishawaka, Indiana, or Los Angeles, California, but two days after your plane lands you will be reeling across the centuries at Hampton Court and Westminster Abbey. The English have more history than practically anybody else, none of it trivial. And why should Americans be expected to know that Richard II double-crossed Wat Tyler at Smithfield, and who was Robert Curthose? On the other hand, England is no fun without Edward II (picked off by his wife and a friend of hers), or what happened to St. Cuthbert after he died (he traveled). How can you make sense out of a *Decorated* window or a *Norman* barrel vault if you do not have a few under-pinnings on Gothic? No wonder American tourists begin to look dazed after their fourteenth English cathedral, and not a word from anybody on what is a rood screen, and why.

We feel sad and indignant about the American face to face with a rood screen or a flying buttress. After all, we Americans have spent a lot of money, come a long way to see Westminster Abbey and the Tower of London. The American is eager to see everything and to have a wonderful time; it is hardly his fault that he knows all about Abraham Lincoln, and who shot Mc-Kinley, and the Empire State Building, instead of having the latest news on Richard, Duke of York, the sad fate of James II, and Durham Cathedral. Englishmen do not know a thing about Daniel Boone or the Missouri Compromise either.

However, you cannot have a good time in England or make head or tail of what you are seeing and doing without a few pointers here and there on Henry II and the like. So we have tried to explain rood screens, on a strictly amateur basis. This is not a history book (which fact I fear will be obvious). We have jotted down a few points we found handy in our own wander-ings about England. Besides the Tourist's-Eye View of history in the front part of the book, we have put two history charts in the back; these are for a quick look when the guide has his back turned. The first is the Kings of England. British schoolboys learn them backward as well as forward, and every time you turn around at Hampton Court or Chatsworth somebody will remark, in a chatty way, "In the last year of the reign of James the First . . ." At this point you flip over the book to the chart, after which you reply, smooth as butter, "Ah, yes, 1624–25, that would be?"

But it is the second chart, we think, that will be the most useful. This one lists the Kings, tells what they did, if anything, matches up *Decorated* arches with Edward I, Abraham Lincoln with Queen Victoria.

On the *Decorated* arch situation, we have tried to make architecture an open book, more or less. Again, we operated on the basis that the standard American tourist when he arrives in England has (like me) a rough idea about Gothic, but is not too firm on the passwords that guidebooks use for *Perpendicular* and Sir Christopher Wren. As a matter of fact, we think architecture is fascinating, and hope you will too. There is certainly a lot of it in England. We have two charts on architecture in Part III—one is a glossary, and the other a brief outline of when was *Early English* and what is *Regency.*

This covers the intellectual approach. But the tourist does not feed on history alone. We think cathedrals are exciting, but you can digest just so many flying buttresses, and then the mind caves in.

How about having a good time in England? We cover that topic too, especially cricket. Cricket is *wonderful.* It is not true that no American can understand it. We have explained the whole thing here; well, maybe not the details, but enough to rush around to Lord's in London, or turn up cheering at the village cricket green.

We loved England; and this book is our "favour" for that green and pleasant land, that other Eden, that demi-Paradise.

We are deeply grateful for the expert assistance we had in preparing the manuscript of *Here's England* for publication. On matters as various as Henry VIII's love letters, L.B.W., toad-in-the-hole, and rood screens, we sought the advice of learned friends. Of course errors of fact, opinion, and omission in *Here's England* are entirely our own responsibility. With this understood, we are eager to acknowledge our debt for wise and painstaking counsel, to Sir Geoffrey and Lady Vickers, Mrs. Gerstley, Mr. William Blake, Miss Naomi Burton, Mr. Graham Watson, Mr. Rupert Hart-Davis, Mr. George W. Jones, Jr., Mr. and Mrs. Peter Cochrane, and Mr. Gerstle Mack.

RUTH MCKENNEY AND RICHARD BRANSTEN

PART I: TWO WEEKS IN LONDON

This Is London

For an American, the quality of London is subtle and, in the beginning, difficult. This is a high-toned way of saying that the first time I saw London I was shocked by anticlimax. But now, like most converts, I am didactic. I think London is the most beautiful and the most fascinating city in the world. Bar none.

The day we arrived at Victoria Station, my husband was aflame to show his wife the city he had remembered fondly across twenty-one years. As we chugged along in our matronly, high-slung taxi, he announced, in a voice charged with emotion, "Look, darling! London! The greatest city in the world!"

"Where?" I cried, hanging out the taxi window.

"Where! What-do-you-mean-where?"

I should have caught a coldness in my husband's tones, but I was too excited for domestic nuance. I thought we had arrived at some dingy suburban station, and were even now driving through the flat, unappetizing fringes of the English metropolis. "How far is it? To the main part, I mean?"

"This," Richard replied between his teeth, "is Piccadilly Circus."

I gaped. Piccadilly Circus has all the charm of Columbus Circle, New York City, and not half the pomp of Public Square in Cleveland, Ohio. There is a small statue of Eros and a large but inferior beer sign.

"Oxford Street," Richard said presently.

"Oh?"

Richard became exasperated. "What do you want, the Empire State Building? Or the Arc de Triomphe? Listen, this is the most sophisticated, civilized city in history; don't be so damned provincial."

Provincial is not a word which, in my opinion, can be bandied about lightly. We arrived at our hotel, after my first taxicab tour of the capital of the British Commonwealth, in an icy mood.

But later on we started out for a stroll, came to Westminster Bridge, walked halfway across the Thames, and turned back. It was a warm summer night. In this northern city, twilight lingers late into the August evenings. On our left, we could see, rising from the darkened waters of the river, the great mass of the Houses of Parliament, magnificent against the pearly sky. Before us was the Clock Tower—Big Ben; and in the background were the shadowed towers of Westminster Abbey.

The great clock struck ten.

Richard and I heard this clock chiming long ago, on another August night. The clock struck, across three thousand miles. Then a voice: "This is London. The Nazi bombers came over in wave after wave tonight. As I speak to you, the whole sky is bright with fire. But the people of London, steadfast in this hour of their peril, defend their city with their lives. . . ."

Nothing in London evokes more sharply for the American the splendor of this great city's history than the scene from Westminster Bridge on a twilight in August.

Triumphant and lovely, London awaits the traveler on the banks of the River Thames; here, in its beauty and pride, is the ancient city of the British people; this, for Americans, was the first home of our language, our laws, our liberty, our culture; and from this Clock Tower rang the chimes that for all those years told people everywhere that the bastion of freedom, the capital of the Commonwealth, still stood against the enemy, un-bowed, unconquered, and unafraid.

All the same, London is difficult for Americans. Cities have a style. For a Roman, a city meant a forum, a bath, paved streets laid out in neat geometric pattern, and a collection of marble villas; without these essential items, a city was not a city at all, but some rude outpost fit only for barbarians. The Romans put up forums in far-off settlements where there was nobody to make speeches, except some second-rate governor and to an audience of backward provincials; they ran up fancy baths all over Britain, and had to invent central heating to make them practical in an outlandish climate. The Romans laid out paved streets across lonely moors, to the general astonishment of the local population, sunk in the tom-tom and glass-bead era. No doubt there were critics who remarked on the plentiful waste of marble in far-flung forums, and laughed their heads off at chilly British bathing pools. But the Romans felt nervous with-out a forum. In the same way, when an American town gradu-ates into a city, the event is marked by a skyscraper (usually the First National Bank and Trust Company of Kansas or Alabama, twenty-six stories and observation porch), Needless to argue, as Mr. Lewis Mumford and other prophets crying logic in the wilderness are constantly doing, that a skyscraper which makes economic sense in narrow Manhattan is laughable in the rude open spaces of Texas or Wyoming. Preposterous or not, the steel tower is the trademark, the style, of urban America. The natural, ordinary familiar look of a city—for an American— is vertical; and the higher the buildings, the bigger and more important the metropolis. The American feels nervous without elevators.

I do not mean to suggest that we Americans are narrow-minded about cities. We have another kind of urban style we know very well indeed. Washington, D.C., was laid out by a French architect. The manner of modern Paris—its grand sweep of broad avenues, its glorious framed vistas, its stately stone pomp—is a nobler example of a city style Americans learn in the fifth grade. Paris is obvious for an American; he can be awed by its grandeur on the way from the railroad station to the hotel.

On the other hand, you have London. It has no geometric

design, no sweep of noble avenues, no drama of great vistas. For an American, at least, it is not vertical. Even the postwar office buildings seem, to put it politely, understated. Understatement is not a city style that I was brought up to respect at first glance; until I fell in love with London, its understatement seemed a paradox. I had supposed that the very nature of a city, its essence, was stupendous, gaudy, overwhelming. There is nothing overwhelming about London. The city does not take you by the throat and shake you with its ferocious size, noise, glory, and speed. At first, London seems limp. Americans have to learn understatement the hard way—walking and walking, up and down the quiet streets, peering earnestly at the lovely Georgian squares.

Everything about London is difficult, in the beginning. It appears to have no logic, no solid center, no starting point. In Paris, you soon learn to know where you are in relation to the Champs Elysées, the Louvre, the Boul' Mich'. The middle of Chicago is, obviously, the Loop. The Grand' Place is the heart of Brussels; and in Cleveland you start with Public Square, after which things are east or west, north or south.

But London! London is a series of medieval towns strung together along both sides of the Thames. The river, when you peer at it from bridges and embankments, seems reasonably straight. It isn't. The Thames makes two bends, dislocating geography for miles. Westminster Abbey and the Royal Hospital, Chelsea, are both on the left-hand bank of the Thames; but a straight line drawn from the Abbey would end you up in Clapham Common, after which you must hire native guides to get back to Trafalgar Square. The glorious dome of St. Paul's is visible from great distances; but it is hardly what I would call a landmark. From Victoria Embankment, the dome appears to be nobly shining across the Thames; a few blocks farther along, it has shifted and now glitters straight ahead, definitely on the left-hand river bank. This is dubious behavior for a landmark. I say nothing of the fact that London streets change names as they go along, so that what is The Strand (definite article) suddenly turns into Fleet Street, to the consternation of the excitable bus traveler, who starts ringing bells and throwing himself off platforms under the delusion that he has somehow started going in the wrong direction.

Londoners, who acquire the geography of their city as a sixth sense, the way Americans learn baseball batting averages, are fond of identifying Piccadilly Circus as the "heart" of the metropolis. I think this is an unprofitable concept for the visitor, who discovers that the Bank of England is a long, long way from Eros. Indeed, I lived in London for months before I was sure how to get from Trafalgar Square to Leicester Square. If you look at the map, this project seems laughably easy—a quick jog down two side streets. In real life, Leicester Square is slippery. I finally got it pinned down. After you get off the bus at Charing Cross, you turn back, and walk past the beautiful church of St. Martin-in-the-Fields. Some architects think the lantern spire is wrong, humpbacked, or awkward, but (for me, at least) it is lovely, especially on a foggy Sunday afternoon in winter. Besides, St. Martin's is queer, for an American; it is the handsome stone model for half the little white wooden churches in New England. I remember an old church in Litchfield, Connecticut—set on the brow of a dark-green hill, surrounded by silence; a small white wooden church, with a clapboard spire, as exact a copy as the settlers could make with their saws and home-forged nails. I expect it is sentimental, but the first time I saw St. Martin's in Trafalgar Square, my heart ached for the men who built the white wooden church in Litchfield so long ago. For I never realized before how homesick they must have been; how, all alone in the forbidding forests, they must have yearned after the dear places they would never see again. The church in Litchfield is wholly different from St. Martin's—it is innocent, simple, rude; St. Martin's is exquisitely sophisticated. But when you see the mannered elegance of the spire you will remember the white wooden steeple in Litchfield, Connecticut.

Trafalgar Square, I remarked. Charing Cross is next to Trafalgar Square—an important point. St. Martin-in-the-Fields is across the street from the National Gallery. The National Gallery has one of the greatest collections of paintings under any roof in the world; there are so many splendid art collections in London that the natives are blasé on the subject. "Oh, yes, the National Gallery," they say, "fine collection." You wander in some Sunday afternoon and discover Michelangelos and Leonardos and Van Dycks and Titians to make the mind reel. However, let us not get bemused. We are now progressing from

Charing Cross (that is, Trafalgar Square, you see) to Leicester Square.

We have crossed the street to the National Gallery; we turn our back on the fountains and, with Nelson in the rear, march smartly forward, for a short block. Now comes a tricky bit. One must be on the alert or everything will go stupendously wrong, and the next thing one will be in Covent Garden.

I suppose everybody works out his own private street guide to London. For many years, I groped my way from Charing Cross to Leicester Square by the sackmen, who operated behind the National Gallery and to the left of Sir Henry Irving's statue. The first sackman wriggled into a long, tight, very dirty canvas sack—what else? His manager secured the sack at the ankles with a thick rope, and at the neck with a heavy steel chain, while bawling at passersby, "Strangle 'im! Come on, strangle 'im!" Sightless, helpless, hideous, the sack hopped around, providing the stuff of which nightmares are made.

The sackmen are gone, leaving us stranded there behind the National Gallery. But bear to the left. Go down a little side street. If you see an immense Auto Association sign, that's Leicester Square. Simple.

All this may suggest the quality of London geography, which is dreamy and improbable, like a Dali painting. There are other and more important mysteries about England's capital. Here is an item: Greater London has a population of more than eight million; another four million inhabit the outskirts. There seems to be considerable controversy as to whether London is bigger than New York or vice versa. If you count in Jersey City, Newark, N.J., and Yonkers, New York City wins the palm, but then surely that is going a little far? People who live in Newark do not regard with any enthusiasm the idea that they are citizens of Greater New York. If you leave out Newark, et cetera, and count the Home Counties as part of London, the English city is out in front by a few odd million. Yet to put the Home Counties in the London total is like Los Angeles counting everything down to the Mexican border. I am afraid there is no clearcut answer to this interesting contest. To sum up, Greater London is either bigger than New York City or almost as big.

This is interesting news for an American. Americans (including me) are fascinated by the size of things. Europeans re-gard our national passion for the tallest building, the longest bridge, the deepest coal mine as the mark of a naïve culture. Perhaps—but it is an American attitude so profound as to be unconscious. I can no more prevent myself from noticing rela-tive sizes than I can suppress annoyance at machinery that does not work, or nostalgia for the taste of sweet corn fresh from a farmer's field. It is part of my national outlook, sunk deep in my bones, to regard with interest the statement: "The popula-tion of metropolitan London is twelve million, which represents approximately one-quarter of the population of the British Isles."

Twelve million, I thought, that day I first came into Victoria. Twelve million! Well!

I arrived in London awed in advance by its statistical gran-deur—to discover that it does not show. English writers compose breathless essays about London's "awful roar" and "teeming bustle" and "madding crowds." But "awful roars" and the like are relative matters. Maybe London does roar for a poet fresh from the Kentish countryside, but for an American, London makes a hum, or buzz. Of course the traffic jams are monumental, and the street-level air pollution must be taking a dreadful toll, but it is all managed in a decent, patient sort of way.

It is the manner of London life which puzzles visitors. Urban Americans are fierce, savage, swift, and embattled. New Yorkers yell in public, taxicabs honk, radios blare, people run wildly for buses, thousands throw themselves at subway doors in one passionate, intense swoop for a seat uptown to the Bronx. The Londoner is quiet, polite, orderly, and slow; as a matter of fact, the Englishman is an experienced urban type. He has learned, across the centuries, how to manage life in the city with a minimum of nervous strain.

English poets have for so long celebrated their love of the British countryside that we Americans, raised on English litera-ture, are apt to think of the Briton as rural. The opposite is true. This island is nearly the most crowded space on earth. One out of four in the British Isles inhabits the London area; but one out of two lives in a big city: London, but also Birmingham, Man-chester, Glasgow, and so on. Even the remaining half, the so-called "countrymen," do not live in the country, not as we Americans think of it. There is no such thing as a "great open space" in England—there are a few moors and the like, but no sooner do you settle down on a patch of heather, alone with yourself and nature, than six birdwatchers appear, or a girls' school, gamboling joyously uphill, arrives for the view. The English farmer does not raise his pigs fourteen miles from the nearest neighbor; he lives in a village, goes to the pub every night for a glass of beer, while his wife belongs to the Women's Institute and campaigns for a sewer system. All Englishmen live perpetually in a crowd. The Briton is not rural; he is urban and sophisticated.

London is the civilized Englishman's answer to the intolerable pressures and strains of metropolitan life. Most American cities are, until you reach the suburbs, deserts of steel and stone, with noise singing like a cruel wind across the sunless, treeless, grassless caverns and towers. London is a city of parks and green squares; Hyde Park, Kensington Gardens, Regent's Park, Clapham Common, Kew Gardens, the Embankment Gardens, dozens more. The London parks are delightful, different from parks anywhere else. Here are no neat gravel walks, geometric flower beds, seesaws embedded in concrete, the whole decorated with loud-mouthed signs: KEEP OFF THE GRASS, THIS MEANS YOU! Hyde Park is a country meadow, Kensington Gardens a grove of trees. London parks are cunningly arranged to give the city dweller the illusion of space and sweet, green liberty. The London squares interrupt the stretches of stone and brick, refresh the eye, make quiet the city nights. Londoners do not sleep with earplugs and eyeguards.

This may be one of the reasons for the Londoner's civilized manners. But do not mistake him. Beneath his amiability, the Londoner is a swashbuckling, passionate romantic. Half his life is lived with fist brandished against the sky. He is forever dedicating himself to some incredible proposition, such as holding out against the Nazi war machine single-handed, beating the Spanish Armada, or pulling a war-wounded Britain up by its patched and mended bootstraps to its rightful place in the world. I have deliberately mixed up a few hundred years' history, not for rhetoric but because the Londoner lives, serenely, in an atmosphere compounded of the past and the future.

It is a shock to an American to discover how near and how familiar English history is to the Londoner. Americans have a present and a future; our past, however, is embalmed for ritual use on the Fourth of July and such occasions. But Henry VIII is knit into the Londoner's bones; Cromwell is part of his way of looking at life; the Duke (that would be Wellington, of course) and Queen Victoria make his hope for the future. Londoners take their little boys to the Temple, where they regard, gravely, the spot where the Wars of the Roses began—most unfortunate affair. London survived it. This leads the little boys to form the opinion that violence is not a suitable or safe way of solving political questions, and that London, having lasted out the Wars of the Roses, will no doubt triumph over other distressing historical items, such as atom bombs.

I remark on the Londoner's living connection with his city's history because Americans often feel that they are missing the "real" London; that, while they brood over guidebooks, life, elusive and swift, is passing them by. In London, nothing is more real than the Tower or St. Paul's or Westminster Abbey. These are the landmarks of the Londoner's true existence. If you want in a brief visit to touch London life, you must acquire a feeling for its vivid, ever-present past. No one understands a Londoner until he has stood, side by side with a horde of English schoolboys, peering in awed silence at Henry VIII, massive, secretive, splendid, astride his great plaster horse in the White Tower.

To the Tower

I THINK the Tower is the best place to begin, whether you have ten days or ten years to explore London. The Tower has the virtue of logic, for it is the oldest monument in this ancient city.

I confess I feel jealous about the Tower of London. Richard and I fell in love with the Tower one dark, gloomy afternoon in December, and since then we have many times returned, enchanted by this extraordinary stone memory of the past. The Tower is unique. There is no other place in Europe where so much of history survives unbroken, unruined, unchanged, hauntingly evocative of passing time. An immense drama was played on these stones, and not for three or five hundred years —but for nine hundred. In this place was enacted the pageant of a nation's history, bawdy, ferocious, bloody, pitiful, and glorious; nine hundred years of history behind a single gate. I am counting back to William the Conqueror; before that Harold and Edward the Confessor and Alfred the Great had some sort of a fort here, and before these worthy Saxons there were (a matter of a thousand years or so) the Romans. Inside the gate of the Tower stands one of the largest physical relics of Londinium; the traveler may stand and regard masonry erected A.D. 56–100.

I recite these bits of information to arouse respect. My blood boils when I note sightseeing buses depositing unfortunate customers with the cry, "One hour for the Tower of London." Nine hundred years at a dog trot! One day, one whole day, is a comfortable introduction to the Tower; and historians have profitably spent a lifetime in these thirteen acres. I do not suggest to the nervous American traveler, with Canterbury, Winchester, Paris, and Switzerland on his agenda, that he should pitch his tent in the Tower and abandon plane tickets and passport forever. But Richard and I are in favor of quality, not quantity, when it comes to sightseeing; there is a balance to be found, surely, between olde curiosity shoppes, minor poets, Swiss castles, and the Tower. I have often thought that it is unfortunate the Tower is so handily located on the London Underground; and included, too, in the Comprehensive Complete Tour of Modern and Historic London—leaves 2 P.M., returns 5 P.M. In Paris you have to take the whole afternoon for Versailles—willy-nilly, the buses leave after lunch and come back to late dinner. For the better part of four hours you are face to face with the glories of French history. The Tower, however, is fifteen minutes from Charing Cross; and it is so famous as to be thought banal, a careless landmark taken for granted, instead of to be examined in respectful and delighted leisure. After all, plenty of Americans take a two-day detour in Switzerland to see the Castle of Chillon—a first-class pile, and positively worth a detour. But Chillon is small beer compared to the Tower. Byron wrote about Chillon; Shakespeare wrote about the Tower. If prisoners intrigue you, the Tower housed hundreds, indeed thousands—people of distinction and tragedy. Sir Walter Raleigh, that queer, dark, morbid adventurer, for thirteen years paced these moonlit stone walls; Lady Jane Grey and Richard II and Henry VI; Elizabeth before she became Queen; Edward V and his brother Richard, Duke of York (their uncle, you will remember, was Richard III); and the old lady, the Countess of Salisbury, who, when her time came, would not hold still to have her head cut off, but ran around and around the block protesting. The Beefeaters at the Tower take a critical view of the Countess; they feel she behaved in a low, shocking, unhistorical sort of way. For my part, the Countess is my favorite Tower prisoner; I think it is inhuman to hold still while somebody cuts off your head, and across four hundred years, I feel strong, sad, indignant admiration for the Countess. She was no stoic, but full of blistering, blazing life, right up until the moment they murdered her. She made her death a murder, not a ceremony; there was no stately, sorrowful pageantry about her end—only shameful, bloody injustice. There is something heartening about the Countess of Salisbury. The other Tower victims go pacing slowly, decently off to the block; you see them in a tragic, mournful procession, each one almost acquiescing, at least bowing, before his intolerable fate. Young (very young) and old, they share this same attitude of rigidity; paralyzed by wicked force, they bow their heads meekly across the centuries. All of a sudden comes the Countess, screeching her indignation, galloping furiously around and around while the headsmen, and finally half the guard, chase after her. I like that. Good for her!

I am skipping. One ought to start at the beginning with the Tower—not with the Countess of Salisbury. Here it is, your first morning in London. You have sampled a kipper for breakfast (with what emotions I leave you to find out for yourself), and you are costumed in something comfortable, plus a stout pair

of walking shoes (as they say in the guidebooks). I hope you
will proceed from your hotel to Westminster Pier (probably by
taxi; it is far safer your first morning) and take the river boat
to Tower Bridge. I feel strongly that the Tower should be first
approached by water—you can take the Underground back to
your hotel. But the Tower is a fortress; for nine hundred years
it has guarded the approach to London, and you will never feel
its beauty, its ancient, chilling power, until you see the gray-
white stones rising from the tidal waters of the Thames. Not
only is the view better, but it is something of a tradition to take
a boat to the Tower. In the old days, kings, courtiers, soldiers,
and prisoners alike nearly always arrived by river. There was
a causeway, built (1278) by Edward I across the outer moat,
and this was used for processions from the City of London.
But there have been times, a good many of them, when it was
distinctly unsafe for the King of England to approach his chief
fortress by land—surrounded on all sides by loving, dutiful
subjects. Moreover, it was quite a journey from Westminster
or Whitehall, let alone Hampton Court, through the filthy,
muddy streets of old London; it was quicker, as well as less
eventful, to come to the Tower by water. Kings have sailed up
to the Tower in flower-laden barges (Charles II, George I, and
of course Henry VIII) with minions energetically squirting
perfume on the night breezes, court ladies languishing in low-
cut silken costumes, and boatloads of musicians front and rear
to serenade the conquering Majesty. Some kings (Richard II,
poor soul, and the wretched Henry VI) arrived at the Tower
in melancholy style, and no nonsense about perfume on the
breeze.

Kings mostly arrived at the Tower in broad daylight; but
there was also a good deal of night traffic downstream to the
Traitors' Gate; muffled oars, clank of swords, victim weighted
down in irons, staring through the clammy, river-misted darkness for a last look at London, city of his triumph, and now of
his death. Then the iron gate, creaking slowly up, torches
flickering in the damp, the flight of steps moss-grown, slippery.
The end. The prisoner went up those wet stone steps, and presently died. Princess Elizabeth, twenty-one years old, made that
journey to the Traitors' Gate; but she did not weep—on the

contrary, she flew into a royal Tudor rage; she sat down on the steps and refused to move. Queen Mary had ordered her half-sister's arrest. (This was sad, for the lonely young Mary had loved her little sister, and told her fairy stories under the peach trees at Hampton Court. But time had effaced the tenderness. Mary was a Queen; Elizabeth was no longer a precocious baby, enchanting and winsome; she was a danger.)

The Princess came to the Traitors' Gate on the Queen's orders—but the Princess sat on the stones and defied the soldiery to lay a finger on her royal person. This slender girl, with the hair blazing red-gold under the torches, was the daughter of Henry VIII, a Tudor. One thought twice, orders or no orders, before rudely prodding a Tudor. The Tudors were magic—they considered (with not much logic but compelling conviction) that God had chosen them to rule England for its own greater glory. A large number of English kings, before and after, cherished this theory, but few ever persuaded Englishmen to share it with them. English kings, across the centuries, have suffered spectacular careers, especially later kings who insisted overmuch on their Divine Right. The Tudors were different. They never doubted their ability to rule a disorderly, spirited people. Across hundreds of years, one can feel yet their formidable quality. No wonder people fainted when Henry VIII rode by; and no wonder the warders of the Tower turned pale when the Princess Elizabeth, screaming with Tudor wrath, sat on the steps of the Traitors' Gate and defied them.

The Constable of the Tower argued (respectfully) for more than two hours before, in return for what she considered concessions to her dignity, she consented to sweep proudly off to her prison. She was two months within the Tower; and for every hour of this time she was in mortal danger. She saw her friends tortured and executed. Day after day she was subtly, persistently, cunningly questioned by her jailors; at night they sent lady spies into her bedchamber, and in the darkness she could hear them breathing, alert, wakeful, hoping for some fatal cry to be wrung from her dreams. She never faltered—not Elizabeth. She faced them all, and triumphed. She was a Tudor; and it sustained her through an ordeal, remembered yet in the stones of this Tower where her mother was married in ecstatic triumph, and buried in headless ignominy; where she herself came, as a beautiful child, laughing in her father's arms, and finally as England's most splendid Queen.

The trip down from Westminster to the Tower takes about twenty minutes, and, as an introduction to London, cannot be rivaled. It is a fascinating journey, thick with history. London is a river city; its spires and domes and palaces rise gracefully from the tidal waters. Until the early nineteenth century, the river was London's chief avenue. Chaucer and Shakespeare alike boated up and down the Thames; Francis Bacon was always going bankrupt buying new and gaudier costumes for his private boatmen; Pepys bargained with watermen for a ride up or across the Thames; Nell Gwyn rowed here, full of splendor and intrigue. On the trip, a man with a megaphone points out the various sights; gas works (formerly the Globe Theatre), Post Office Tower, Monument (to the Great Fire), and dome of St. Paul's. Presently the boat makes a sweeping circle into the Pool of London (the ancient harbor, used alike by Sir Francis Drake and the Cunard Line) and back, past the White Tower, to the Pier.

The Tower is an all-day project. After buying your ticket at the entrance, inquire from the Yeoman Warder (Beefeater) at the moat when the next tour of the Tower begins. I expect Richard and I have the usual prejudice against conducted jaunts, especially of castles. But the Yeomen Warders of the Tower are different; they are well informed, witty, brisk, delightful. It is worthwhile waiting a few minutes to begin at the entrance gate with the next round trip of the various buildings; the standard tour will give you a chance to orientate yourself in the thirteen acres. The Beefeaters will lead you past the Traitors' Gate, the Roman Wall, to the Church of St. Peter ad Vincula—"the saddest spot on earth." They will show you the Queen's ravens, wonderful, morbid birds, which stroll about the Tower lawns with an air insolent and evil. Sir Walter Raleigh's prison, the fatal cell where the little Princes are thought to have been murdered, the window where Lady Jane Grey was made to stand and watch the headless body of her young husband being brought back from Tower Hill—these and many, many other silent stones, mute, senseless witnesses for history, are pointed out by the Tower guides.

When you have finished with the tour, I suppose you will want to see the Crown Jewels. Really, the Crown Jewels are second-rate. All the good ones were stolen or lost during Cromwell's time, and I do not understand why hordes of people line up on a hot summer's day and solemnly file past a glassed-in collection of gaudy red, white, and blue stones, none of them having any distinction beyond their cost. Still, there is a certain fascination in a decoration valued at half a million dollars and up. The Crown Jewels are one of those things you will find yourself doing as a tourist, which you will never conceivably do again. Like the Queen's Doll House, at Windsor. You keep wondering how you got trapped. However, the Crown Jewels take but a moment—you march in and out. On to the White Tower.

William the Conqueror put up the White Tower. He brought over from Normandy a monk of Bec called Gundulf, who started operations on the London fortress. Gundulf afterward became Bishop of Rochester, and built the charming cathedral which I hope you manage to see on your way to Canterbury. Gundulf was one of that tribe of swift, opinionated, excitable Norman builders who came storming into England after 1066 and in two generations transformed the rude Saxon landscape with towers and spires, churches and castles and bridges. It must have been a delirious time—castles going up in every neighborhood, ships arriving with stone from Caen, serfs mixing batches of cement instead of getting in the hay, monks arguing about the size of bell towers, masons (the architects of the day) wandering around with rules clenched in their teeth, carpenters' levels stuck in their back breeches pockets, and wearing that fierce, fixed, abstracted look of men trying to decide whether to run up a good-sized cathedral by the fork of the river or farther upstream, on top of that rise in the land. The Saxons were apparently flabbergasted by this Norman fever. Wooden halls had been good enough for Harold and Alfred the Great.

"Who's going to pay for this sort of thing?" elderly Saxons asked each other, in severe, irritated tones.

The answer was, naturally, they were; and if the Normans

could not collect in gold coin, or sheep, they were cheerfully ready to take it out in hard labor. The White Tower, for instance, is a good, solid piece of work, built to last. In fact, it has lasted nine hundred years, and there seems no reason why it should not last nine hundred more. Gundulf's city fortifications escaped the Nazi bombers in the last war, and it seems that nothing short of atoms is likely to dislodge the Norman monk's carefully arranged walls; fifteen feet thick in the foundations. It may be surmised that a large number of Saxons, grumblers to the last man, were employed for the heavier work, such as toting the stone. Within the walls, buried in chunks of cement, is Roman stone, left over from Londinium, a flourishing good-sized colonial town, complete with baths, bookshops, villas, temples, forums, perfume shops, restaurants, theatres, central heating, running water, and plumbing.

Londinium! In A.D. 450 people were sending their sons to school, haggling about villa rent with the real-estate agent, and going to the theatre to see the latest play, straight from Rome. Business was bad and there was a good deal of going up to Colchester in the chariot to complain to the governor, and incidentally pick up a new piece of table silver, or a handsome tunic for the next wedding in the family. That was A.D. 450; two hundred years later, savages in bearskins were poking about the ruins which littered the bank of the Thames. Now and then some bright-eyed lad, digging in the rubbish, would come across a silver vase, cunningly wrought, and peering at this lonely relic, the child in the bearskin would cry, in his pig-German dialect, "Oh, pretty!"

What happened to Roman civilization in Britain, and to Londinium in particular, never fails to give me a turn. Every time I go to the British Museum, I hang around the silver plates and cups dug up from various London backyards. The worst thing is not the ruins, but the silence. In A.D. 450 Londinium was very much part of the world; people wrote letters back and forth to Rome, historians got up commentaries on military campaigns. Then the Roman legions were withdrawn to southern France to hold the Italian peninsula against the invading barbarians. For a few years Londinium continued; the home guard repaired the city walls, merchants shipped tin and ordered linen from Rome. Then, silence. All the researches of scholars at Oxford and Cambridge have never disclosed what happened to the great civilized city of Londinium.

All we know is that once, on the bank of the Thames, there was a city. History stops. Two hundred years later the city was gone. How did it die? In flames? Or slowly, year by year, generation after generation? Historians imagine that this slow rot was the fate of Londinium; they think that the imposing city walls and the commanding site of Londinium, upstream on the great river, probably discouraged the first wave of savages. The elegant, learned Roman-Britons sat, at first smugly, behind their fortifications; but little by little the population died off. Merchants abandoned their counting houses—trade stopped—and planted corn in terraced gardens. Schools closed, for there were no teachers, and the half-starved children went foraging for game instead of learning their letters. The water mains choked up with refuse, and nobody could remember how to repair them. The central heating fell apart, and fires were kindled on the exquisite mosaic floors. Perhaps a few of the braver spirits slipped away from Londinium, fought their way through the hostile forests, and finally reached that legendary Arthur, who, far away in Glastonbury, made his last, sad stand for Christianity and British civilization before he fled, with a broken remnant of followers, to the mountains of Wales, and darkness. The barbarians came out of their forests, and attacked the crumbling city walls of Londinium. They made a good job of slaughtering these last citizens of Londinium; by A.D. 650, in the place where there was once a city, there was not even a tradition, not even a faint memory of learning. The savages did not live in the remnants of Roman splendor; they were afraid of the marble ruins; at night they heard the wind howling through the broken columns, or the rain beating down on a sagging roof—spirits, they said, the ghosts of the old enemy. The earliest Saxons pitched their skin tents upstream, and it was not for another two hundred years that Alfred the Great (886) began to patch up the walls of London, and build rude wooden houses over foundations of broken marble and chipped Roman brick. Alfred was a learned man, greatly gifted; in the intervals of policing his rude subjects, he translated Latin epics into Saxon, drew up a code of laws, and introduced some measures of enlightenment into the darkness of the land. It was uphill work, and it should be noted that Alfred was educated in Rome; he did not inherit even a vague tradition of British civilization—for the good reason that British civilization was dead. Of all the wealth, splendor, and learning that had once graced the great town of Londinium, nothing remained.

The White Tower, A.D. 1080. At long last things are looking up. Gundulf is bossing around his master masons, figuring out the clerestory for his chapel of St. John, arguing about buttresses, erecting a model Norman keep which is to stand for nine hundred years (and much more, we hope) as a solid souvenir of that gaudy, passionate medieval genius Duke William Bastard, the first bona-fide King of England. Of course, you had Alfred the Great, and Ethelred the Unready, and all those Edmunds and people like that; and Edward the Confessor and the Noble Harold. They were English kings. But the situation was haphazard before 1066. Even Alfred the Great had trouble with Kent; Northumberland was always declaring war on East Anglia. There was constant warring with the Danes; the Danes moved over (because Ethelred was Unready) and put in a king of their own, Canute, who was supposed to have defied the tides. In real life, Canute was an uncommonly good king, intelligent and a great believer in law and order. The Danes, however, were a restless, backward, unwashed lot. Canute was an exception, and when he died, the Danes lost interest in the English kingdom. They could loot and burn, but colonial administration bored them. With Canute dead, the English pulled themselves together, and sent over to Normandy, where they had a king, named Edward, in exile.

Edward the Confessor answered his country's call with either saintly or weak-minded reluctance. Opinions differ about Edward. He spoke French, loved Normandy, despised the Saxons for backward peasants, and was pitifully homesick for the land of his youth. In general, he was a poor king. He had better things on his mind—he was busy putting up Westminster Abbey, which he meant to be a bit of old Normandy in England. He lived long enough to see the Abbey completed (his version of it, that is), after which he died, and was the first person to be buried, before the plaster was dry, in his own church.

William the Conqueror has never been a popular character in English history. He won the battle, but Harold has won the literary palms, from Dickens's *Child's History of England,* to *The Golden Warrior.* I was brought up on Harold (via Dickens and Sir Walter Scott) and I never thought of the Noble Harold or the brave Rowena without shedding a mental tear—until the first time I took a look at the Chapel of St. John in the White Tower. It occurred to me that William I of England built churches, conquered kingdoms, loved his wife, made wily plots, transformed England, argued theology, and saw the world. He understood the logic of a strong central (and secular) government six hundred years before the same notion took root in his native France, and three hundred and fifty years before the Tudors made it stick in England. Harold was the melancholy child of bad luck, acute mismanagement, and inferior battle weapons. William had twice the nerve of the last of the Saxons (who was brave but lugubrious) and five times the brains. One ought to remember that he landed, like Cortez, on a hostile shore. One false move and William would have been cut down where he stood on the English beach. People feel sorry for Harold; they forget the victory William won against long odds and impossible weather. William not only won the battle; he kept it won—nobody has invaded England since 1066, and the present Queen, Elizabeth II, is a direct lineal descendant of that remarkable William, who finished off Harold and marched up to London, where he had himself crowned (in Edward's Abbey), settled down, and built the White Tower.

The White Tower today is not greatly different from the White Tower William saw (with intense personal satisfaction) in A.D. 1080. The outside windows are Christopher Wren, in an unfortunate moment, but inside the décor is strictly William I. You can spend a whole afternoon, bemused, inside the White Tower, but there are two items which Richard and I especially cherish. The first is Henry VIII, in his golden armor, on the third floor; the second is St. John's Chapel.

Henry is easy. Go upstairs and peer at the massive, barrel-chested Henry VIII in his steel armor. There is a queer, heavy feeling about Henry VIII, silent on his plaster horse. It is the current fashion among historians to remember Henry the poet, Henry the gallant, beautiful prince; Henry, musician and tender lover, art patron and architect; Henry, scholar, theologian, statesman; Henry, who broke the power of the European

Church and with his own two hands made the beginning of modern Britain—Henry, Renaissance genius, great King, and great Englishman.

Yet he was also a wicked, cruel, and sinister human being. He ruthlessly murdered two of his wives (maybe three), plus a large number of other innocent, helpless victims. People make excuses for Henry: it was a violent age; Anne Boleyn turned out to be a shrew; little Kate Howard broke Henry's heart; Renaissance theologians always burned thinkers who did not agree with them. True enough. But, for all the violence of the age, Henry's own ministers regarded him with terror, which they often had difficulty in concealing in the royal presence. Maybe Anne Boleyn's temper soured, and she was impolitic to nag a Tudor. But surely the punishment did not quite fit the crime? Kate may have wrung Henry's heart, but he cut off her head all the same, and she was only sixteen years old, a little girl, forlorn and frightened. The Inquisition did burn heretics in gross lots, but Henry was far from dull-witted, and it must have occurred to him that he himself had made a few shifts in standard theology? One cannot expect Henry to have been broad-minded— tolerance was not an attribute of the age or of Henry. Undoubtedly he sincerely held the view that kings had the right to fiddle about with theology, but not the common people. Even so, among Henry's theological victims burned alive was a fourteen-year-old boy.

Religious disputes were for Henry impersonal; he gave an order or two, and maybe he cannot be blamed if the judges acted with excessive enthusiasm. Anne Boleyn, however, was no stranger; once she was his "awne darling." And Kate was sixteen years old.

These points occurred to me when I saw Henry VIII in his gilded armor in the White Tower. There is an atmosphere about that plaster figure; you forget the love songs and the theology; you remember Queen Catherine Howard, crying for mercy, and Queen Anne Boleyn, and Shakespeare's Wolsey, dying, saying with all the bitterness of his soul, "Had I but served my God with half the zeal I served my King . . ."

The Chapel of St. John is the chief architectural glory of the Tower and one of the loveliest places in England. It is on the second floor of the White Tower, and one mounts by a winding stair; bevies of small boys, on their way to the armor museum, will try to carry you along in the stream of traffic past the little chapel. Stand your ground; the Chapel of St. John is one of the best examples of Norman architecture still in the world; it merits time, attention, and delight.

The Chapel brings us to an important and curious topic: Architecture.

Europeans live with architecture. Most Englishmen are born next door to a *Regency* terrace, or around the corner from a nice bit of *Perpendicular* in the local parish church; they go to Sunday school in the *Decorated* Lady Chapel and buy their first "sweets" in the shadow of a *broach spire*. At the age of ten, English boys are lined up by schoolteachers, bullied into silence (broken only by a giggle or two), and trotted through the nearest cathedral.

I never saw anything more Gothic than the Woolworth Building until I came to Europe; at which point I "did" (thoroughly) eleven large cathedrals in fourteen days. I remember dragging through St. Vincent's in Vienna, my feet on fire, my eyes bulging, and my whole soul protesting. "Baroque," people said to me, "Middle Gothic, fenestration, Renaissance, Romanesque, spatial concepts, Ravenna influence, Greek revival, triforium, Palladian . . ."

"Ah, yes," I used to say, flashing my persecutors a Uriah Heep smile. "Middle Gothic? Of course."

In the end I became dreamy; flying buttresses floated by overhead, gargoyles were wafted gently about in Byzantine spatial concepts, I could not remember why Baroque was supposed to be beautiful. In conclusion, I am violently opposed to eleven cathedrals in fourteen days, and especially for the American tourist who did not grow up around the corner from a Palladian façade or a triforium. Why on earth should it be assumed that a short plane flight makes a Middle Gothic fanatic out of somebody who has yet to see his first *Decorated* choir? Architecture requires time, and a good stout pair of walking shoes; then it can be delightful, the most exciting part of your English journey. But cathedrals, like drink, should be imbibed in moderation. No work of art can give pleasure without some discipline; Canterbury is sublime, but not to somebody innocent of medieval philosophy. Architecture, like music, has its idiom; Mozart will be only sweet sounds without some grasp of musical form, and St. Paul's is a forest of marble until you discover the Renaissance.

Which is not to say that you should spend your entire time in England holed up in your hotel room with the *Cambridge History of Architecture,* or nervously memorizing the tables at the back of this book. Be calm. After your first four Gothic cathedrals (providing you take them in slow, easy, thoughtful stages) you will recognize a *Perpendicular* window and a *Decorated* arch without severe mental strain; almost before you notice, you will develop taste, and above all pleasure, in architecture. If you give yourself a chance, there is no reason why one of the most poignant experiences in your life should not be the lantern tower at Ely, or the choir at Canterbury, or the lovely city of Bath.

Pleasure is subjective. Aesthetic experience can be described but not transmitted. There is no point in telling a tone-deaf listener that a Mozart sonata is beautiful; perhaps it is, but not for him. The same with Durham Cathedral. Durham is a magnificent building—I think. So do a large number of critics, poets, architects, and laymen. But you may feel no pleasure when you walk into Durham Cathedral, and it is pointless to insist that you should; joy cannot be compelled. Moreover, age and experience, knowledge and mood, can affect aesthetic reactions; nobody can feel too great delight at Hampton Court with a large blister on his heel. There is no need to creep about in hangdog style if Westminster Abbey leaves you blank; aesthetic pleasure is like happiness—a by-product, an accident, a bonus.

All buildings, from the Empire State to St. John's Chapel in the White Tower, must be approached from two angles: their physical history and their aesthetic value. The first can be learned, briskly, but the second is acquired by understanding, time, and good luck. If you know enough about the Tower Chapel, it is probable you will think it beautiful and find joy in looking at it; then again, as you peer at the Norman arches, you may simply wonder (uneasily) what date it is. So far as Richard and I are concerned, we think it profitless to labor the question of aesthetic pleasure in this book; as we go along we shall remark, from time to time, that Canterbury (in our opinion) is breathtaking. For the rest we shall stick to dates and facts, in the hope that one day, as you trot about making mental notes on façade and vaulting, you will feel a queer sensation—which will be you, shaken with joy by a work of art.

To gallop from the general to the specific, the Chapel of St. John is considered by critics to be one of England's brightest architectural jewels. The Normans were vast and wonderful builders, but unfortunately most of their work has been hopelessly damaged by nine hundred years of weather and neglect, or blown up in various wars, especially the last one (as befell Caen in 1944), or razed to the ground when Henry VIII "dissolved" the monasteries, or remodeled out of existence by Gothic and Renaissance architects. England has the grandest Norman architecture standing in the world today, at Norwich and Durham; also the purest and most perfect, in the little Tower Chapel. It was built inside Gundulf's thick Tower walls, so neither rain, nor ice, nor modern smoke has ruined these ancient stones; as a royal chapel, St. John's escaped the Dissolution wrecking crews; finally (a bit of good luck) the Chapel seems to have been too small and too trivial an affair to have attracted the attention of the various builders who blithely tore down Edward the Confessor's Westminster Abbey, transformed Winchester, and remodeled Ely. The Chapel of St. John stands today as it stood in 1080, a small but perfect example of pure Norman.

I remark on the size of the Chapel because it would be a mistake to suppose that the Normans specialized in pocket-sized building. The energetic Normans went in for grandiose castles and enormous cathedrals, the bigger the better. The Chapel of St. John is a miniature, because it had to be fitted inside the fortress walls, and, in any case, it was designed for domestic use. Gundulf used the space available in a cunning fashion; on a small scale, the Tower Chapel repeats all the major themes of Norman architecture: the massive columns, the round arches, the geometric ornamentation, the triforium arcade. Here, in the Chapel of St. John, you may see, as you can also see at Durham, or at Arles in France, or in Italy, the origins of what is called Western Culture.

At first glance, you may think I am pretentious in assigning so much virtue to the Chapel of St. John. But architecture was the first of the arts and sciences to come to life again after the Fall of the Roman Empire. For hundreds of years after Roman civilization gave up the ghost in Europe, the barbarians camped out in Italy, Spain, and France; they tilled the soil in a primitive sort of way, and occupied themselves with squalid brawls; when someone wanted to write a letter or count up to forty-seven he had to send around to the local monastery. Charlemagne's brief reign was a premature rift in the general darkness; after he died, France went downhill again; in England the locals were murdering Christian missionaries and wearing skins. Civilization, such as it was, tottered along in Constantinople. Western Civilization was not deeply influenced by the Byzantine, but started by limps and halts and detours, in Sicily, Italy, southern France, Normandy, and various other spots where the ex-barbarians, after hundreds of years, finally settled down to the task of building a new world where their ancestors had destroyed the old.

Architecture was the chief activity in this flickering dawn—the chief cultural activity. We live in a world so rich with variety and anxiety that it is hard to wrench our minds away from a climate of organized crime, Shakespeare, Saul Bellow, overpopulation, ecology, archaeology, atomic warheads, and the great question, Will we survive? But in A.D. 800, nobody expected to survive very long; even love was too simple to take up more than ten minutes a month of anybody's time (this was long before poetry, chivalry, women's rights, complexes, or other refinements). Religion, for the layman, was a matter of faith, and wars were nasty affairs—a sharp ax in the back of your neighbor's neck when he wasn't looking. There was little literature, because nobody outside the scattered monasteries could read; there was no science, because nobody could count or took any interest in natural phenomena; there were no politics to mention, because government largely consisted of making away with the duke around the corner before he made away with you; there was scarcely any painting or dress design (ladies inherited a belted wool sack which they wore until they had time laboriously to weave another), no music (except something in the nature of a hideous bagpipe bleating on state occasions), no fine cuisine, no news, no knowledge, and, in general, no fun.

As the sap rose in the springtime of our Western World, men began to build; architecture was, for a time, the only European art. All the creative impulses of society, all the half-unconscious drive to knowledge, all the scientific curiosity, most of the energies and wealth of embryonic Europe went into architecture. What you see in the Chapel of St. John at the White Tower is the knowledge, skill, passion, and intellect of our ancestors, translated into stone. Shakespeare and Einstein, Michelangelo and Picasso are implicit in these barrel vaults, in the cunning of this fenestration—that is to say, in the artful arrangement of the windows. Norman architecture was the beginning of the world we know.

Norman architecture is called Romanesque on the Continent of Europe, and for a reason that will be immediately obvious to you. As you will remember, the Normans were sea raiders, Vikings, from the North; they came helling out of the chilly Scandinavian oceans in their longboats, and after a sortie to Paris, settled in that part of France which still bears their name. Sicily was thick with the ruins of Roman grandeur; and when the Normans began to build, it was natural that they should try to imitate what they had seen. The Saxons, over in England, for that matter, also had a try at putting up something along the lines of the Roman ruins in the neighborhood. But the Saxons never got far with their building projects; they could not figure out how to make an arch; they generally worked in wood and were satisfied to erect simple wooden halls, which generally burned down, owing to their habit of starting fires under a bit of thatched roof. The Normans were different; they knew little about stresses and strains and buttresses and vaulting, but they were experimenters—they tried first one thing and then another until they got the hang of a round arch; next they tackled the barrel vault; and little by little they evolved a style which, while obviously a memory of the Roman past, was also fresh and original. By the time Duke William moved over to England (that green and pleasant land!) the Norman style was at its peak, and the Normans evidently had an obsession for building. When one considers the possible Norman popu-

lation of England, 1066–1154, it is staggering to find how many
castles, churches, chapels, cathedrals, monasteries, and the like
they built over the countryside. Edward the Confessor (a
transplanted Norman in exile) could think or talk of little else
except his Westminster Abbey—to the annoyance of his Saxon
subjects. William the Conqueror, who had a good deal on his
mind, found time to take a lively interest in any number of new
projects, such as dozens of castle keeps, Winchester, Durham,
and so on. His worthless son, William Rufus, one of the wicked-
est kings in English history, nevertheless subsidized several
good-sized churches. All Norman bishops, without exception,
started big building projects the moment they arrived at their
new appointments. Norman style transformed itself rapidly
into English Gothic; there was no pause between the round
arch and barrel vault, and the new soaring, daring, pointed
style—one merged into another, and the passion for architecture
went on and on for hundreds of years. A word of caution: dates
given for architectural styles are always arbitrary; in real life, one
style overlapped or blended into another. What you see in the
Chapel of St. John is the perfection of the beginning, the moment of ripeness before change. I think the Chapel of St. John
is lovely because it is serene and fresh and full of vigor; aside
from its merits as a work of art, implicit in these stones is the
beginning of our world. More specifically, here is Chapter One
in the history of modern England.

Transport and Newsprint

AFTER A brisk day's work peering at Norman architecture, you
probably will not linger on Tower Hill—which raises the problem of transport in London, i.e., how to get back to your hotel
for a chance to take your shoes off.

I am an immoderate admirer of London taxicabs. London
taxis are relatively cheap, comfortable, and driven by a tribe of

staid, solid, respectable gentry who do not amuse themselves
(as their colleagues do in Paris and New York) by beating
traffic lights, taking corners on two wheels, missing trucks by
a hair, and engaging in altercations with pedestrians or cops.
A ride in a London taxicab is not an adventure, I am happy
to say.

Taxicabs bring up that delicate question of interest to tourists: Are the Natives Cheating Me? The answer to that question
in England (for that matter, in most of Europe) is No. I am
not a partisan of the American who arrives across the Atlantic
with the firm intention of tipping ten percent and arguing over
every dinner check. Do not believe the ancient chestnut that
porters and guides will depise you if you "throw your money
around." A taxicab driver expects to be paid the charge on his
meter, plus about fifteen percent tip, in round figures. If English money confuses you (I can't say the decimal system makes
it any easier, not for me, at least) ask the driver what you
should give him; if in doubt, tip too much. No waiter or London
cabby is going to put you down for an arrogant, rich American
if you give him an extra sixpence. Always offer guides, church
vergers, chambermaids, hall porters, and anyone else who does
you a service some sort of payment; in the event they do not
wish an extra half crown, they will tell you so politely. You
cannot blacken the fair name of our country by being generous.
Do not listen to horror stories from characters lounging about
your hotel lobby. I suppose, in a city as big as London, there
are taxicab drivers who will drive the unwary traveler three
times around Hyde Park to run up a charge on the meter; or
"antique" dealers who will sell you "Georgian" silver nickel-
plated yesterday in Granny's back parlor. But London is one
of the safest and nicest cities in the world—you are running
small risk of being robbed or cheated. If a salesgirl says an
article is real leather or real silver, you may be sure she is telling the truth; if the hotel adds ten percent to your bill, you can
be certain it is the law; if the taxicab driver tells you a shilling
would be about right for his tip, it is what he expects to get
from his English passengers. You can trust the average Londoner: at least about money. Street directions are something
else again.

If you have decided to eschew the enervating luxuries of a

taxi and to take the Underground from the Tower to your hotel —beware! London transport, both buses and subways, is splendid; the Underground trains are cushioned and comfortable, and you can smoke. The best way to see large chunks of sprawling London is from the upper deck of a bus. But the ordinary man-in-the-street has little idea of how to get from Stepney to Charing Cross, though he is cheerfully ready to take a stab at advising you. No Londoner (as no New Yorker) admits he does not know the nuances of his own city; challenged by a stranger with a Yankee accent to provide advice on how to proceed from Tower Hill to Marble Arch, the Londoner will briskly outline a wonderful program. Two hours later you will end up on Hampstead Heath or in Kew Gardens, much bedraggled. Here is a solid rule for using public transport in London: *Never ask directions from a layman.* Get your information firsthand from authority—ticket sellers in Underground stations, bus conductors, or policemen. With these precautions, the London transport system is superb; there is no better way to learn the immense proportions of London than by the bus ride to Hampstead Heath. The Underground is quicker, but there is nothing to see, except your fellow passengers and the newspaper headlines.

Newspaper headlines, incidentally, are important. Every now and then I run across an American tourist in London who tells me solemnly he wants to know the real England; he fears he is wasting his time inspecting Hampton Court and such sights. When I ask if he read the letters in the *Times* that morning, or what he thinks about the *Daily Mail*, he gives me a childlike stare. Any tourist worth his salt should read two or three London newspapers each day, and as many weekly magazines as he can gulp down between cathedrals and cricket games. The English are a fabulously literate people; the number of books, newspapers, weekly and monthly journals consumed per head in London is startling compared to what we Americans absorb. If you want to catch some of the flavor of the real London (and the real England) you will have to explore the delightful contradictions, the cock-eyed gamut of the London Fourth Estate. Most Americans are flabbergasted to discover that London is the home not only of the *Times*, but also of the raciest, loudest, juiciest tabloids in history. The English press lords invented what is politely called the Popular Press, and I must say, on the whole, London newspapers are a good deal more "popular" than journals published on the other side of the Atlantic. I don't remember anything quite like the *News of the World*, even in Chicago; and for what is still an unfrivolous, Puritan nation, English magazines (I do not mean the ones sold under the counter to furtive old men) publish photographs to make an American's hair stand on end. Public *mores* are always fascinating. *Tobacco Road* was banned here for a decade, but respectable English magazines with a sound home circulation print lush photographs of stark-naked ladies— generally dancing on the greensward, or making ineffectual gestures at a bird.

The *Times* no longer wears its classic Victorian dress. The type is bigger (readable, in fact), the headlines frequent, and the personals have been shifted from the front to the back page. But the foreign correspondence is still distinguished, the editorials erudite and the letters to the editor unique. The personals may have lost status, but not substance. For instance:

> CHIEF WANTED. Have skins toward envisaged rural wigwam uniting two lost tribes for permanent security. —Box . . .

Obviously this is code. On Her Majesty's service, perhaps? Or a thief, smoke signaling location of booty? You can (that is to say, I can) waste the better part of a morning worrying about why Chief is wanted, if the advertiser already has the skins?

Then there is a Mrs. Raphael, whose correspondent wishes her a happy, happy day, begs her to remember "stroke of nine," and signs himself "Tiger One." Sinister, that "stroke of nine," but it could be an advertisement for a new detective novel.

Besides the weekday newspapers, the visitor to London should read the *Sunday Times* (no relation to the daily institution) and the *Observer*, which are the better products of Fleet Street. The high standard of writing in the *Sunday Times* and the *Observer* has no counterpart in American newspapers, and the weekly magazines, the *New Statesman and Nation*, the *Economist*, and the *Spectator* make similar publications in the

United States look immature. *Punch* is as English as kippers. A standard sight in a London summertime is an American sitting on a chair in Hyde Park, peering incredulously at a copy of *Punch*. Richard and I subscribed to this most sacred of English publications; it is required reading if you want to know England. On a totally different level, no visitor should let a Sunday go by without the *News of the World* and one or two of the Sunday tabloids. Fleet Street is like the little girl who had a curl on her forehead; when the London press is good, it is very, very good; when it is bad, it is—well—spectacular.

While I am exploring the matter of the printed word in London, I should mention the bookshops. You might stop off for a glance at Charing Cross Road, and some of the best second-hand bookshops in the world. The bookshops are clustered together, although you will run into wonderful, musty old establishments here and there in the City, or sparkling, handsome outfits on Piccadilly and Oxford Street. But an exciting and thoroughly satisfactory occupation for any visitor in London is a slow, brooding progress up Charing Cross Road. You will discover that you are more than welcome to settle into any bookshop, sample the stock at your leisure, and buy or not as suits your fancy. It often seems that the proprietors of some of the most enchanting shops are downright reluctant to part with their treasures; they like to talk about bindings or literature, Keats or type faces, bird calls or first editions—but when it comes to taking your money and wrapping up an 1814 edition of Swift, edited by Sir Walter Scott, you feel they are saddened.

Foyle's is one of the standard London sights—like Big Ben. It is an immense, untidy warren of buildings; the management remarks, in a casual, not a boasting way, that Foyle's stocks any book published in English, besides thousands of volumes in French and German. It is an experience diving in the door and emerging two hours later, dazed and dazzled, the proud owner of a volume on Roman false teeth or an eighteenth-century atlas, along with the latest novel. I wonder why more tourists do not hit on books as a solution to the souvenir and presents-for-back-home problem. The infinite variety of price and subject, binding and topic solves everybody from Aunt Mamie, who has everything but must be remembered, to Cousin Joe, aged six, who will not care for Bristol glass, and

Grandpa, who probably does not want another woolen scarf, even a hand-made scarf from England.

Interlude

IT IS seven o'clock, your first night in London. You have recovered from your bout at the Tower; your hotel room is littered with newspapers, postcards, and trophies of your Charing Cross Road expedition—and now, surely, you are going to the theatre?

I confess that, as a noisy, slam-bang American, English understatement often baffles me. The French have let everyone in the whole world know, from babes in South American arms to tottering old ladies in Alaska, that the tourist in Paris spends his evening in restaurants, ceremoniously sampling the famous cuisine. Citizens in Mishawaka, Indiana, and Melbourne, Australia, trade Paris restaurant addresses. Tour d'Argent is at least as famous, in international American Express circles, as the Luxembourg Gardens. But nobody tells the eager tourist that the theatre in London is what the cuisine is in France— unique, special, and wonderful. The Englishman, if pressed, will shyly agree that the London theatre is not uninteresting; but too often the visiting American is left to discover the English stage by accident, and perhaps (tragically) on his last night in town. I urge you to plan your theatre program before you stop to unpack. The hall porter at your hotel can arrange your schedule; or there are dozens of ticket agencies within striking distance of any hotel district. You will want to see six or seven West End productions, from Shakespeare to comedy to a revue; book seats for one of the old-fashioned music halls (they are something like American vaudeville thirty years ago, only livelier), but also plan on at least one ballet (English ballet is famous), a symphony concert at the Albert Hall (or the Festival Hall), and an opera. These last events depend on the season, but if you miss the regular program, there are often summer "galas" well worth attending, or open-air theatres, particularly in Regent's Park. The West End theatres operate briskly all summer, and if you book your seats on your first afternoon in London, you will have no trouble seeing even the big hits. Theatre and music are agreeably inexpensive for Americans, which is all the more reason for collecting a batch of tickets in advance.

If I had two weeks in London, I would book seats for at least ten of the evenings, and look up the movie schedules to fill out the remainder of the time. London theatres and concerts begin at odd hours, often as early as seven or seven-thirty. West End successes may sometimes be sold out for a week, but usually you will be able to get seats for a whole gamut of plays, if you order tickets as you arrive. Plan ahead for your evenings; otherwise—unless, of course, you are a patron of gambling clubs and night clubs—time is going to creak heavily on your hands.

You cannot gaily wander the streets of London at night. There is nothing to do and little to see after dark, even in Leicester Square or Piccadilly Circus. People do not linger over coffee in cafés—for the excellent reason that there are no cafés, only the pubs, which are crowded and close early. Your hotel lobby can look mighty bleak the third night running. There is nothing sadder than a disconsolate American, poking about Trafalgar Square after nine on a summer's evening, with nothing to do in this immense city but to go to bed.

But you are agog to hear Mozart sung in English in an open-air performance; you are booked for a music hall for tomorrow night and theatre the next, and here it is seven o'clock on your first evening in London. You are off to see *Richard III*. The curtain is early; if you missed tea, a glass of lager and a crab sandwich on your way to the theatre is a good idea.

I hope your first London theatre is an Old Vic performance; many West End productions are as good or better, but the Old Vic is a famous company, a landmark, a growing tradition. If you see the Old Vic do Shakespeare, you will be enchanted; there is nothing quite like it. The great plays come vividly alive; the poetry comes to you fresh, with electric force; the characters breathe and suffer and triumph and die before your eyes. Shakespeare by the Old Vic is an experience. When the last curtain comes down, and the orchestra plays "God Save the Queen," you will find yourself exhausted and shaken—and hungry.

Where to have dinner? Answer: if you are feeling rich and grand, at one of the West End hotels, such as the Dorchester, the Savoy, the Ritz, the Mayfair, and so on. Otherwise, in Soho.

Soho is, in a vague way, the Greenwich Village of London; also it is Bohemian Italy, France, and Greece. As a foreign district, Soho will not seem spectacular to Americans, who are accustomed to four hundred thousand Italians established in

A CORNER IN SOHO

one city, two hundred thousand Poles in another, and so on. But to Englishmen Soho is romantic—spaghetti is sold in the grocery shops, French pastry or a reasonable approximation to it is found in the bakeries, and the streets are lined with French, Italian, and Greek restaurants. There are good restaurants outside of Soho, too, and some of them are very good indeed. English food has gradually improved over the decades.

So, when the curtain comes down on your first London play, you can look forward to a good supper, excellent service, and a long wine list.

The Fossil Called Westminster

WESTMINSTER Abbey and the Houses of Parliament logically come next after the Tower, on your program for London.

You will have noticed that we lurch about violently from theatres, taxi rides, and the *Times* to towers and abbeys. Our theory of travel, especially for London, is a nice balance between flying buttresses and music halls. We hold that the human mind, however willing, can absorb only a certain budget of triforiums and fan-vaulted cloisters at one whack. London is a dangerous city. There are more sights per square foot in London than in any other place in the world, with the exception of Rome. Many an upright American, haunted by the theory that he has come three thousand miles to see the immortal glories of London, drives himself remorsely from the Temple to St. Paul's to Westminster, from Hampton Court to Windsor. Three weeks later, shattered in limb and mind, he collapses on the airplane and spends the next nine weeks recuperating from the rigors of his London "holiday."

London is an enchanting city, but Easy Does It should be written in letters of fire on the walls of the American Express Company, and Relax Or You Won't Really Like It emblazoned over every hotel lobby favored by the transatlantic trade.

We thought, for your second day in London, you might explore the Gothic splendors, real and imitation, of the Abbey and the Houses of Parliament. This would be in the morning. After lunch, you could see your first cricket game at Lord's.

Westminster Abbey has suffered a curious fate; it is too famous for its own good. People tramp up and down the nave, mill about the choir and transepts, crying, "Oh, look, Tennyson!" and lose their grip on the fact that Westminster Abbey is a glorious example of *Early English* (Gothic) architecture. Guides explain how King James I had his mother, Mary Queen of Scots, dug up and reburied just across the aisle from Queen Elizabeth; they show you the throne where English kings are crowned (liberally decorated with the initials of naughty English schoolboys, circa 1704) and the great black tomb of Edward the Confessor. Frankly, it is hard to concentrate on clerestories of *Perpendicular* when you keep running across tombstones of Dickens, Anne of Cleves, Henry II, and Chaucer.

I think the best way to approach Westminster Abbey is to divide the project into two sections: Item A: the tombs, memorials, and monuments. Item B: the Abbey itself, the beautiful stone relic of medieval life in England.

Tombs appear to exercise a universal fascination. Every time I go back to the Abbey to study the fan vaulting in the Henry VII Chapel, I find myself making a detour for Jenny Lind, or Edmund Crouchback, or Dr. Johnson. I don't know why it should be interesting to peer at some indifferent marble memorial to Darwin or Mrs. Siddons; yet even my husband (who has a severe, refined taste) lingers over the stone which is carved with the four words "O Rare Ben Jonson," or makes remarks and says, "H'mmmm, H'mmmm," about Lord Castlereagh.

Students of post-Waterloo Europe or the works of Shelley will remember that Lord Castlereagh was a spectacularly unpopular cabinet minister. He committed suicide for reasons unknown, and his funeral was enlivened by dancing in the streets. Citizens of London joyously greeted the black-draped coffin with hoots of mirth and overripe cabbages. The last rites for Lord Castlereagh were nearly as uproarious as the unconfined celebrations held at the funeral of His Grace, the Duke of Buckingham. Modern historians sometimes defend Lord Castlereagh (he did much for Anglo-American friendship), but they are fighting a lost battle. Poets are dangerous enemies. The terrible lines of Shelley have made the cabinet minister immortal. The epitaph on the Abbey tomb is fulsome; however, what people remember is not the eulogy, but the poem, "The Mask of Anarchy."

I

As I lay asleep in Italy,
There came a voice from over the Sea,
And with great power it forth led me
To walk in the visions of Poesy.

II

I met Murder on the way—
He had a mask like Castlereagh—
Very smooth he looked, yet grim;
Seven blood-hounds followed him:

III

All were fat; and well they might
Be in admirable plight,
For one by one, and two by two,
He tossed them human hearts to chew,
Which from his wide cloak he drew.

This is the sort of thing that happens at Westminster Abbey; you start out to glance at a tomb or two, and end up quoting Shelley.

In defense of people (like myself) who can idle away a whole morning with the Abbey tombs, many of these Westminster monuments and especially the surviving medieval sculptures are of artistic importance, and taken separately would be the chief glory of any museum lucky enough to have them. The Elizabethan tombs provide historians with invaluable documentation; the eighteenth-century monuments illustrate a change in English taste; the Victorian absurdities have a kind of gruesome interest. But it is the general sum of all these Abbey memorials that excites my greatest admiration. You can begin with Edward the Confessor and trace the fortunes of the English nation in Westminster Abbey; here are displayed the incomparable vigor and variety, sin and glory of an immensely daring, energetic, curious, and passionate people. Think of a nation that produced Chaucer, Shakespeare, and Darwin; or the wicked Duke of Buckingham and Gladstone; Richard II, poor wretch, and Henry VII, that wily master mind, that foxy, slippery, brilliant first of the Tudors. There is such a wealth of tragedy and triumph in the Abbey tombs. I remember coming across Henry V, in the chantry just off the Chapel of Edward the Confessor. Henry lost his solid silver head and silver-plated robes during the later Henry's Reformation; battered and black, the fifth Henry lies in effigy now, very old, very long ago, very dim. Next to him is his Queen. Passing by, I glanced at the inscription on the tomb. *Katherine of Valois.* Henry's "beautiful Kate"! His "fair Katherine, and most fair," his enchanting little French princess, who had "witchcraft in her lips" and spoke in "broken music"—for her "voice was music" and her English broken. Alas, one feels a pang, across five hundred years, for the sweet maiden who made Shakespeare's Harry of England (drinking companion of the incomparable Sir John Falstaff) love her so "cruelly." It is sobering to reflect that she was the mother of Henry VI.

The tombs in the Chapel of Edward the Confessor, and those in the transept crossing, just before the altar rails, are considered the most interesting of the medieval sculpture in the Abbey, or for that matter in England; very little French work of the period is so fine. Edward himself is a sad remnant of his former glory; until the Reformation his shrine was the most gorgeous in the Abbey. There was a complete outer tomb in pure gold, profusely decorated with statues of fellow saints, also in gold; and the whole tomb was thickly covered with diamonds, rubies, and sapphires. Henry VIII, not to put too fine an edge on it, stole the lot. For that matter, Henry coolly packed up the most famous shrine in England, Thomas Becket's at Canterbury, lock, stock, and barrel—and carted it away in twelve wagons to the royal treasury. Henry did not even leave St. Thomas's bones; but as Edward was an English king (and Henry thought highly of English kings, though far less of saints) the Abbey's most gorgeous tomb was simply stripped of its convertible treasure, and Edward's mortal remains were left to molder decently in the plain block stone coffin.

Henry had the courage of his convictions. For five hundred

years Edward the Confessor had been credited with formidable miracles—lepers were cured after a night spent praying at the diamond-studded shrine, cripples walked again, the blind saw. Public opinion considered Edward a powerful saint; the most wicked and strong-minded of robbers thought twice about lifting a ruby from St. Edward's canopy, or chipping off a bit of gold. Suppose the loss of the ruby were resented? One would not like to come down with leprosy or contract the dropsy. . . . And then Henry VIII issued a brisk royal announcement: from now on, his loyal subjects were not to believe in saints. To prove the point (and add to the royal revenues), Henry destroyed the shrines, where and when he found them. Edward the Confessor went first. People waited around (hopefully?) to see if Henry VIII came down with anything. Nothing happened. Art critics bitterly deplore Henry VIII, and no doubt Edward's shrine was a great loss. Still, Henry broke the back of the medieval Church in England, and revolutions of that profound nature are not made with unborn museum curators in mind. Superstition rarely yields to reasoned arguments: when the Tudor citizenry saw the great Edward's shrine knocked down and carried off for secular use, there is no doubt the demonstration was a practical success. The English have not been great believers in such saints since.

Edward's tomb rises black and bare in the center of his chapel. Fortunately for the twentieth-century traveler, no other English king, among those buried at the Abbey, worked miracles from his grave; the circle of royal tombs in the Confessor's chapel for the most part escaped the Reformation and the Cromwell troubles later on. All are beautiful; I like best the bronze effigies (the earliest ever cast in England) on Henry III's and Eleanor of Castile's tombs. The detail on Edward III's handsome monument is worth attention. Originally Edward's twelve children were spaced out in niches around their royal father's tomb, but six of the twelve children have been lost. His eldest son you will see again at Canterbury—the mighty Black Prince.

This is the merest sampling of the Abbey tombs; if you fall in love with medieval sculptures or Elizabethan effigies, you may well come back to the Abbey another morning and, armed with a detailed chart, settle down to a closer study of the Westminster monuments. For the time being we will leave the tombs and consider the Abbey itself, the Henry VII chapel, and the cloisters.

Westminster Abbey is like a pyramid, a Roman forum, and the Empire State Building. It is also a fossil. Its stones describe the nature of the medieval Englishman, as the pyramid reveals the essence of Egyptian culture, and the Empire State Building provides an index to modern American life. The Empire State, for instance, proves that the twentieth-century American has a high degree of scientific control over nature; it shows that Americans are able to manufacture steel in great quantities, and are competent to use it at daring heights. Moreover, the Empire State reveals the character of twentieth-century American civilization. This immense steel structure is not a temple, a tomb, or a cathedral; it is not the seat of government or even a factory. The Empire State is an office building. It was designed for the use of the financial and technical organizers of American production; it was built as a stronghold for the men who owned the factories, the experts who controlled the distribution of manufactured goods. It is characteristic that even rebels in modern America see nothing wrong or peculiar in an office building of such imposing size. The function of the Empire State Building appears natural to Americans, proper and inevitable; it is taken for granted, although a church of such proportions, even a factory, would seem shocking, queer.

But Westminster Abbey is also a fossil. As the steel girders in the skyscraper describe modern science, so the pointed window arches in the nave at Westminster (*Early English*, they are called—1245) tell how much medieval man had learned since 1080 and the Chapel of St. John in the White Tower, and how far he had to go before Columbus and Galileo, before the daring walls of glass, the intricate stone vaulting (*Perpendicular*, 1519) in the Henry VII chapel on the east end. I hope I shall not be laboring the obvious if I remark that as the Empire State is an office building, so Westminster is an abbey.

The nature of a civilization is laid bare in the function of its buildings: the primitive rigidity and quietism of Egyptian society are implicit in the pyramids. The pyramids were tombs, not temples; and their function (however imposing their size) was to celebrate a death cult surviving from the Bronze Age. The Romans built roads, forums, forts, baths, coliseums, palaces —but no factories or office buildings, not of a size or importance to outlast the passing of time; and this says all there is to say, both of the richness of Roman culture and the dead end to which its economic system finally reduced it.

Medieval England built for the Church.

Between 1100 and 1500 the English built monasteries, chapels, parish churches by the thousand, great abbeys and cathedrals. To be sure, they built castles here and there, but the castles were crude affairs compared with the gigantic glories of Westminster and Canterbury, York, Wells, Lincoln, Winchester, Salisbury—the list is enormous. Across modern England darkly rise the immense stone fossils of medieval man. But after 1550 (roughly) almost the only imposing churches built in England were the ones put up to replace those lost in the Great Fire of London and World War II. After 1550, English architects built palaces for their secular rulers; then roads and banks and factories and government buildings; then Georgian spas and Regency town houses; then railroads and bridges and steel mills—but few distinguished churches.

The most important observation to be made about Westminster Abbey, as you enter its great west doors, is the purpose for which it was designed. This is not so simple as it sounds. Today, Westminster Abbey is a church in the modern sense of the word; but if you mean by a church a gathering place where people come together and worship, that was not the original purpose of Westminster, nor indeed of any medieval abbey or cathedral. Westminster was built, first of all, as an offering; every stone, every bit of carving, every altar and window was meant (by the kings and abbots who put up the Abbey) as Abraham meant the lamb—to be a personal sacrifice. We are so separated by time and habit of thought from the medieval world that it requires a wrench of the imagination to grasp the primary purpose of Westminster Abbey. Think of the facts:

Henry III (Richard the Lion-Hearted was his uncle, and the wicked King John his father) chose Edward the Confessor as his patron saint—an intimate connection in 1216. Henry expected a good deal of his patron saint: the wars with France must be won, local barons must be defeated in their plots against the Throne, healthy sons must be produced to carry on the royal line. On the other side of the ledger, St. Edward required something more than an occasional prayer or a pilgrim's candle from the King. Lesser men might give jewels or gold for St. Edward's shrine; Henry III rebuilt the whole of what was then a Norman church (like the chapel at the Tower, but much larger) and made what is, with a few changes in design and some important additions, the great Westminster Abbey you see today.

Incidentally, it was Edward the Confessor's own work, the beloved church he spent his whole life building, which Henry briskly tore down to make way for the pointed arches and slender shafts of the *Early English* Abbey. It apparently never crossed Henry's mind that his patron saint might be piqued by the wholesale destruction of the round arches and massive columns he had designed with such loving attention . To Henry's thirteenth-century eyes, Edward's Norman church was old-fashioned, dark and low and crude. It was taken for granted that St. Edward would much prefer a brand-new Abbey, with plenty of light from the big, pointed windows, and fine carving on the stonework. The best, Henry felt, was none too good for St. Edward, his patron saint. The nave at Westminster (to the annoyance of the Thomas Becket clique at Canterbury and the canons up at York) was the loftiest Gothic in all England; the pointed arches were surmounted by an exquisitely carved triforium, and above that came an even finer clerestory. St. Edward, in Henry's opinion, had the finest abbey, the most glorious shrine, in the Kingdom.

Westminster Abbey was built for St. Edward; and for St. Edward alone. It is important to understand that Henry III did not build his Abbey as a public meeting place where the faithful could assemble to worship; such an idea was as impossible for Henry as theories on the equality of man, or the conception of an airplane. Henry built Westminster to delight and flatter his patron saint. The elaborate ornamentation on the lofty roof —not ten human beings in fifty years would see these gargoyles, these rich and fanciful carvings hidden along the rain spouts. But St. Edward did not need a ladder to examine the detail on the ceiling vaults at Westminster, or field glasses to admire the delicate traceries on the triforium. Gargoyles were meant to amuse the saint, not to edify the citizens of thirteenth-century London; the whole of Westminster Abbey was designed to please Heaven, not the populace.

This may seem like splitting hairs; but neither Westminster nor any other medieval church can possibly make sense if its true function is not understood. Take the nave. At first glance, the nave looks as though it had been planned to seat a vast congregation at a religious service, as in fact it does today. But if the nave at Westminster was built for an auditorium, then the planning was crude and foolish, and does not speak highly for the good sense or technical skill of the architects who designed it. Rows of pillars shut off the view, screens hide the altar, and only a modern loudspeaker system can make the choir heard beyond the transept crossing. The nave was bitterly cold in winter (it still is, in spite of central heating) and had no provision for seats of any kind; the congregation must have stood in freezing dampness for the whole length of the service. The chief attraction of Westminster, St. Edward's shrine, was located behind the choir, so that the faithful in the nave would have been excluded from the most interesting and important ceremonies of all. The men who were capable of erecting the loftiest clerestory in England, the architects who worked out the intricate engineering details of the pointed arches, had contrived a nave which, if it was meant as an auditorium, was certainly a complete failure.

The point is, the nave at Westminster Abbey was never intended to be an auditorium. It had a theological and symbolic, not a practical, purpose. Medieval churches were built in the shape of the Cross, and always ran east and west. The altar was at the east end, pointing toward Jerusalem. The choir, with seats for the monks or priests to sing the services (thus the word *choir*), was the short, top vertical head of the cross. The transepts ran north and south, and the nave was the long, vertical stem of the cross. The nave was always the west end of a Gothic church; and since the altar was at the east end, the business of the church—the services and ceremonies—did not take place in the nave at all. The nave was an elaborate vestibule. On feast days, big processions formed there (although ordinarily the transepts were used for this purpose) and pilgrims lined up waiting their turn to visit St. Edward's shrine. The nave was not an especially hallowed area of the church—it was often crowded with the wicked, or in any case secular, citizenry, who moved in from the market square on rainy days, exchanged grain or gossip, and peddled charms, medals, bread and red silk shoes to visiting pilgrims. The screens between the choir and the nave shielded the monks, who were conducting private services at their sacred altar, from the impious uproar in the nave. However, the nave was only by accident a meeting place for the citizens of medieval London; Henry III did not lavish his treasure on clerestories and arched bays to accommodate a market-day crowd. The nave at Westminster must be understood as part of an immense stone model of the Crucifix, richly decorated and cunningly designed.

I remark on the size of Westminster, because, to be understood as a fossil, the proportions of the Abbey deserve some thought. The Empire State Building is also large; but it was a relatively simple matter for American society to find the steel and stone and manpower to build it. No great community effort was needed to put up the Empire State, and only a minute percentage of the American national wealth was spent on it. But Westminster represented an enormous outpouring of medieval treasure. A primitive agricultural and wool-trading society spent its entire surplus wealth on Westminster, and on the dozens of other great cathedrals and abbeys going up at the same time. The population of thirteenth-century London was about twenty or thirty thousand souls. Although some expert labor—stone masons, stone carvers, and the like—was imported from France or other parts of England, for the most part the Abbey was built by the wretched serfs from the countryside near London, and by the people of London themselves. The effort required was staggering; not only the community's wealth, but its manpower was concentrated on this one fabulous monument.

This suggests, I think, the nature of society in England, the character of its civilization, A.D. 1100–1500.

Here is a building which cost medieval London its bread, its treasure, its men, and whose sole function was an offering to God. It seems natural to Americans that the Empire State is an office building; natural, but not urgent. If the population of the United States had paid two-thirds of its income, not for one year, but for two decades, if the whole manpower of the city of New York had been drafted, to the exclusion of other tasks, for the building of the Empire State, no doubt its function would have been more narrowly examined by those making such a sacrifice. The function of Westminster Abbey takes on greater importance when its relative cost is understood. The power of the Church, the force of religion in medieval life, is revealed by the fossil of Westminster. The soaring arches, the great pillars, the lofty clerestory of this Gothic building express a way of life, a kind of society profoundly strange to modern minds. Medieval man lived for Heaven; and here is Westminster to prove it.

Yet every society nourishes the seeds of its own destruction. How inconceivable to Henry III that one day another Henry, of his own blood, would steal the rubies from St. Edward's shrine! Westminster bears the scars of the Reformation, which destroyed medieval society in England; it displays, in the lovely chapel of Henry VII, the restless intelligence, the curious, searching, probing minds which undid the Gothic mold. *Perpendicular*, as an architectural style, is medieval—but the end of Gothic. The windows, pointed in *Early English*, wider and segmented in *Decorated*, have spread out to become walls of glass; and the engineering problems which so often baffled the thirteenth-century architects are, in *Perpendicular*, easily, almost recklessly solved. Look at the Henry VII chapel, the most developed and elaborate phase of *Perpendicular*. A heavy, stone-vaulted ceiling is apparently supported by glass. Sixteenth-century stone masons have almost a swagger, compared to the staid designers of the nave. A glass wall? Easy. A flying buttress to take the stress of the vaulting piers, slap on decoration across the ceiling—why arch your windows? More glass, more light . . .

Henry VII was pious, and his chapel was built to the glory of God. But he had other things on his mind besides Heaven; and the stone masons who designed his beautiful addition to Westminster were bold thinkers, ready to break away from the designs of the past, strike out in unknown, untried ideas. The Henry VII chapel is the end of Gothic, and the beginning of our modern way of life.

Do not leave Westminster Abbey bemused with *Perpendicular*; reflect that the Henry VII chapel did not spring, disembodied, from the sixteenth-century mind. It is easy to think of the medieval world as rigid, gripped by the force of its religious principle; and it is true that change was slow across those centuries, sometimes almost imperceptible. All the same, medieval man was alive, thinking, daring. The monks who built the Westminster triforium, flung up the roof of the nave higher than any other roof in the Kingdom, challenged all the dead past and made the soil ripe for the seed of the future. *Early English* came out of the Norman arches you saw at the Tower; and the *Perpendicular* glass walls of the chapel have their origins in Westminster's glorious nave.

I abandon *Perpendicular* and Westminster Abbey to trot across the street to the Houses of Parliament. They are, let us face it, phony. Mind you, I think the Houses of Parliament are a great success. From almost any angle, on the bridge, in a boat going along the river, from the green open square across the avenue, the Houses of Parliament, with the Clock Tower alongside, are an impressive pile, and beautiful. Indeed, the seat of the English government is eminently satisfactory. Yet the style is overripe Gothic, and the Houses of Parliament were built in 1840–1867. If Henry III's *Early English* arches led, in due course, to the triumph of Henry VII's *Perpendicular,* Sir Charles Barry's mighty masterpiece along the banks of the Thames led directly to the Prince Albert Memorial and the old Union Station in Cleveland. The English government buildings were the first massive attempt to reproduce in Europe the dead Gothic past; and no sooner were all these edifices finished than architects and laymen all over the world caught the disease. Twenty years later, a building without a synthetic turret or a carved arch was old-fashioned. A stylish block of flats, 1875, featured Henry III's windows, including mass-produced stained glass to shut out the light, a Norman water tower in iron on the roof, and a *Perpendicular* vestibule.

The vast collection of masonry entitled the Houses of Parliament includes Westminster Hall. The Hall was built in 1097 by William Rufus, and remodeled by Richard II. From the thirteenth century until 1882 the chief English law courts sat in Westminster Hall, and the place is thick with history. No sooner had Richard II put on the new roof than his barons assembled under it (1399) and deposed him. Charles I was tried in Westminster Hall, and shortly afterward Oliver Cromwell was installed there as Lord Protector. The guided tour of the Houses of Parliament includes a survey of Westminster Hall, St. Stephen's Chapel, where Parliament met from 1547 until 1834, and, if Parliament is not in session, various buildings inside the pseudo-Gothic courtyard. If you are one of those tourists who Bring Letters and Call at the American Embassy, you may be able to wangle a seat in the Strangers' Gallery when the House of Commons is sitting; or even, in the case of exalted personalities, get yourself invited to tea on the famous terrace overlooking the river. Run-of-the-mill Americans (such as myself) can trot around the corner for a midday snack; after which, as a violent change from Gothic, whether fake or *Early English*—cricket.

Time Out for Cricket

BEFORE I get down to solid facts about cricket, a tourist who does not see at least one cricket match at Lord's is, in my opinion, no tourist at all, and ought to be stripped of traveler's checks and passport and ignominiously cashiered back to the United States by slow freight. Cricket is fundamental to England like canals in Venice, or snails in Paris, or glaciers in Switzerland. I know that cricket is scorned in American circles. There is a theory that cricket is (a) dull, and (b) impossible to understand, except for 50,000,000 Englishmen, 8,000,000 Australians, 400,000,000 (about) Indians, and assorted West Indians and New Zealanders. Anybody not hopelessly dim-witted can get a reasonable grip on cricket, enough for a delightful afternoon at Lord's. Naturally, cricket, a profound, subtle game, cannot be probed to its depths by the casual visitor—but then, you don't have to know batting averages by heart to watch the World Series.

Furthermore, cricket is not dull. It is fascinating.

Americans are constantly making dreary, ignorant jokes about cricket. They say that cricket is played in slow motion. Nothing ever happens. It goes on and on. They even stop the game for tea! (Mad hilarity, although Americans see nothing humorous about the half at a football game. "Oh, well, that's different," the heckler announces. "Besides, you ought to see the crowd at a cricket match. Every now and then the stands go simply wild—and somebody claps.")

As it happens, the uproar at an English soccer match would terrify an American baseball fan; if public frenzy at a sporting event is a measure of national virility (a theory to which I do not subscribe), then the American is effete compared to the rough, tough, muscle-bound, manly Britisher who goes to a first-division football match. Customs vary. The American who thinks cricket fans are too quiet does not usually scream the place down at a tennis match, or throw bottles during a golf tournament. Cricket is not supposed to be hysterical; it is meant to be restful to watch and fun to play. Loud noises, at a cricket match, are bad form. Little boys, carried away by emotion, sometimes cheer out loud, but a brisk round of applause is the most noise countenanced at Lord's—or on the village cricket green. It is this easy, relaxed, pleasant atmosphere that makes cricket delightful.

So much for preliminary points. Here we are, off to Lord's—probably by taxi. Lord's, I ought to explain, has nothing to do with the English nobility. The field was built by a Mr. Lord, some hundred years ago. It is the home of the Marylebone Cricket Club (the M.C.C.) and also of the Middlesex (County) cricket team. The match you will see will be Middlesex against Yorkshire or Surrey or some other first-class county team.

A few succinct words for the Marylebone (pronounced "Marrerbn") Cricket Club. Candidates for the M.C.C. are registered at birth, or at least before they are out of rompers; usually they are thirty-one or thirty-three before there is a vacancy in the Club—if their lives have been reasonably blameless, and they meet with the grudging approval of the Older

Generation, M.C.C. candidates may make the grade before they go totally bald. Or there is a quicker way of getting in: brilliant cricketers may be elected to the M.C.C. as young as twenty-one or -two.

What happens after you belong to the M.C.C.? You can wear the famous yellow-and-red-striped "Marrer-bn" necktie, and sit in the M.C.C. Pavilion at Lord's, behind the wickets. This last is no small privilege during Test Matches (the World Series of cricket), when the seats at Lord's are sold out for weeks in advance; all you have to do on the great day is to stroll luxuriously into the Pavilion, sniffing at the madding crowds.

The M.C.C. owns cricket, lock, stock, and barrel. It makes the rules, schedules the games, picks the officials, decides disputes, registers the scores, collects and spends the gate receipts, chooses the England team for Test Matches, and in general keeps a keen but benevolent eye on cricket clubs as far-flung as Durham County or Hong Kong. The M.C.C. was never elected to be the collective czar of cricket; it happened, like cabinet government, or common law. But it works well. Cricket is nonprofit—gate receipts go for the common (cricket) weal and little boys are admitted to Lord's for half price to encourage the younger generation. Now and then sports writers for the London newspapers blast the M.C.C. choices for Test Matches —but the M.C.C. cannot be blasted out of its majestic calm. The M.C.C. has picked the England teams ever since there were Test Matches, and they propose to keep right on doing so, which, on the whole, seems to suit most cricket fans.

This may give you a rough idea of the organization of English cricket. County cricket teams play each other for the English championship—the big counties, with powerful teams, play in a major league, and small counties have a bush-league circuit of their own. International championship games are not played between the winning English League team and the challenge from abroad. The M.C.C. picks an all-star, all-county aggregation which it stacks against a similarly brilliant team from Australia, or India, or some other such team. Amateurs play in the same teams as professional cricketers. In the old days, most of the leading players were amateurs, but now, with the high income taxes, there are more professional than unpaid cricketers.

You have bought your ticket at Lord's, hired a cushion (soft seat) at the gate, located yourself in a stand, and looked around. It is a lovely summer's day (I hope) and the sun is shining brightly in a blue sky. In the sacred Pavilion, yellow-and-red neckties flutter in a soft breeze; the nearby seats show a sprinkling of ladies in bright-colored dresses, and at the edge of the field, rows of solemn little boys.

The grandstands run along three sides of the cricket field, an expanse of bright green grass, a rich, delicious green; moving gracefully across this background are the players in spotless white. I do not know any English scene more charming, more refreshing to the eye or soothing to the soul than this lyric in blue sky and sunlight, green grass and fluid white figures. It is like a Renoir painting—smiling, timeless, delightful.

The players are moving across the green oval. They are not warming up; the match has already started. Don't be alarmed: only fanatics, small boys, and the unemployed ever see an ordinary cricket match at Lord's all the way through. (Test Matches are different: people bring box lunches and settle in for the duration.) First-class cricket matches last three days, from midday until six each afternoon, with short intervals for lunch and tea. Cricket, like football or basketball, limits play to a measured number of hours, though village cricket is more elastic—a local game can start on Saturday afternoon after lunch, when the star bowler finally arrives, and ends when the visiting team quits to catch the bus back home.

Umpires keep time at Lord's. As the six-o'clock deadline on the third day approaches, the situation is apt to get feverish. Cricket is a chancy game—matches are not postponed because of bad weather, and if a team is suddenly rained out on the third afternoon, alas, the match goes down as a draw in the Championship Table. Draws count as a zero. But, no matter who wins, that team ahead at the end of the first innings of a match scores four points—even if it subsequently loses the match, or gets rained out. Winning a match counts twelve points; and at the end of the season the county with the highest score is champion. Each team has the same number of matches scheduled for the year, but rain does not always fall on the just and unjust, or on Middlesex and Yorkshire, alike. The season runs from May 1 to August 31. You can understand why

Middlesex fans, with their team running neck and neck against Yorkshire, take an acute interest in weather reports for northern England round about August 28. How sad it would be if Yorkshire, which is sure to win against Derbyshire, should happen to run into a cloudburst—a local cloudburst—while in London, under a sunny sky, Middlesex valiantly battles Surrey to a triumphant win!

Cricket is played with a time limit—unlike baseball. Baseball keeps right on, until nine innings, or in the case of a tie score until one side emerges as the bruised and battered victor. Cricket stops at six o'clock sharp on the third day; this time limit makes cricket a subtle sort of a ball game. I used to play first base on the all-boy (except me) East Cleveland Junior Hyenas, and I stand second to no woman in my admiration for the great and glorious game of baseball. Yet I fear baseball does look the merest touch crass compared to the art of cricket. Let me illustrate:

Cricket is played by two teams of eleven men (instead of nine, as in baseball). Both sides must come up to bat to make an innings (the same as in baseball, except the word is plural at Lord's), but in cricket there are only two innings played over the three-day match against the nine or more in one day of the American game. Three outs retire a side in baseball; it takes ten outs to send a cricket club to the showers.

If the Cleveland Indians come up to bat in the first half of the ninth, strike a run of luck, and stay in there, slugging out runs until six or seven o'clock, it does not matter. The audience may go home, surfeited, but when the Indians are finally retired, the Tigers finish the last half of the ninth inning. All very simple.

But if Middlesex has an equally colossal triumph in the first half of the second innings, people in the Pavilion begin to bite their nails. Say it is three o'clock on the afternoon of the third day. Middlesex is in there, happily batting them over the fence. Score: Middlesex 125, Surrey a miserable 87. However, this game ends at six o'clock sharp; and before zero hour the second innings must be finished. That is to say: Surrey must come up to bat and Middlesex has got to put ten men out. Otherwise, the watch is a draw, and Middlesex is confounded.

The Middlesex captain may "declare his innings closed"—retire his team before Surrey puts out ten of his men. But when?

That's the rub. Suppose Middlesex stays at bat until teatime, piling up a hefty score of 150. Then Surrey comes in and, not to put too fine a point on it, stalls. At six o'clock there are only nine men out for Surrey, and there is no joy in London. Mighty Middlesex has finished the day's work with a goose egg, while up Yorkshire way, the enemy has piled up a rich twelve points.

Evidently, you are saying, that's what comes of being greedy. If Middlesex had not stayed at bat all afternoon, slugging extra runs, they would be in clover with twelve points of their own.

But take it the other way around. Suppose Middlesex declares its innings at three o'clock, with a score of 125 and plenty of time to knock out Surrey, stalling or no stalling. Surrey trots up to the wickets, seizes the bats, and stages a big comeback. At teatime the score is Middlesex 125, Surrey 118. By five-fifteen Surrey has reached 126 to Middlesex's 125. Terrible, eh?

This may suggest why the captain of a cricket team needs a streak of second sight. I bring this up because, as you settle into your grandstand seats at Lord's, the first thing you need to check on your program is what innings? and what time is it? If it is first innings on the second day, you have arrived in the middle of the match; second innings on the third day—you will see the grand finale.

A few more fundamental points. Cricket is scored differently from baseball, which should clear up the mystery of why so many runs. Even the East Cleveland Junior Hyenas counted the day a big success when we made 20 runs, and in Big League baseball a score of 8 or 9 is colossal. But in the New Zealand Test Matches both sides hung up tallies above 300; in 1938 England scored over 900 in one innings.

In cricket, an ordinary hit in the class of a safe-on-first brings one run; a decent hit collects at least two runs; a grounder to the fence around the field is automatically four runs; and a ball hit over the fence is six. The fence at Lord's is a low white wooden barrier with a thick chalk line underneath it. Obviously a good batsman does not make singles; he bangs the ball up and over the fence and scores a six, or at least he slams the pill for a grounder to the chalk line and a four. Another detail: in baseball, a player must sling away the bat as he connects, and physically touch the base with some part of his person—toe, elbow, or eyebrows—as he runs. In cricket, the base may be touched with the tip-end of the long bat—which saves a lot of time and trouble, as you can see, and helps pile up the score.

So much for grand principles. If you look down on the grass at Lord's, you will see thirteen players, in white flannel trousers, white shirts and sweaters, plus two parties in dark trousers and long white cotton coats—like the family butcher. These picturesque types are the umpires.

But why thirteen players? If each team has eleven players, and Middlesex is up at bat, why not twelve? Answer: because two batsmen are up at a time—two. This is fundamental for Americans watching their virgin cricket match. In baseball you have one batter operating on the diamond, and lots of people from Ohio, et cetera, become very baffled by two batsmen. It is not really so difficult: two batsmen; two bowlers; and two wickets.

What is a wicket? A wicket is three slender shafts of wood, like chair legs, knee-high, and stuck firmly into the ground four inches apart. Two small wooden crosspieces, called bails, fit on top of the three vertical spindles, held in place by shallow grooves. If a ball hits the wicket, the bails fall off, the wicket is "broken" and the batsman is out.

Does this sound complicated? Actually, it is easy, and sort of fun. In baseball, a batter is out if he swings three times at the ball and misses; or if the umpire (amid the catcalls of the multitude) calls three strikes on him. (And for various other reasons that do not concern us here.) Suppose you had a wicket between home plate and the catcher, and our batter would be back to the dugout, not if he swung and missed three times, but rather, if the pitcher hit the wicket once. The batter would have to be on the alert; none of this letting a fast one go by for Strike One, and swinging a little slow on Strike Two—he would have to stop every ball that looked as though it might connect with the wicket behind him; otherwise, he would be out.

There are two wickets on the grass at Lord's. They are placed directly opposite each other in a straight line, more or less in the middle of the field. (They have to move them a little for each match, because the grass gets worn, and cricket, like lawn tennis, is played on green turf.) In front of each wicket is a crease (base), and that's all the bases there are in cricket—two. You have a cricket bowling alley, instead of a baseball diamond.

The batsman stands at the base in front of the wicket, the bowler opposite, and the catcher behind the wicket. Let us pretend it is the first half of the second inning, the batsmen are up for Middlesex, the bowlers and catcher are playing for Surrey.

Batsmen, bowlers, catcher. Who are all those other people? Obviously, the Surrey fielders. However, cricket defense is much more fluid than baseball field play. A right fielder at Shea Stadium operates within fairly definite limits—you would not suddenly find him backing up the catcher. But cricket fielders are all over the place—rather like slower-motion basketball, or hockey. The captain of a cricket team "places the field"— the code phrase for distributing his players around the grass oval as Heaven and his intellect suggest. Say Middlesex puts in a notorious southpaw, famous for slugging them over the right fence. The Surrey captain rushes four of his bravest lads out right fence way, and prays them to look alert. Whereupon lefty belts a mean grounder to the opposite chalk line. "H'mm," the Surrey captain mutters, and revises his calculations slightly— two men over to left oval! This, naturally, provides our Middlesex batsman with a delightful opening on the right fence—and so it goes.

Placing the field is a fine, if not black, art. All you need to know for your first look at cricket is why seven of the Surrey players move from one side of the field to another, or restlessly back up, run forward, close in, and spread out.

So much for the fielders. Now for the bowler and the batsman. Why do they call him a bowler? An American baseball is pitched; and a cricket ball (small, round, leather-covered) is bowled. What's the difference? you inquire, baffled. Pick up a ball, any ball; aim it at something, and let fly. You aimed the ball with your fingers and wrist, and threw it with your shoulder muscles. That's the natural, normal way to throw anything short of a piano; little boys, aged three (even in England), pick up a ball, aim it with their wrists, and throw it with their shoulder muscles.

Now try this: clutch the ball with your fingers. Stiffen your arm, make a circle, sweep your rigid arm down, and up, and over—and let fly with the ball. This is called overarm bowling. The ball is aimed and propelled by the whole body.

That is what you are watching on the field at Lord's—overarm bowling. The bowlers take a long, swift running start, and bowl the slippery leather cricket ball overarm with such deadly accuracy that they can calculate how many feet and in what direction it will bounce out of the batsman's eager reach. A good bowler can deliver high curves, low curves, fast and slow balls, bounced curves, full pitches (when the ball does not bounce), and mean surprise thuds, to foil the batsman. All the time, you understand, the bowler is trying to get past the batsman's guard to break that wicket and put him out; and, as if he didn't have enough on his mind, there is the condition of the "pitch." In baseball, the pill goes over the plate full speed ahead; the pitcher does not have to worry about what is underfoot. But the bowler usually, and preferably, bounces the ball in front of the wicket—for cricket bats are wide, heavy, and flat. What a good batsman can do to a full pitch is not pretty (for the bowler) to see—he is likely to hit the ball out for a six. What if it rained last night? A cricket ball bouncing on a soggy patch of wet grass is one thing; and the same on a hard, dry spot of ground is a totally different kettle of fish. The bowler must have enough control to deliver his favorite bounced curves whatever the weather, come cloudburst or drought.

What of the batsman? Presumably the odds are on this fellow with the shin guards (pads) and the oversize bat; the bowler is an artist—all the batsman has to do is to give the ball a few vulgar slugs. The batsman's lot is not a happy one; he is menaced on all sides; one false move, and he is finished. I mentioned above that in cricket there is no such thing as three strikes; if the bowler gets past the batsman's guard once, it is curtains. There are all sorts of ways the batsman can be got out. As follows:

1. He can be Bowled: as above, when the bowler actually breaks the wicket, knocks the crosspieces off, and scores a clean-cut triumph.

2. The batsman can be Caught Out on a fly ball, as in base-

ball—the fielder catches the ball before it touches the ground.

3. The batsman can be Run Out: something like baseball. The batsman gets a hit, and runs for the opposite base. The fielder scoops up the ball, and throws for the wicket. If the bails fall off before the batsman is safe on base, he is out.

4. The batsman can be Stumped—he is lured out of the batter's box, and before he can return, the catcher breaks the wicket with the ball.

5. Best of all, the batsman can be Got Out by Leg Before Wicket. Leg Before Wicket is always abbreviated, L.B.W. You will see it often on your program. (The program lists the players and how they were Got Out. For instance: Mr. Jones, Bowled; Mr. Smith, Stumped; Mr. Robinson, L.B.W.)

The theory of an L.B.W. is this: a ball which in the opinion of the umpire would have broken the wicket, but which hits the batsman instead, is an L.B.W. The cricket ball is not large, and the batsman wears heavy shin guards. If there were no L.B.W.s, the game would degenerate from a contest of great skill into a mere vulgar battle of brute strength—how hard the bowler could bowl, as against how many bruises the batsman was willing to suffer.

Therefore, the L.B.W. But not all balls that hit a batsman would have broken the wicket. What if the bowler (presumably) loses control and gets the batsman a nasty one in the jaw? That is not an L.B.W.

Take this example: the wicket is knee high, you recall. A ball gets the batsman on his right shoulder and bounces off, ninety degrees away from the wicket. Is that an L.B.W.?

Remember: only a ball that would have broken the wicket can be called against the batsman.

When is the ball that hits a batsman an L.B.W.? Response: When the umpire says it is.

When a cricket ball connects with a batsman, the fielding side instantly appeals to the umpire. They cry out, in a sudden yell: "Howzzz—th-at?" Baseball fans may be interested to know that the only thing a cricket player may ever (ever!) say to an umpire is: "How's that?" It is unthinkable that an umpire's decision should be challenged by so much as a raised eyebrow.

. . .

Cricket is an illuminating experience for the American tourist. Here is a game where the umpire's decision takes on much more importance than in baseball. The umpire at Shea Stadium may call one "ball" a strike, but he is hardly likely to call three mistaken strikes in succession and put a man out. Close decisions at the bases, or at home plate, revolve around actual matters of fact—did the man's foot touch home before the ball landed in the catcher's mitt or did it not? A photograph could prove the point one way or the other.

But judging an L.B.W. is theory. A ball that angles off a batsman's ankle, or his elbow, or his right shoulder, might, or might not, have broken the wicket—it is a matter of opinion; the umpire's opinion. There is not even a muffled groan in the stands at Lord's when the umpire puts a Middlesex man out on a queer-looking L.B.W. Now and then, if the fans think the enemy team is stalling against the clock, and trying for a draw on the last day of the match, there may be a round of slow, ironic, rhythmic clapping, but this only happens in extreme cases, under great provocation, and such sounds of disapproval are never directed against the umpire. It is generally held that the umpire does his best. . . .

I think this clears up the L.B.W.

Now the bowler is winding up for his first ball. It bounces slow, and the batsman (Middlesex) gets a puny hit into the pitch. He does not run. The bowler winds up again for a second ball. This time Middlesex nails it for a healthy grounder to left field. Batsman Number One (who hit the ball) and his partner, Batsman Number Two, standing at the opposite wicket, both run—for each other's base. The first batsman tags his partner's base with his cricket bat; meantime Number Two touches the opposite base with *his* bat. They run back to their original positions. Score: two runs.

The bowler lets fly a third time. Nothing. A fourth time—another hit! Two more runs! Our bowler is having a poor afternoon. Ball five. Nothing. Six: again, nothing.

Watch carefully; because it is at this point that most Americans give up cricket. I know that the first game I saw struck me as strictly an exercise in mysterious tribal rites downright infuriating for the outlander. Just as I was beginning to get the hang of the game, batsmen, two bases not four, wickets, and so on, and settling down to figure out who was winning, every man on the field (so it looked) changed places. A major upheaval.

There are two bowlers, and two batsmen. When the match starts, Bowler Number One bowls six balls to Batsman Number One—and that is what is called an "over." Then Bowler Number One fields, for the time being.

Bowler Number Two bowls six balls to Batsman Number Two from the other end; and that is another over.

Back to Number One for the third over. And so on.

In effect, the bowlers simply take turns, every six balls the pitchers alternate.

What is the big upheaval on the field at the end of every over? Why do all the players mill about, running from one end of the field to the other?

The two bowlers stand behind opposite wickets. At the end of an over, the bowlers do not change places; the ball is thrown in the opposite direction. As in tennis, first one side serves, then the other. The second batsman hits in the opposite direction from Batsman Number One. Therefore, the fielders shift from one side of the oval to the other at the end of each over—and that is the upheaval you see at regular intervals in a cricket match.

Another point about overs: the bowlers take turns. Bowler Number One pitches six balls; Bowler Number Two pitches the next six; then back to Bowler Number One, and so on. In theory, the batsmen also take turns. But that is theory. For example: Middlesex has a strong batsman, the star of the team (we will call him Mr. Brown), on one wicket, and a good bowler but a mighty poor batter (Mr. Green) on the second wicket. Every time Green gets up, it is a sure out for Middlesex. In our game, Mr. Brown is batting and it is nearly the end of the over. Brown is hitting one six after another. But in one more ball the over will be finished and bowler Number Two will be winding up to murder Mr. Green. Can nothing be done?

Watch closely. Ball six comes across the plate. Mr. Brown gives it a careful tap, not too hard, because he must not hit it beyond the fence for an automatic six, or to the chalk line for an automatic four—that would be fatal, because in either case he would remain where he is, on base Number One. He must not hit too softly, because Mr. Brown has got to make a run. He hits it—medium, you might say.

Brown and Green jog across the cricket pitch. But when Brown gets to Green's base, he holds it. Green freezes onto Brown's sack. Score: one run. The over is finished and Bowler Number Two winds up—and look who is up to bat: Mr. Brown, the invincible, who has changed places with Green. The star Middlesex batsman carries right on, through one over after another until he is finally Got Out.

This is how famous cricketers make their "centuries." A century is a score of one hundred runs in one innings, a tremendous feat. If the word goes around London that some Middlesex hopeful has passed the fifty mark, the stands at Lord's magically begin to fill—publishers bid hasty goodbyes to their latest authors, brokers abandon the stock market, house painters stop painting houses, and little boys assemble like robins in spring. All of London holds its breath. Will he? Won't he?

Eighty! The bowler sends a slow, tricky bounced curve to the wicket. And Williams picks it up for a six over the fence!

Eighty-six!

The bowler winds up. A hush falls over the stands.

A pitch with a high, fast bounce! Williams connects! A grounder . . . all the way to the fence! A four!

Ninety! Ninety on his first century!

But this is the last ball of the over. The batsman dares not hit the ball over a fence for a six, or even send a grounder to the chalk line for a four. He *must* change places with the batsman on the opposite wicket.

The bowler runs forward—the fielders close in. It is a low bounce! The batsman connects—a high one, to right field. A fellow runs down under the ball. Is the sun in his eyes? Make the sun be in his eyes, three hundred little boys openly pray.

The ball comes down, hard and fast. The fielder lunges forward. He's got it, he's got the ball! The batsman walks slowly off the field. Ninety. Ninety runs.

In the Pavilion somebody makes a gigantic effort, and says bravely, "Well caught!"

Several gentlemen aged ten break into tears.

This painful episode will indicate why, when a century does

happen, the rejoicing is intense. Batsmen are not the only heroes in cricket, any more than home-run artists are the only kings of baseball. Bowlers are famous for their repertoire and styles, as pitchers are back home. Specifically, bowlers can pitch maiden overs—a no-run over, like a no-hit inning in baseball. Finally, there is that rare and beautiful episode in the career of a cricket hero: the Hat Trick.

The Hat Trick is done as follows: The bowler dismisses three batsmen—in successive balls, one, two, three. These unlucky victims may be bowled, stumped, caught out, or L.B.W.

Why is it called the Hat Trick? Because in the nineteenth century gentlemen played cricket in high silk toppers and full beards. When a bowler bowled three batsmen in succession, his teammates bought him a new silk hat: ergo, the Hat Trick.

This concludes our once over lightly on the great and noble game of cricket. Cricket, as I remarked in the beginning, is profound. People are constantly writing (and reading) books about it. The branch library around the corner from our flat in Chelsea had eighty-nine books on cricket listed in its catalogue, and I understand the cricket titles at the British Museum are enough to make the mind of even a fanatic reel. In New York publishing circles there is a saying that a book about a doctor—for, by, "agin," exploring, denouncing, praising—is certain to sell well; in England, cricket is a sure thing, especially in winter. Millions of Englishmen spend January and February happily reading their Christmas books on *Some Aspects of Preparing the Pitch* or *Bowlers of the Twentieth Century*. It is a comfortable picture.

The American tourist can admire from afar. An afternoon at Lord's is the merest introduction, but if you fall in love with the game (as I did, at one fell swoop) you can spend your English Saturday afternoons watching Village Cricket. The true cricket fancier is rather pained by local matches; awful things happen. Bowlers go wild and hit the umpires, batsmen get bowled by mistake, when they are looking the other way, and so on. But Village Cricket is like sand-lot baseball, energetic if not refined, and fun, especially for the amateur, spectator as well as player. Or maybe, between museums and cathedrals, you will take another afternoon off before you leave London, to visit the sacred Home of Cricket—Lord's.

Hampton Court and St. Paul's

HAMPTON COURT should come after Westminster, on the third day or so of your London visit. You must also see Windsor Castle, but I suggest Hampton Court—which is Tudor—to follow the great Gothic of the Abbey. Windsor (partly Norman, partly *Perpendicular,* and partly Queen Victoria) can come later on in your second week; by that time you will be a cunning hand with English architecture and English history, and Windsor will make sense.

The expedition to Hampton Court is an all-day affair. Hampton Court is one of the marvels of England, and of Europe; it takes time to savor. First of all, there is the great red-brick and stone palace itself. Cardinal Wolsey started building in 1514; England's noble lords (including the King) were still inhabiting dirty, drafty, and inconvenient Gothic castles, complete with moats, drawbridges, stony keeps, and hardly any windows. Cardinal Wolsey had other ideas for his private residence. The Cardinal was not for nothing the richest, the most splendid, and the most powerful lord in the kingdom, after Henry, and on the side, something of a hypochondriac. He went so far as to consider dirt unhealthy, and fresh air delightful. These heresies were met with sour disapproval by the English nobility, who hated Cardinal Wolsey anyway; but the Cardinal did not care—he planned to show them a thing or two, at Hampton Court.

Hampton Court was England's first palace. The stone masons were withdrawn from the cathedrals, the artists and craftsmen came from Italy and France and Yorkshire and London. The court buzzed with gossip; the Cardinal had no turrets on his new castle! In fact, it was not a castle at all. The glass in the windows—acres of it! Bedrooms and banqueting halls, fireplaces in every room. (Most people in England went to bed to keep warm, or built a fire in the middle of the room. The smoke filtered out, maybe, through the cracks in the stone walls.)

Cardinal Wolsey began Hampton Court as a health resort.

London did not agree with him—too damp. The Cardinal thought a pleasant country retreat would be good for his chest. But Hampton Court grew on the Cardinal. He could not let it alone. Architects in England had concentrated for four hundred years on cathedrals; other men, when they felt a building fever, added a new chapel to the local parish church, or ordered something grandiose in the way of a family tomb. But the Cardinal was bored with flying buttresses and *Perpendicular* windows. Wolsey was a prince of the Church and wore the red hat, but he was the first Englishman in history (or at least since the unfortunate Roman Britons, A.D. 400) to make architecture secular in the grand manner. After Hampton Court, Englishmen built palaces, not churches. The Cardinal went about sneering at Gothic: his palace was different; it was new, up to date, the most splendid palace in England, in Christendom.

It seems odd that the Cardinal, who knew his master King Henry VIII so well, did not reflect on the character of the formidable man he served. Surely it was hardly tactful to boast to a Tudor that one of his subjects was building the grandest palace in Europe? Perhaps the gods make into architects those they wish to destroy? Wolsey made the mistake of building a palace bigger than anything Henry could call his own; he added fuel to the fire by abandoning Gothic and designing his residence in the new Italianate fashion. Henry, we have seen, was an all-around man, an intellectual, a poet, a scholar. Before Hampton Court, he had not given much thought to architecture, but Cardinal Wolsey's views on flying buttresses and fireplaces interested Henry deeply—when he thought them over.

In 1524, Hampton Court (Wolsey's version of it) was finished; and the Cardinal celebrated by giving a tremendous housewarming. Torches burned in the graceful courtyard, ladies in their best jewels admired the glass in the many windows—and Henry looked around carefully and found the palace good.

In 1526, Henry took it.

There was some jiggery-pokery about Cardinal Wolsey giving Hampton Court to the King as a present. His Majesty was graciously pleased to receive the palace from his loyal subject.

HAMPTON COUR

To show his gratitude, Henry arranged a state trial, at which Cardinal Wolsey was to be convicted of treason. The Cardinal died, abandoned, at Leicester Abbey.

For his part, Henry had a clear title to the most splendid palace in Christendom; he moved in, court, child, and first wife, and started building operations on his own. Henry was no backward layman; he intended to prove he was every inch the architect his Cardinal had been, and indeed Henry's great hall and chapel at Hampton Court are delightful additions to Wolsey's master plan. Moreover, Henry paid his dead minister the compliment any architect would have cherished: he fell in love with Hampton Court, not for a year, but for his lifetime. The Gothic glories of his castles and his London quarters filled Henry with distaste after the Cardinal's charming palace on the Thames. It was at Hampton Court that Henry courted Anne Boleyn, at Hampton Court that Henry's beloved son Edward was born, at Hampton Court that little Kate Howard's tragedy was played out. After Henry, Hampton Court was the favorite residence of England's monarchs for two hundred years, until George III, who had spent too much of his childhood in the Tudor palace on the Thames. George's father, Prince Frederick, beat his royal son savagely inside his historic brick walls, and when at last both the Prince and the second George were dead, the third George announced he never intended to set foot in the royal residence again. This story touched me until I discovered that George III had his son, George Number IV, regularly and brutally flogged by the royal tutors. This was at homely old Kew Gardens; perhaps George III thought scenery made a difference.

Henry was not the only royal builder at Hampton Court. William III (Prince of Orange, he is usually called in American history books) engaged Christopher Wren to rebuild the east and south wings; after you inspect the Tudor windows and courtyards of Henry VIII and his great Cardinal, you may walk through the courtyard archway and come upon the work of England's greatest architect in his warmest, sunniest, most delightful mood.

Christopher Wren could be (as you will see at St. Paul's) overwhelming; he reached summits of grandeur not touched since Gothic, and some think never afterward. But at Hampton

Court he is serene; his graceful courtyards have a grave but charming dignity—they must have suited exactly the court life that Pope celebrated in his poems. William III loved Hampton Court; and alas, he died in its great gardens after a fall from his horse.

There are four things to see at Hampton Court. The palace itself; its remarkable art gallery and collection of historic English furniture; the Mantegna "cartoons," which are separately housed in a small gallery of their own; and finally, the glorious gardens. Of the art collection there is nothing for a book of this kind, or an author of my limited powers, to say. The Mantegna "cartoons"—drawings or sketches made for an intended fresco—are unique.

Hampton Court is a tremendous experience, in itself; perhaps you will be tired and hot and a little surfeited by the time you pass the Orangery, get your ticket and line up with the crowds. But you may not come this way again, not soon at any rate, and what you will see in the gallery of the Mantegna cartoons is (in the middle of fairest England) the miracle of the High Italian Renaissance. It will be a sort of wrench; for the genius of the Italian and English peoples is disparate. From the cool, mannered grace of Wolsey and Wren and the idyllic dignity of the gardens, you will plunge into a different world—hot, intense, impassioned. How Italian is this Crucifixion, all the agony explicit, the tragedy savored as part of life, the pain seen as drama! How lovely, how haunting, how sensual this drawing!

If the Mantegna cartoons are not English, you ought to reflect that it was an Englishman who fell in love with their beauty, and brought them all the way across Europe to Hampton Court. The English know how to cherish great art, however alien. They also know how to create, in their own several manners. The gardens at Hampton Court are no less cunning, inspired, or enchanting because, instead of marble or oils, they are composed in grass and living, vibrant colors. The garden is an English art; Hampton Court comes as a shock to most Americans; at least until I saw the walled perfection of the little Tudor Privy Garden, until I stared astonished, at the green avenue of the Fountain Gardens, I had no idea a park could be a work of art, as true as any cathedral, as exciting as any painting. The English work in shrubbery and groups of trees, lawns, and profusions of flowers as a painter works on canvas, or an architect in stone. They are masters of many garden styles, and at Hampton Court you may see a succession of Elizabethan walled flower beds, French formal box hedges, mazes, wildernesses, romantic "Gothick" avenues, dramatic with shadow and silence—and, above all, the great English style of rolling lawn, framed in "natural" groups of oaks, and colored richly with splashes of bright, flamelike flowers.

Hampton Court is the National Gallery of English gardens; the museum of artists who work in living materials. The many great gardens in England echo, repeat, develop, the themes you see at the top of their elegance and perfection at the palace on the Thames. Newstead Abbey, in the Midlands, develops water vistas beyond Hampton Court; Haddon Hall displays the Elizabethan walled garden in acres of glorious rose terraces; at Chatsworth an eighteenth-century duke razed whole villages to make miles of low hills covered with lawn and gracefully grouped trees. But each of these ideas you may see at Hampton Court, and more besides. As an introduction to the art of the English garden, Hampton Court is peerless.

The space is put in, as they say in theatre programs, to mark the passage of twenty-four hours. It is the morning of your fourth day in London, and we think that the glories of Hampton Court should be the preface to England's masterpiece of Renaissance art: the Cathedral of St. Paul's.

St. Paul's is very different from Westminster Abbey. A revolution, indeed two revolutions, happened between the Gothic Abbey and the Renaissance Cathedral. You saw change beginning at Hampton Court, in the very secular designs of Cardinal Wolsey. England's Tudor palaces were both an echo of the medieval past and the harbingers of the brave new world. The Reformation broke the political power of the Church in England; the restless, inquiring mind of the Elizabethan swept away the dead formalism of medieval discipline.

English history is fascinating. After Henry VIII and Elizabeth there are no pauses, no long dead empty spaces. In France, after the monarchy at last compromised the feudal power of the nobles, there followed almost a century of relative stability, a ripening, and a long decaying of royal state power. The French Revolution did not happen until 1789; the English Revolution came in 1649. The Elizabethan flowering was hardly finished before Cromwell's armies destroyed the nascent absolute monarchy, and destroyed it, despite the pageant of the Restoration, forever. The English middle classes, those reckless, greedy, juicy merchant-adventurers, those bankers ready to gamble on India or shipyards, cotton factories or opium, those flinty squires, sitting on the fertile acres only a century ago the property of the Church—these middle classes challenged royal power before it had hardened into lifeless tyranny. From Henry VIII to Cromwell is little more than a hundred years. Perhaps it is sentimental to attribute to nations special aptitudes or characteristics; yet surely it is not inexact to remark on the political genius of modern England. French merchants were still stifling under the clammy weight of absolute monarchy, while the English middle classes, having long since consolidated their political power, were comfortably free to pursue at their leisure the exciting and dangerous prospcts of the new capitalism.

The Restoration, I remarked, was a pageant; Charles II took good care not to challenge the Parliamentary authority his father had died fighting. No one knew better than the second Charles the source of the political power in the state he professed to rule; and no one was more prepared intelligently, if sulkily, to accept the shadow for the substance of authority. A long and impecunious exile had cured Charles II of any stubborn addiction to principle; if the English wanted a king for Sunday's show and a Parliament for Monday's work, Charles was delighted to oblige. A job was a job, and Charles was not choosy—he had been unemployed too long. He was much too intelligent not to understand that the cause for which his poor father had died was lost indeed; the lessons of catastrophe were not wasted on this second Charles, who, perhaps, had less character, but definitely more brains than his sire. Indeed Charles II, always canny, was forever counseling his dimmer-witted relatives against exasperating the English people—a king could never be sure of what came next, not with the English! But Charles had the lion's share of the family cunning. No sooner was he dead than his feather-brained brother, James II, exasperated the Protestant nation; the English were perfectly willing to have a dissolute King, but a proselytizing Catholic monarch was dangerous. It was luck that James II lived to tell the tale of his miscalculations in dealing with his loyal subjects; meanwhile the Glorious Revolution installed William and Mary, who profited from the experiences of the lamented first Charles and of his unwary second son, James. The English never had serious trouble with kings again.

While the Restoration was, in one respect, an elaborate political comedy, in another it served a liberating, fertilizing purpose. Two generations of Englishmen had been deeply absorbed in religious and revolutionary dogmas; at first these were profoundly creative, finding their greatest voice in Milton; but at length the search for theological and political truth withered into sterility. History decided the issues: a united Protestant England began the long evolution to Parliamentary democracy. The giants moved off the stage, and left the shrill bickering of the pygmies. The Restoration swept away this empty aftermath to glory. A fresh wind blew across English life. Men forgot government and theology, and turned their attention to banking, commerce, building, mining coal, science, painting pictures, and writing poetry.

There has been so much nonsense written about Nell Gwyn and similar irrelevant but indelicate foibles of the time, that people forget the Restoration period (1660–1688) led to the Augustan Age in poetry and prose; the foundations of the English banking system were laid and the beginning made of British world trade; and in politics the soil was watered for the great Whig ascendancy of the eighteenth century. The last decades of the seventeenth century were rich with creative impulse in the arts, animated by scientific research, prosperous after the wars, sunny and comfortable, now that political decision, with attendant passion and fanfare, was in the past. The artist does not easily flourish in disturbance; he needs the moment of peace, to summarize the new world won on battlefield or rostrum. Shakespeare came two generations after Henry VIII broke the Church—and St. Paul's was the ripened fruit of a Revolution absorbed in time.

Indeed, Cromwell's battles were so very much won that Christopher Wren's England could cheerfully call them lost;

and this is no French paradox. In 1690 Englishmen (at least middle-class Englishmen, the poor were a different matter)— in 1690 English poets and bankers, merchants and squires took for granted, as their natural right, the political freedom, the brisk, grasping, winy hope of the future which the despised Roundheads gained in the bloody struggles of 1648. During the ensuing century far more would be won, before Frenchmen, let alone Germans or Italians or Poles or Russians, acquired the same confidence in the modern world that the British enjoyed as a matter of course in the post-Cromwell years. Genius is the flowering of an age. England in 1669 was the one country which could have produced Christopher Wren. He was scientist, engineer, practical building contractor, and artist; proud in the company of kings, passionate, tenacious, fierce, but able to compromise; in spirit serene, in imagination daring. His art was free, his style was closely disciplined by an informed and balanced intelligence. Christopher Wren was neither despairing in revolt nor servile under tyranny. He was a free-born Englishman; and the great cathedral church of St. Paul's on Ludgate Hill in London stands as a monument to that humane, enlightened happy hour in English history.

Christopher Wren's masterpiece is a cathedral by accident, a famous accident. It was not a religious age, the last half of the seventeenth century. Medieval faith had been followed by the religious controversies of the Reformation and the Revolution; the Restoration brought a general apathy. Quakers and Calvinists largely emigrated to a sterner soil; in England men were glad to conform to a Protestant state church, or forget the prickly thorns of conscience in commerce or quiet dissent. The impulse which had produced the glories of Westminster had been dead these hundreds of years.

But on September 2, 1666, the Great Fire of London broke out in Pudding Lane; on September 3 it reached Old St. Paul's, the medieval church of London. Old St. Paul's, which had been much rebuilt, had a great central tower, surmounted, until the reign of Queen Elizabeth, by the highest steeple in Christendom. I mention the steeple of Old St. Paul's because it inspired the beautiful dome of the new cathedral. Wren determined that his church should also be crowned by a landmark rising above the crowded streets of London, and, as the steeple had done for the medieval city, provide a proud focus for the modern capital of the English people. Two and a half centuries later, the citizens of London awoke each morning after the Nazi bombings and looked first to see if the dome of St. Paul's still stood on Ludgate Hill. Symbols are usually sentimental; but for more than five years the shining dome of St. Paul's spelled hope to the embattled people of London.

The Great Fire of London destroyed more than the old Cathedral; it laid waste the whole of the City. It might be thought that this catastrophe, coming immediately after the tragic outbreak of plague, would have reduced the citizens of London to despair. Not so. The age was full of vitality and bounce. The rebuilding started on the cooling ashes of the Great Fire—much to the annoyance of Christopher Wren and a number of other city planners. The artists had hoped to make a new London, with wide avenues radiating from central circles, and decorative embankments along the Thames, a city, in fact, not unlike modern Paris.

Alas, the anarchy of private enterprise defeated the architects; before they could put their schemes to Parliament, merchants were moving into new houses, shipowners were hammering up new docks, warehouses were rising where warehouses had stood before. The street plan of the modern "City" was therefore the ancient pattern of medieval London—until September, 1940. The Nazi bombers laid in ruins a great part of the City which Wren saw growing up around his half-finished Cathedral.

For many years after World War II, while city planners and real-estate moguls wrangled, visitors enjoyed "one of the most splendid views in any city—St. Paul's, from across the ruins. For two hundred and fifty years, Wren's great Cathedral was hemmed in by crowded acres of mean office buildings. Now it is free, lonely, tremendous on the dramatic skyline."

The quotation is from the earlier editions of *Here's England*. I regret to report that the real-estate barons won the battle of St. Paul's just as they did in the seventeenth century. This time the office buildings are not so much mean as they are feeble—cubes of glass, steel, and faced stone, in a limp imitation of New York's Park Avenue, or midtown Chicago.

One immense city planner's warren, called Barbican, features chunks of the old London city wall, dug up in excavations, gardens here and there, pedestrian malls, bridges spanning through-traffic routes, and a careful mix of twelve-story "towers" with four-story houses and schools. The effect is American urban renewal, not bad. But Barbican (and the rest of the bombed-out City) could have been a great park, preserving for the centuries to come the Cathedral of St. Paul's as Wren meant it to be seen.

There remain a few distant views of St. Paul's, but they will appear and disappear on the afternoon's inspection of Wren's remaining City churches.

The best way to begin with St. Paul's now is to walk around the narrow strip of park which surrounds the great Cathedral. Walking up Ludgate Hill you can study its front elevation—the double order of columns, surmounted by the twin towers. From the sides and back you can look at the mighty dome, the stately march of great windows below. You should make a complete circle of the church, peering at the ornamental detail; then up the ceremonial sweep of shallow steps, cross the portico, and enter St. Paul's by the nave.

There is no other church in Europe like this; no Italian or French architect used Renaissance in the manner of Christopher Wren. However, before we consider his personal genius, we ought to get fairly clear the idiom he was using.

What is the Renaissance style in architecture? As you walk into St. Paul's, you will make one immediate (and probably shocking) discovery: Renaissance is not the least like Gothic. After Westminster, St. Paul's hardly looks like a cathedral at all; and it is true, this is a monument to reason, not mystical faith. Gothic was dead when Wren built St. Paul's. Henry III tore down the Norman work of Edward the Confessor to make the *Early English* nave at Westminster; in exactly the same fashion, when Wren came to replace Old St. Paul's, he worked in the style which had supplanted the past.

Before Wren the Gothic style had been fading, transformed by new ideas and new needs. Tudor England, as we found at Hampton Court, evolved secular building out of Gothic church style; the Elizabethans built more palaces, elaborating, adding classic details to Gothic forms; the Jacobeans (in the time of James I, that vain and pedantic monarch with an unshakable confidence in his own supreme virtue) added more decoration and elaboration to Tudor domestication of church building. England produced its first great Renaissance architect, a man of severe and precise taste who broke completely with the medieval and brought to England from his studies abroad a new vocabulary of building. Inigo Jones roamed widely through Italy in the last years of the sixteenth and the first years of the seventeenth centuries. He studied the ruins of Rome with the eyes of a discoverer, learning a fresh conception of architecture. Like all his fellow discoverers of the Renaissance, he reinterpreted what he saw in the light of his own inheritance and prejudices. In northern Italy, in Vicenza, he was overwhelmingly convinced by the designs and proportions of that great originator Andrea Palladio, who stamped his own original idea of the classic on architecture, the Palladian motive.

Back in England in 1619, Jones built the Banqueting Hall in Whitehall, in which he introduced the Renaissance style to England, and with it, a predilection for the porticoes and purity of Palladio. Most of Jones's work has perished or has been altered out of recognition. But the Banqueting Hall remains, along with parts of the Greenwich Hospital down the Thames. Jones was the starting point for the passionate and energetic Wren, who learned from the work of his predecessor and pressed on to make English Renaissance a glory and a triumph.

Just how is Renaissance different from Gothic and its Elizabethan and Jacobean modifications? At St. Paul's you will notice striking details: Gothic is shadowed, but St. Paul's is flooded with light. Westminster is full of pointed arches and vertical lines—St. Paul's is curved and curved and curved again. Gothic is gaunt, forceful; Renaissance is graceful, using Greek orders, Roman colonnades.

This is a key to the Renaissance. As a style it originated in Italy, where Gothic in the French and English variations never fully developed. In the fifteenth-century Revival of Learning —in that sudden and wonderful Italian flowering—Florentine architects discovered the technical treatises of their Roman predecessors. Classical orders were "revived" and symmetry became for the architect both aim and ideal. I put "revived" in quotation marks because it would be wrong to think that the new Italian architects slavishly imitated the past.

There is perhaps a superficial similarity between Michelangelo's designs for St. Peter's and antique Rome, just as there appears in St. Paul's an echo of the Ancient World. But only superficial, only an echo. The Florentines rediscovered yet thoroughly misunderstood Roman building techniques, Roman rules of ordering space; and armed with new vision, they developed a new philosophy of building.

I am always impatient with writers on architecture, because they keep talking about "ordering of space" which cannot be supposed to make sense to somebody not in their line of work. However, now that I get down to writing about St. Paul's, I see it is not so easy to remark on Wren's ideas without a fancy language. Take "ordering of space." When Henry III (or the stone masons he directed) planned Westminster, Henry did not think of the area of the nave as space or how to fill it, surround it, and divide it. He may have had a dim notion of what we call symmetry, but it is unlikely. Henry wanted a large number of bays—pillars surmounted by arches, in his case, pointed arches—because the longer the nave, the grander the Cathedral and the more honor to St. Edward. He wanted a high roof, to let in light through the raised triforium and clerestory; and because the higher the roof, the more impressive the building. The Westminster nave is as long as Henry had money to build; the proportions between the Westminster nave and the choir and transepts are haphazard, rule of thumb; chapels and shrines at Westminster were simply added on to the existing building. Henry and his Gothic followers had no interest in balance, or in proportion between one part of a building and another; the shape of a cross was a symbol, a religious convention, rather than an architect's choice of design.

When Renaissance architects set out to design a building, they thought first of the space it was going to occupy; Wren planned the height of his roof in proportion to the width of nave and choir and transepts. In fact, Wren did not want a long nave at all; his original design for St. Paul's was in the shape of a Greek cross—equal arms, with the great dome in the center of his building. This would have been a logical, symmetrical way of using the space St. Paul's was to occupy; however, in the seventeenth century, as now and earlier, architects must make concessions to backward clients. In this case, the Bishop of

London and his Cathedral Chapter bitterly protested; a cathedral wasn't a cathedral, in their opinion, if it did not have a long nave, shorter transepts, and a choir. Wren argued, but he had to give in. As a Renaissance architect, he was faced with problems Henry III blithely ignored. How could a long nave be used in a harmonious, symmetrical composition with choir and transepts? Wren solved this—as you can see if you look closely—by cheating the eye, diminishing the seeming length of the nave at St. Paul's by a succession of shallow saucer domes above the ordered pillars. The effect is to slow down space, divide it, make it hesitate, until it is breathtakingly joined in the choir and transepts by the great central dome. This dome unites all the space in St. Paul's; it is the heart of the whole building, and it unifies transepts, choir, and nave—as they never are united in Gothic.

Another illustration of Renaissance, and its approach to space: Wren had to determine how high the dome should be in proportion to the length of nave, the size of the transepts and the choir. If it was too low, it could not unite the building; if it was too high, it would rise out of sight, and make a sort of a cavern where there ought to be a grand central focus. It was easy enough (for Wren) to decide on the height of the dome; but what about such a dome as the great landmark of London City? Wren's ideal inside dome would result in a flattish mushroom when seen from the outside; it would be hardly visible from the foot of Ludgate Hill, let alone for miles. Yet he could not put a steeple on top of a dome, and Wren needed a dome for the interior of his Cathedral. A nice problem, and Wren's solution of it was brilliant.

It is ironic that the dome of St. Paul's is sometimes derided as a fake—as though Wren could not have spanned his interior with any elevation of dome he chose to design! There are two domes at St. Paul's because the lower inside dome is the correct and felicitous height needed to adorn and unite the several parts of the interior Cathedral; and the magnificent outer dome rises 365 feet above Ludgate Hill to dominate all of London. The engineering problems involved in imposing one dome over the other were greater than the problem of elevating a single dome to no matter what dizzy heights. Wren had to find radiant light for the interior crossing of his Cathedral; yet the inside dome was to be covered over completely. The huge outer dome—how was it to be supported? Where was its immense weight to rest?

Fortunately Wren was not only a great artist, he was also the most expert building engineer in seventeenth-century Europe. His ingenious solution of the engineering difficulties of a double dome still awes modern building engineers who can solve their problems in structural steel. Wren's building materials—stone, wood, lead, masonry-filled rubble—were no different from Henry III's at Westminster. But another great difference between Gothic and Renaissance is that medieval architects worked almost without benefit of mathematics. They could not calculate the exact weight of a roof, and how this weight would be distributed—thus the massive pillars in the Westminster nave, capable of bearing twice the weight they support. Again, twelfth- and thirteenth-century monks could not resist the intoxicating notion of a beautiful central tower (preferably bigger and more beautiful than the next cathedral's) over the crossing of their splendid naves and glorious choirs. Throwing caution to the winds, and having no idea of what would now be high-school dynamics, they ran up a whole series of exquisite stone towers—which fell down ten or fifty or seventy years later. Half the cathedrals of England have an X Marks the Spot of one of these miscalculations; the distribution of stresses on an immense hollow square pile of stone is a delicate problem; Newton helped solve it. It must have been exciting being a medieval architect. You never knew; and the monks were ready to try anything once or even twice.

Between the dismal collapse of the Gothic towers in England and the building of the dome of St. Paul's, modern mathematics was born. Galileo and Newton invented a new kind of approach to the physical world, and Renaissance architects in Italy were able to calculate, with increasing precision, the stresses and strains of their pillars and domes. It was characteristic of the seventeenth century that Wren himself was a great mathematician before he ever turned to architecture at all. He held two chairs of astronomy (at Gresham College, London, and at Oxford) before he was thirty. He first attracted the attention of Charles II by his brilliant contributions to the Royal Society. (Charles II, between gallantries, was a talented amateur astronomer fascinated by scientific experiment.)

Wren's massive dome on St. Paul's was not put up by guess-work; algebraic formulae, not medieval faith, inspired this triumph of engineering and art. If you have the physical energy, you can climb to the roof of St. Paul's and examine the cunning hidden pillars which bear the weight of the outer dome; on the inside you may see the graceful windows which light the cathedral crossing, and appear, on the outside, as part of the handsome decoration on the base of the outer dome. An erudite but not athletic friend (he got his training during elevator strikes and power failures in New York City) reports the climb to the Golden Gallery, which circles the very top of the dome, is definitely worth the 426 steps. Not only can you inspect, with satisfaction, Wren's architecture, but the views are superb.

Of course, the double dome is not the only ingenious engineering idea at St. Paul's. You need only crane your neck to ask yourself, why does the Wren Cathedral look so different, on the outside, from a medieval church? English Gothic is built on two levels; as a rule a high narrow roof in the middle is flanked by two sloping lower roofs on each side. This rather homely, barnlike arrangement existed because medieval architects could not span a wide roof. The massive double row of pillars of Westminster run up the narrow central area of the nave; the clerestory and triforium rise above the pillars to light this middle aisle, and then comes the lofty roof. On the right and left of the center nave are two very much lower aisles; their steeply pitched roofs are seen from the outside. *Early English* windows (to a lesser extent—more with *Decorated* and *Perpendicular*) pierced the solid walls of the Cathedral and so weakened the support the walls might (as in *Norman*) have given the room. Therefore the walls are strengthened—propped up—by the buttresses, so characteristic of Gothic architecture.

As you examine the exterior of St. Paul's, you will notice that the walls rise straight to the lofty elevation of the towers and dome. You see no roof, let alone three of different heights. These nobly proportioned, unbroken, rising walls give the Cathedral its imposing grandeur.

Walk back into the nave, and the design is Westminster's—here a lofty center aisle and on each side lower aisles lit by immense windows. Pillars march up the center of St. Paul's nave, as they do at the Abbey. They are Renaissance pillars, but the

idea is the same. In effect, St. Paul's is Renaissance on the outside and, in its arrangement in the nave, medieval on the inside. How is this possible? Where are the flying buttresses to
prop up the window-pierced walls?

You will recall the Court and Cathedral Chapter of St. Paul's
insisted on an old-fashioned medieval nave. They were willing
to have a dome (St. Peter's in Rome had made domes fashionable), but they were not willing to have the rest of Wren's
original design, which they considered new-fangled, if not
dangerous to public morals. If you examine the beautiful model
Wren built in 1673, you will see that he conceived the new St.
Paul's shaped as a Greek cross, with four equal-length halls
leading into the center circular area under the dome. A hall
has a flat roof across its whole area instead of a lofty narrow
center aisle flanked by lower aisles. In vain Wren argued that,
unlike the architects of Westminster, he was perfectly capable
of spanning any-sized roof; his clients were not interested in
structural engineering, and were shocked when it was suggested that Gothic design grew out of an imperfect ability to
put a roof across large areas. So far as the Cathedral Chapter
was concerned, a church was not a church unless it had a nave,
and a nave had a high center aisle and lower right and left ones.

Wren gave in; the nave at St. Paul's is designed in what Sir
Christopher scornfully called "Gothick." But he was no mean
fighter; because he was forced to a Renaissance version of
Westminster for the interior, that was no reason for making
the exterior of his beautiful building look like a hay barn! Yet
the problem was difficult. He needed buttresses for the medieval nave, and how could he have buttresses without breaking
the smooth lines of the outer walls? How could he have an
unbroken outer wall when he had these low aisles on either side
of the high middle aisle?

Wren turned this problem over for several years. Work on
the choir of the new building had been long in progress before
the architect developed the major aspects of the Cathedral's
design.

If you look closely at the outer walls of St. Paul's, you will
see the great windows of the nave. Above, the graceful design
of these windows is repeated in another row of, not windows,
but blank stone niches. If you go up on the roof (or comfortably

examine an air-view of the Cathedral), you will see that the whole top half of the outer walls of St. Paul's is a mask— a fake, if you like—to conceal the shape of the interior nave. Behind those smooth, unbroken walls rising to the dome and towers are the roofs of the low-pitched outer nave aisles, and the higher center nave aisle. In fact, the Renaissance walls of St. Paul's completely cover up the medieval interior.

But Wren's work, like that of all great architects, modern or otherwise, was always functional. The outer walls of St. Paul's are an effective screen for the medieval nave; they are also but- tresses. An air photograph of St. Paul's will show you the stone bridges Wren built from the solid outer walls to the piers of the nave. The Renaissance walls of St. Paul's are a cunning piece of modern engineering. The calculation of the stresses from the nave on the outer walls is a neat problem to tease the minds and challenge the learning of any modern scholar.

The design for St. Paul's illustrates the difference between medieval and Renaissance architecture; the manner of its building indicates the chasm between thirteenth- and seven- teenth-century England. St. Paul's was designed and built by one man in forty-three years; the medieval world created its masterpieces, the abbeys and cathedrals, over many genera- tions. Westminster cost the wealth of the English Crown and the English nation; but if the serfs groaned under the weight of taxes, if city artisans paid for Westminster with the rags off their backs, they did not complain.

The situation was different in 1675. It was all very well to have a new cathedral—everyone was agreed that Old St. Paul's had to be replaced. Civic pride, more than religious fervor, animated the decision. The great City of London without a cathedral of its own? Westminster was only an Abbey, not the seat of a bishop, and if York and Lincoln and a village like Wells could boast mighty cathedrals, not to speak of Paris with its Notre Dame, London must certainly have a cathedral worthy of its position as capital of England and, more or less, of the world.

Who was going to pay for it? That was a very different ques- tion. The Cathedral Chapter could not raise the cash by tithes (church taxes, that is to say); the faithful of the seventeenth century already grumbled their heads off about supporting a few fox-hunting clergymen, let alone paying for a full-sized cathedral. The merchants of London declined the honor of building St. Paul's to the Glory of God and the good of their immortal souls. Charles II, unlike his revered ancestor Henry III, was bankrupt, and every time he asked Parliament for some small sum to support an aging relative or to build a new palace at Greenwich, there was ominous talk about how little a Cromwell had cost compared to a king. Parliament balked outright at building St. Paul's from the public treasury. Squander taxes on a cathedral? Politicians shuddered.

Things had changed in England when it came to cathedrals. Westminster rose in the midst of an impoverished, primitive, agricultural people, counted in handfuls; in 1675 a large, prosperous city of merchants and bankers could not see its way to afford a new cathedral. "Very expensive proposition," everybody said; people shook their heads, and looked grave when St. Paul's was mentioned. Then some genius of government finance thought up the levy on sea-borne coal. In the days before railroads and highways, London's coal arrived in coastal sailing ships—why not a tax on every ton brought into the Pool? St. Paul's was built on the coals from Newcastle, and the magnificent towers and domes are a measure of the growing prosperity of seventeenth-century London. It might be added that Parliament, dazzled by its success with the coal tax, handed over the cash for St. Paul's with the greatest reluctance, and tried to cheat Wren out of part of his architect's fee. No client likes to pay an architect, and Wren, in the immemorial tradition of all building contractors, had spent four or five times the amount of his original estimates. It made Parliament's blood boil, the way Wren threw around other people's money! Stone carvings, domes—what next? In the end (like most clients) Parliament paid for the carvings and the architect, and after the shock wore off, all England proudly rejoiced in its incomparable new cathedral.

St. Paul's was—and is—without compare. The design is unique. Wren composed in the Renaissance style, but his great work is original and personal. Forced to the Gothick for his nave, Wren contrived to make a triumph of his difficulty—. the succession of saucer domes and grouped pillars gives nobility to the whole of the interior. His inner central dome makes a solemn and imposing focus for the Cathedral, and the magnificent outer dome crowns the whole composition. Two lovely *Baroque* towers are skillfully used to surmount the severe classic orders of the front elevation. (*Baroque* followed *Renaissance*; it interrupted the severe antique symmetry with broken curves, allowing light and shadow to play across bare surfaces.) Above all, Wren's display of virtuosity in stone never forgot the fundamentals: St. Paul's rises on the summit of Ludgate Hill, perfectly proportioned to its site, so exquisitely fitted to its space that the eye cannot conceive it a foot longer, shorter, wider, higher. Old St. Paul's was considerably longer, its transepts wider, its roofs lower. Wren had another of his tremendous struggles on the size of his design. That battle he won, perhaps because even a client could see that Wren's St. Paul's belonged on Ludgate Hill.

The master design for St. Paul's is unique; the smallest details are carefully studied and exquisitely executed. Between making blueprints for palaces and hospitals, City churches and Cathedral, Wren also gathered together on Ludgate Hill Europe's finest stone cutters and woodcarvers, masons and sculptors. At first he hunted his talent in France and Italy, but during the thirty-six years St. Paul's was building, Wren trained a whole generation of English artists. The modern tradition of English craftsmanship had its origins on the scaffolds and ladders of London's new Cathedral. Wren's designs for the low, restrained bas-relief on the outside of St. Paul's required stone carvers of the greatest skill; his *Baroque* towers demanded the artist stone cutter. There was always a place at St. Paul's for a talented young English lad, and Wren took pride in his cathedral "graduates" as they went out from Ludgate Hill to tutor the taste, ornament the buildings, and delight the eye of a whole nation. If you journey around England, you will see the work of half a dozen great craftsmen, trained at St. Paul's. Grinling Gibbons did the handsome carvings at Windsor Castle —and the choir stalls at the Cathedral. Christopher Kempster, Samuel Fulkes, Edward Pearce, Thomas Wise, Jonathan Maine learned *Renaissance* and *Baroque* from the great master Wren, and within a generation were transforming the Tudor mansions of the new Whig rulers into the eighteenth-century "stately homes" of England. St. Paul's made a revolution in English taste and design. The delightful style called *Georgian* (echoed in our American "New England" and "Southern Colonial") grew directly out of St. Paul's. Sir Christopher Wren was father both of Bath and the White House in Washington, D.C.— grandfather is probably more exact—but the style developed directly, without pause, from St. Paul's in 1716 to its corruption into *Regency,* a hundred years later.

The Cathedral Church of St. Paul's is a building of the greatest importance; it is history, architecture, drama. Although I have forsworn remarks of this kind, I cannot resist adding that surely one of the greatest moments of your journey to England will be on the day you walk into the nave of London's Cathedral, and look upon what Sir Christopher Wren made, not so much for the Glory of God, but more for the Triumph of Man.

Wren's City Churches

Within the walls of medieval London City, crowded into the narrow lanes, often two or three in the same short block, stood ninety-seven churches. Even allowing for the Heaven-oriented society of the period, ninety-seven seems an uncommon number of churches for something less than a square mile. But there was a reason for all those St. Mary's and St. Dunstan's.

To begin with, a few of the City's ninety-seven churches were homely parish affairs, convenient for morning mass and prayers at evensong. Most of the City's churches, however, were built by London's livery companies, called "guilds" in other parts of Christendom. You will recall dimly, from high-school history books or *Die Meistersinger,* guilds were associations of merchants, or bankers, or craftsmen of endless variety—fishmongers, goldsmiths, vintners, all that sort of thing.

But why livery companies in London, not guilds? Because Edward III was wily. In France, Italy, Germany, and the Lowlands, guilds cornered the gold bullion, the spices, the salted fish, the wine, the armor, anything a medieval king might have in mind. Smug behind their city walls, the guilds drove cruel bargains with tattered majesties of a dozen different kingdoms.

By 1350, Edward III was feeling rather tattered himself. He had just started the Hundred Years' War, with the glorious victory at Crécy, won by his son, the glorious Black Prince. But, as everyone knows, victories, especially of the glorious variety, are very expensive. Edward III brooded over those rich, rich guilds in London City. One would think that true-born Englishmen, even if lowly, would take more of an interest in glorious victory. But no. They did not seem to care.

Edward III pondered. (Or someone on his staff pondered; one never knows with kings and presidents.) The first half of the fourteenth century, before the Black Death struck, was a period of pomp and gauds. Earls swanked about with rubies sewed to their velvet shoes, and even underwear. But those London burghers—it was bad enough to *be* lowly, without *looking* the part, too.

So Edward III chartered the guilds, and dubbed them, from that day forward, His Majesty's Liveried Companies. Each of the new liveried companies was graciously permitted an ornate coat-of-arms, suitably embroidered on gold cloth, with plenty of costly fringe, should they wish to pay for it. (They did.) Members of the companies had the King's assent to distinctive uniforms—thus "livery"—something really eye-popping for use "on ceremonial occasions."

His Majesty's Liveried Companies did not start handing over gold bullion by the fistfuls to Edward III. Fishmongers still wanted cash for their fish. But on the other hand, English monarchs never had real guild trouble again. Across the Channel, guilds were starting uprisings and foreclosing crown jewels—shocking deeds. In London, the liveried companies paraded in outfits to make an earl look drab; and they put up, or took over, most of the City's ninety-seven churches, in order to hang their glorious gold-fringed banners over their own altars.

The City churches were destroyed by the Great Fire. The liveried companies had long since withered into ceremonial marching societies. Of the ninety-seven medieval churches, only fifty-one were rebuilt after the fire—by Wren himself, who, during the same years he created St. Paul's, designed and watched over the smallest details of his new City churches. Each was different, each cunningly fitted to its small, often awkwardly shaped site, each adorned with lantern, spire, bell tower, even dome, and each echoed one or another of the themes of St. Paul's. Yet the sum of these Wren churches was not the soaring grandeur of St. Paul's. These little churches were very light, graceful, even fanciful—happy.

In September, 1940, the Nazi bombers destroyed Wren's City churches. Or so I thought, walking in the ruins from 1947 to 1955. But I underestimated Englishmen or, more exactly, Wren-ites. Between fighting off fire bombs on the roof of St. Paul's and digging out victims from rubble, the London City air-raid wardens and their valiant crews, aged under seventeen or over fifty, saved what they could of Wren's City churches. They spent weeks patiently dismantling a sagging lantern tower, or cautiously, carefully, taking down the spire precariously bal-anced on a broken stairway. They sifted the ruins, foot by square foot, unearthing a smoke-charred pulpit in one church, an exquisitely carved pillar from another. The stones were num-bered, packed up in weather-proof cases, and lowered into the church crypts. No wonder that, for a time, the ruins looked so desolate—so total.

Today, there are eleven towers, free-standing, and forty City churches, thirty-nine of them in the immediate neighborhood of St. Paul's. St. Mary Aldermanbury, however, was shipped to the State of Missouri, United States of America, to mark the very spot where Winston Churchill made his "iron curtain" speech. The reconstruction of St. Mary's is said to be quite good.

Thirty-nine churches and eleven towers sound a formidable program for one afternoon. In fact, the surviving Wren churches are delightful, and easy. Many of them have charming small gardens, formerly churchyards, where you may sit down, listen to lunch-hour concerts, eat a sandwich, and admire Wren's façades, spires, lanterns, and bell towers.

For this foray into the ghost of Wren's City, arm yourself with the latest information, either from the British Travel Asso-ciation, or for sale at the literature stand in St. Paul's. The thirty-nine churches are sometimes open, sometimes closed to visitors. Concert schedules change from month to month.

Everyone has his own favorites among the saved, restored, or rebuilt Wren masterpieces. I like the tower and steeple of Christ Church, on Newgate Street, both for the elegance of its diminishing stone turrets, and because it affords a splendid view of St. Paul's.

The view from the simple—but very subtle—tower and steeple of St. Vedast-Alias-Foster, on Foster Lane, is another superb frame for St. Paul's. St. Vedast itself is more rebuilt than restored, but it shelters several rescued splendors, the organ, the pulpit, and the baptismal font, from other Wren churches. Then there is the interesting point—why "Alias"?

St. Vedast was originally a Bishop of Arras, in a period when being a bishop was an extremely hazardous occupation, especially in northern France. After some years of fleeing the blood-thirsty heathen, Bishop Vedast managed to turn the tables in A.D. 540 and baptize Clovis, Emperor of the Franks, for which feat of faith and valor he was promoted to Saint.

Nothing much happened to St. Vedast between 540 and the late twelfth century, when a pride of international bankers happened to locate at Arras. They took St. Vedast along with them when they went over to London City to do a little inter-national business: coin clipping, increasing the base metal in the gold bullion mix, and foreclosing mortgages. They needed a reliable saint.

The bankers went away, but St. Vedast had settled in, on Vedast Lane. The only trouble with this imported saint—his name was Latin, probably for some rude Germanic original. It certainly did not come trippingly to honest English tongues. So, after a few decades, Vedast became Vastes; another century, and he was Faster, then Faister, Fuaster, and finally, St. Foster, on Foster Lane.

At this point some spoilsport pedant, newly appointed to the parish, reversed the whole process, to the bewilderment of the faithful, who supposed the priest had changed saints on them. Thus, St. Vedast-Alias-Foster, on Foster Lane.

The French are not nearly so blunt. Across the Channel, in Arras itself, is an eighteenth-century cloister, heavily restored, and now a museum. It is the Abbey of St. Vaast—Vedast again, with his name slipping.

St. Vedast-Alias-Foster is, I think, a very satisfactory experience, from every point of view; but all of the thirty-nine standing City churches are encrusted with history, a sense of time, past, present, and continuing, and, even though London's traffic and new office buildings are only a few steps away—a tranquil beauty. Together, they make a smiling valedictory for Sir Christopher Wren, the genius of St. Paul's.

Next Day: Whipsnade Zoo

I realize this sounds something like looping the loop; from Hampton Court to St. Paul's to a zoo! Unorthodox; none of our guidebook colleagues recommends spacing out cathedrals with tigers. The Baedeker gentry are professionals; flying buttresses and Baroque towers are their regular line of work. They don't mind how many churches they see, one right after the other. But the tourist is strictly an amateur, and Richard and I are one hundred percent tourists. After all, your journey to England is a pleasure trip, and surfeit can set in, after too much architecture at one fell swoop.

We hope you will ask your hotel porter to look up the time schedule for the Whipsnade Zoo bus. While you are jolting comfortably along, you can digest your first few days in London. You have worked your way up from Londinium through William the Conqueror to George III, a lot of history in a short time, and naturally you feel a little queasy. You are afraid you have lost your grip on Norman dogtooth while peering at Renaissance bas-relief. Be calm, and allow yourself to lie fallow on the sleepy trip to Whipsnade. From now on, what you see will begin to make sense, fall into a pattern. Don't worry if you forget the technical names for this or that kind of Gothic, or get sadly lost in the Wars of the Roses. Flip the pages of this book over to the charts for first aid on *Decorated* or Edward III, and for the rest, use Hampton Court and St. John's Chapel and so on as your touchstones or yardsticks. Most of your second week in London, your whole trip in England, for that matter, will fit into the framework of your first week's sightseeing. You will find pleasure in telling some backward fellow traveler that the Lord Mayor's Mansion House is eighteenth-century Renaissance; Windsor Castle is one part Norman and two-fifths late *Perpendicular*. The reason we have explored Norman and Renaissance and Tudor in such considerable detail is that we hoped to make your first week in England a profitable introduction to the rest of your journey. From now on we shall assume you are old-hat when it comes to Richard II and James I and Henry VII, and we plan to bounce rapidly about from Frederick Prince of Wales to John of Gaunt, and back again.

Why a zoo on a trip to England? There are a lot of zoos in the United States—you may even live around the corner from one. Is this a waste of time? you inquire of yourself. (Tourists always worry about wasting their time; it is a universal neurosis. I suffer from it constantly.)

But Whipsnade is not a waste of time; it is delightful and enchanting. You walk down a quiet country lane and presently you come to a green English meadow, peaceful under the drowsy sun. In the middle of this meadow is a large rhinoceros, browsing—where one would expect a horse or a cow. If you whistle at the rhino, he comes over to the fence and looks at you, thoughtfully.

Or you stop to admire a silvery pond, blue-green, with smooth banks of thick English turf. You think poetic thoughts. You sigh. Ah, England! How peaceful! At this point two seals appear, barking at each other.

Or you see, in the distance, an immense oak tree, its spreading branches shading a pastoral glade. The scenery is suitable for Robin Hood, or village maidens tripping around in the dewy English morn. Close up, the oak tree is found to be inhabited by a large number of monkeys, which perform dizzy aerial acrobatics in the middle of the staid countryside.

The giraffes at Whipsnade are put out to pasture like sheep. You take a turning in the road, and there are a lot of giraffes, munching treetops and peering down at passersby. The hippopotamus lives in a field; he looks queer, gamboling around in the sunshine. He gambols in a stately way, shaking one immense paw after the other. The tigers and other more uninhibited beasts live in caves; they like caves. The elephants, intelligent pachyderms, practically have the run of Whipsnade. They go to bed in comfortable barns, but in the daytime they fool around in their big yard—or sometimes they have to work, trotting children up and down for rides.

I am not sure if I have suggested the astonishing, delightful quality of Whipsnade; it makes me laugh to remember that rhinoceros, idling in an English meadow. The scenery is charming, but expected: meadows and fences and lakes and spreading oak trees. It looks like the poet's standard version; but where there should be the local squire chewing on a straw, the zebras graze; sheep do not dot the peaceful hillside —those are water buffaloes; and in the meadow where Old Dobbin could safely be expected to browse, there browses the savage rhino.

The animals add to the enchantment. They seem easy in their minds, relaxed, and good-natured. There was an ostrich at Whipsnade the last time we visited the place, and he was giving his mating call. It sounded like a tuba player gone mad with sorrow. That is the kind of thing I mean. I never heard an ostrich in a regular zoo give any mating call; this one kept turning bright purple in the neck, after which he deafened everybody for miles with his raucous appeal for love.

What to Do with
a British Sunday

Out of every seven days in London, one is a British Sunday. Frenchmen go all to pieces over a Sunday in Britain. Italians think it must be the Revolution, or at least a general strike. Even the Swiss suspect Doomsday. No other nation in Europe shuts up on Sundays. But for Americans the situation is about the same as New York City, Des Moines, Iowa, or Pittsburgh. Most of the standard tourist sights are closed in London, so are the better restaurants. The movies open late Sunday afternoons as a special concession to the wicked of the metropolis.

What can you do (the standard question of all British visitors since Prince Albert) on Sunday in London? Be of good cheer. You can walk in Kensington Gardens and Hyde Park in the morning, which is delightful. If it is a nice day, the little boys will be sailing their boats on the Round Pond in Kensington Gardens, and the babies' prams will be crowded around the Peter Pan statue—all as you have read so often.

Or you could hear the glorious choirs at either Westminster or St. Paul's. No sightseeing is allowed during the frequent Sunday services, but the music is superb, and the setting is without compare. Be sure to find out the hours of the main morning service (ask your hotel porter), and be there well in advance.

You can take a Sunday-morning walk along the Thames in Chelsea, and explore the winding, narrow back streets. Every fifth house or so is marked with a plaque: Carlyle lived here— or Oscar Wilde or Whistler or Rossetti. The row of houses in Cheyne Walk on the Chelsea Embankment is considered the best example of *Georgian* architecture in London, and is full of historic overtones. Charles II's Queen was supposed to have lived here (she didn't); Rossetti, however, definitely kept his animal collection in the back garden, and George Eliot came to Cheyne Walk before she died.

The Royal Hospital is Chelsea's most famous exhibit. I think it is one of Wren's masterpieces, and its setting, overlooking green gardens and the river, is lovely. The Pensioners, natty old gentlemen rather aggressively quaint in their traditional Red Coats, will show you around the *Doric* porticoes and handsome entrance hall. A minor point: some tourists, discovering that the pensioners are by no means charity cases, but appointed to the Royal Hospital as a great honor and reward for long and faithful Army service, make the mistake of supposing that pensioner guides do not expect tips. They do. All the tips from sightseers are pooled at the end of the year to provide handsome toys for crippled children in the nearby hospital, and it is a matter of honor among the pensioners to be able to turn in a rich haul for the Christmas fête.

At two-thirty, the British Museum.

The British Museum, guidebooks state firmly, is "unrivaled in all the world for the richness of its contents."

We begin with fundamentals and work our way up to superlatives.

Question: What is the British Museum? An art gallery? A library?

Answer: The British Museum was, and probably is, the most famous and important library in the world.

The British Museum is also an art gallery. It has "unrivaled" collections of sculpture, ceramics, drawings, and paintings of the Egyptians, Assyrians, Babylonians, Persians, Greeks, Romans, Normans, Franks, Africans, Chinese, Japanese, Indians, and many other peoples. It has also incomparable collections of Italian drawings (Leonardo, for one), English prints, woodcuts and etchings, French cartoons, medieval jewelry.

The British Museum is the most famous and important museum of archaeological studies anywhere. Its collections of prehistoric relics are—I grope for the *mot juste*—unrivaled.

The Manuscript Room at the British Museum has the most famous and important collection of English documents, *Beowulf*, *Magna Carta*, *Paradise Lost* in the orginal manuscript—to give you an idea.

The British Museum has unrivaled collections of early printed books, music manuscripts, ancient maps, Oriental religious objects, postage stamps. In the manuscript division, it has the first copy of the New Testament in Greek. In the world of archaeology there is the Rosetta Stone, which gave scholars the key to Egyptian hieroglyphics; in the art collection, the Elgin Marbles. As to the library, there are more than six million volumes—all of them catalogued and ready to be used or examined, an important point. Moreover, not only is the British Museum one of the two largest libraries in the world (the Bibliothèque Nationale in Paris is about the same size, the Library of Congress is third), but the collections are various, rare, and important—in every language, not merely English.

Yet I have not really answered, nor in the larger sense, the question: What is the British Museum?

The British Museum is more—much more—than the sum of its "unrivaled" treasures. It is a living, breathing monument to the character of the Englishman. His curiosity: Englishmen in Victorian frock coats and shovel beards, carrying umbrellas, Englishmen in eighteenth-century powdered wigs, English ladies in respectable divided skirts, riding camels across Wildest Araby, pursued relics and manuscrips with hair-raising devotion to their personally appointed missions. No government commission sent these English collectors out into the obscure corners of the world; no Rockefeller paid for an expedition. Curiosity, for an Englishman an itch as great as Destiny, brought many of the British Museum collections home to London.

Or take the Englishman's learning—refined, yet thumpingly vigorous; original, daring, and determined. For three hundred years English scholars have contributed their trophies and their knowledge to make the British Museum the repository of fact beyond the dreams of any university, library, or museum in the world.

Or the Englishman's impassioned love of art. Here in the British Museum are collections of what Englishmen thought was so beautiful they were prepared to spend their fortunes on it, risk their lives to save it, break their health to bring it home, to the British Museum.

Bring it home. Cynics make snide comments on the British Museum. The finest collection of Greek art in the world is here, not in Athens; the most beautiful Chinese vases, not in Peking; the Rosetta Stone in the British Museum, not Cairo. And so on. The list is long. I used to feel it was shocking the way Englishmen looted half the world to fill the British Museum—until I looked at some of the "loot." In the first place, it was not really loot, not in the sense that the Louvre is filled with Italian pictures which Napoleon took. The Elgin Marbles were purchased by Lord Elgin—from the Turkish government. Nobody wanted the Elgin Marbles—not at the time. People (in Athens) thought Lord Elgin was off his head—what did he want with a lot of broken stones from the Parthenon? Englishmen are crazy. The reason Lord Elgin was moved to lay so much cash on the line, in such a hurry, was that the Greeks were having a local war. The Turks had already shelled the Parthenon twice, and threatened to do so again. It was now or never for what little was left of one of the most exquisite works of art in human history. If Lord Elgin had not "looted" the Elgin Marbles, there would be no such marbles today, either in the British Museum or in Athens.

What is true of the Elgin Marbles is true of the Rosetta Stone and most of the other collections of the British Museum. Maybe the men in Cairo feel wistful now about the Rosetta Stone, but when Englishmen transported it, eighty years ago, nobody wanted the trouble of carting it around: too heavy.

I cannot help admiring the Englishmen who ranged the world, a hundred years ago, poking their noses into Chinese hill towns, digging away at Egyptian pyramids, lugging around Greek marbles, hunting Etruscan cooking pots, turning up (to the shock of the natives) in Abyssinia and Tibet, hot on the scent of a fine Bronze Age hatchet or a fourth-century Oriental reed pipe. Half the knowledge we have today of the remote, and not so remote, past we owe to Englishmen pursuing exhibits for the British Museum. If the English shut their treasures up, or carelessly let them go moldy in some obscure shed, one might carp over the trophy hunting of the past. But the British Museum is open to all; the races of the world assemble here to study, admire, and be ravished by joy. To my mind, the British Museum is one of the greatest instances of good luck that has ever happened to civilization: under one roof are assembled the treasures of the past. All you have to do, whether you are from Tibet or Council Bluffs, is to check your umbrella—and you can either see the first manuscript in Greek of the New Testament, that fourth-century musical instrument, or a reconstructed Etruscan hill tomb.

What is the best way for tourists to tackle the British Museum? I take it for granted you are not a tremendous scholar. Scholars take a taxi direct from customs to the British Museum, head like nervous homing pigeons to the Nereid Room or the Bronze Age exhibits, and board the airplane six weeks later, tired but happy. The tourist has to sample and choose, lurch from the early Greeks to the later Romans to Shakespeare; I say lurch advisedly. Having demonstrated my endless admiration and affection for the British Museum, I may surely be permitted to say it has the hardest marble floors in history. It has always been my dearest dream to go through the Museum in a rubber-tired wheelchair, pushed by some stout and willing attendant.

In lieu of wheelchairs, I suggest a catalogue and caution. The best way to tackle any museum, let alone the British, is to invest in a catalogue at the entrance gate, read over the list of treasures, select enough targets for an hour or two of sightseeing, get out the map, take your bearings, and head straight for the Blake drawings or the *Codex Sinaiticus*. If you dawdle about at random, you will not have enough strength left for the Rosetta Stone or the Chinese vases. Most museums have dead spots you can pass up—even the National Gallery, a magnificent collection of major items. But the British Museum is difficult. Everything is fascinating, even the Assyrians. I hardly know what to suggest for one brief afternoon.

If I had only one afternoon, or two, I think I would see the Elgin Marbles, first of all; then the Chinese vases and the Japanese paintings; and then the Manuscript Room and the Early Printed Books. (With maybe a quick look at the Rosetta Stone and Roman jewelry on the way past.) This is rather more than a two-hour program, but tourists must have stamina, and you can always go to the movies afterward.

The City

LONDON, I remarked farther back, is a collection of medieval towns, strung together along the banks of the Thames. You have spent your first week in London peering at the World-Famous Super-Sights, from Westminster to the Tower to the City and back again. The time has come, get out the map, put on stout walking boots, seize cane or furled umbrella, and set out to explore London itself, the most intricate, various, and fascinating metropolis in the world.

The first item on your agenda should surely be the City. I feel nervous writing about London. The natives are not merely born (or attached by loving habit) to London—they are passionate citizens of Chelsea, or Hampstead, or Regent's Park, or Mayfair. They write books, hundreds of books, about side alleys in Stepney, or *The Curious History of Oxford Street*. I would not say the true Londoner is tolerant, either. People get bitter if they discover you are wasting time on Kew Gardens, when you ought to be admiring Bloomsbury. When we started to collect material for this book, we innocently broached the subject at a polite dinner party. People who were capable of chatting mildly about the atom bomb or Whither Germany, began to snarl. One lady said flatly that if we did not tell American tourists to spend three days in Hampstead as an absolute minimum, we were out of our minds, and probably ought to be suppressed.

"Hampstead!" bawled a lawyer at the foot of the table. "My dear, I don't say that if a traveler has all the time in the world, say six months, he shouldn't take an afternoon for Hampstead. But the Regency terraces overlooking the Park . . ."

"Dockland!" somebody roared.

". . . and Knightsbridge played a very curious role in the fourteenth century. It seems that Edward the Third . . ."

People split up into small, narrow-eyed groups; solidarity broke out between Bloomsbury and Regent's Park, but Dockland and Hampstead were lone wolves and went home early, quivering. If we took all the suggestions offered by that one small company of Londoners, we would have a brisk program for the American tourist of approximately ninety-two days, and all of it Shank's pony. As for the literature on the subject, it would take three years to read the standard, unexotic books on London, and Heaven knows how many decades to peruse the specialist publications such as *Chelsea in the Nineteenth Century* or *Chaucer's London* (with maps).

Be of good cheer. You will probably miss the side alleys of Stepney and the finer points of Oxford Street, but you can see solid chunks of London in a week, if you put your mind to it;

and we suggest beginning with a two-day foray into the City, because every Londoner is agreed that from Temple Bar to Aldgate is Fundamental.

After a quiet, relaxing Sunday nosing around the British Museum, we are off to Smithfield by . . . taxi. I realize it is cowardly not to recommend the Underground, but frankly, the last time I tried to hit Smithfield by public transport, I got quite exasperated, to put it mildly. I seemed to be in West Ham, and after a while East Ham. Tell the taxi driver to let you down at the Meat Market, Smithfield. On this historic spot, Wat Tyler was slain by Sir William Walworth, the Mayor, while Richard II stood around grinning. He who laughs last—This was 1381. In 1305 Sir William Wallace, the hero of Scotland, was executed at Smithfield. In 1546 Anne Askew was burned alive (a matter of theology). In 1553 the Protestant Martyrs were burned (more theology). And so on. Smithfield was infamous as the scene of London's more horrible bloodlettings for a matter of some five centuries and more. And why? A good place to torture people to death because it was so centrally located: from 1150 to 1855, Smithfield was the chief horse and cattle market of London. Crowds coming to drive a sharp bargain could stop off to watch the faggots laid for some martyr or other. Colorful spectacle.

The contemplation of man's ferocity to man across the centuries makes me irritable. I think Smithfield is one of the most depressing places in England, and I only suggest your going to peer at it as an antidote to *tourisme*. All last week you have been examining the triumphs of man's spirit; tourists get a strange feeling for the past because they are constantly breathing deep over flying buttresses or Renaissance church domes. But they were still hanging eleven-year-old children for stealing sixpence when Wren built St. Paul's, and Tudor architecture flourished while martyrs roasted alive at Smithfield. History (including English history) is not just a record of *Perpendicular* fan vaulting and *Norman* triforiums; but also a long, bloody, anguished tale of cruelty and pain. The medieval cathedral is one side of the coin; Smithfield is the other—and I suppose historians, c. A.D. 3000 (assuming, of course, that *homo sapiens* survives at all) will say much the same thing of our brave twentieth-century world. George Bernard Shaw, the Wright Brothers, and open-heart surgery on the one hand; Buchenwald and Hiroshima on the other. The grillwork on Smithfield Market is handsome; Holburn Viaduct, nearby, is gorgeously painted in black and scarlet and gold but that never cheers me up much.

We abandon meat markets and Smithfield and proceed to St. Bartholomew's Hospital—which represents the Department of Human Progress, Brotherly Love, etc. The hospital entrance is on the southeast side of Smithfield and it is one of the oldest charitable institutions in England. It was founded in 1123 by one Rahere, a courtier of Henry I. This Rahere fell ill on a trip to Rome with what he feared was a mortal complaint, and vowed a hospital for the worthy poor, if St. Bartholomew would rally round in his hour of need. A few centuries later (1423) Dick Whittington, the Lord Mayor of London, contributed money for the repair of the hospital, and later Henry VIII, who closed down practically every monastery hospital in the country, spared St. Bartholomew's, in grateful token of which narrow escape the hospital calls Henry its "second founder." All of this history is colorful enough, but, for my part, the exciting item about St. Bartholomew's is Harvey, who was Chief of Staff from 1609 to 1643. While James I was getting up his Doctrine of the Divine Rights of Kings, while his lamented son, Charles I, was dying for same, while martyrs perished hideously, Harvey was working at St. Bartholomew's—discovering the circulation of the blood. The world does move.

The buildings inside the hospital quadrangle (as I am sure you recognized at a glance) are not medieval. They were built by James Gibbs, a pupil of Wren, between 1730 and 1770. Poor Gibbs! He is damned with the label "follower of" Sir Christopher. It must be an odd trick for destiny to play on a man—bringing up the rear of an all-time genius, playing ninth moon to somebody else's blazing sun. The same thing happened to Ben Jonson. But Gibbs was a delightful and talented architect in his own right. As you can see at St. Bartholomew's, he developed Wren's grand style into the handsome and quiet *Georgian* which adorns so many of London's graceful squares and pleasant side streets. He was the designer, too, of one of my favorite London churches, St. Martin-in-the-Fields in Trafalgar Square.

St. Bartholomew's Hospital owns—and will let you see, if you ask—two little-known and quite surprising paintings, "The Good Samaritan" and "Bethesda Fountain" done for the hospital in 1736 by William Hogarth, as his contribution to the Gibbs restorations. Critics rather sneer at these two paintings —they are dead serious, use seven-foot figures, and betray none of the savage wit of the great satirist. But I thought they were very interesting. They describe Hogarth's religion—pity. "I would rather have checked the progress of cruelty, by however little, than to have done Raphael's cartoons." Cheers!

The *Georgian* in the hospital quadrangle makes a considerable contrast to the *pièce de résistance* of our trip to Smithfield, the priory church (or what is left of it) of St. Bartholomew the Great. Next to the chapel in the Tower, this is the oldest church in London, partly Norman, partly *Decorated,* partly *Perpendicular,* partly Victorian restored, and partly ruins, both Reformation and Nazi. St. Bartholomew's, in fact, has everything.

This is a good moment to outline the Foolproof System for Peering at Historic English Churches. I do not like to boast, but the Foolproof System will save you time, trouble, and humiliation. If you haphazardly rush into a church, you will find yourself gaping with awe at something which afterward turns out to be Victorian vandalism, or (once bitten, twice wary) sneering at stupid modern carving dated (as the verger corrects you) 1342. Our method for churches follows:

A. As you walk into the church, cathedral, abbey, or ruin, buy the leaflet guide, complete with map. Some churches have a literature table logically located at the nave door, but most cathedrals keep it tucked away in the transepts. On rare occasions you may have to chase the verger through the shadowed depths crying after him, "Do you have a guide? Please?" Persist; even the most remote English parish churches have discovered that guides pay for new altar carpets, and no matter how unrewarding the situation looks at first glance, there is a leaflet guide tucked away somewhere.

Not all guides are accurate or instructive. Schools of thought apparently differ. Some churches, and cathedrals, offer leaflets apparently written for the child or feeble mind. "Legend tells us," such literary gems begin coyly, and five pages later we are still with the murky old Saxons, who had a waterspout or a hurricane or something of that nature on the hallowed ground where, in 1437 (only a matter of six hundred odd years later), some local wool merchants built a *Perpendicular* window. The church is mentioned, briefly, in the last paragraph. Again, there are erudite documents which hash over theological disputes current in 1620 or 1190.

Most of the guides steer between pendantry and Legend Tells Us, and some of the leaflets flourishing in remote parish churches are admirable, models of brisk style, and accurate information. They all have charts or maps of the church. This brings us to:

B. As soon as you have collected the guide, trot to the last pews in the nave, as near the west doors of the church as possible, and sit down. Take up the guide and read it all the way through, mentally checking off silent points as you go: "Fourteenth-century tomb in right aisle of nave . . . Victorian vandalism on altar screen . . . *Decorated* choir . . . pass up the crypt, it is restored . . . Lady Chapel *Perpendicular*, first-class tombs."

When you have the situation in hand, get out the map. Remember you are at the end of the nave, by the west doors. Peer earnestly at your chart, and get your bearings—south, north, transepts, choir.

C. With the map for frequent reference, start off on a round-trip tour: up the right-hand (south) aisle of the nave, around the south transept, choir, and Lady Chapel; back the other (north) side of the choir, around the north transept, down the north aisle of the nave to home base. Then, crypt, altar screen, choir interior, chapter house, cloister if any, towers, and other glories. Do not dip and swoop from one side of the nave to the other like a pigeon. Avoid wandering into one side of the choir and coming out on the other. Cathedrals, even ruins and parish churches, can be slippery. A false move, and you are looking at a Crusader's tomb which is afterward revealed to have been built in 1816 for the local squire.

With the System, the tourist need never be at a loss, or hardly ever, not even at old St. Bartholomew's, which is by no means easy.

THE VERGER

D. Vergers. There are vergers and vergers. The verger at
Hexham Church, Northumberland, is one of the most delightful, original, and learned students of architecture in England.
And then again—look before you leap with vergers. Edge in on
the sightseers' lecture and eavesdrop. If the verger is making
painful little jokes and giving clerical giggles as he says,
"Legend tells us . . ." you can fade away into the shadows. But
if the guide is accurate and interesting, elbow briskly to the
front row. There is no better way of seeing an English church
than in the company of a well-informed and passionate verger.

So much for the System; it is easy, practical, and fun.

This is your first English ruin, and although the effect is different in Yorkshire at Fountains Abbey the theory is the same.
You remember Henry VIII carting away St. Edward's tomb at
Westminster? That was nothing compared to other changes
Henry made at the same time. It cannot be said that the Reformation was a half-hearted approach. When Henry came to the
throne, his revered sire, the wily Henry VII, had already tamed
the feudal secular noblemen. But Henry, who meant to be an

absolute monarch and run an efficient central government in England, was left with the Church. In 1509, the Church was far and away the biggest landlord in England, and in an agricultural society the land was the key to power. In addition to the good earth, the monasteries, cathedral chapters, and the like owned the portable treasures and solid cash. It galled the Tudor sovereign that any first-class monastery could lay its hands on more gold, silver, and precious stones than the King was likely to come by in a month of Sundays. The monks, abbots, priests, and monastery hangers-on, lay or clerical, had an absolute grip on their local neighborhoods. They dispensed justice (rather high-handedly), hired the day labor, decided the land rents, and kept a tight hold on the common people. The monks ran the local hospitals, if any, handed out doles to the hungry, and kept a reasonably benevolent eye on the halt and the lame.

Modern apologists for the monastic system make a good deal of Church charities, but you may judge whether the Church was really popular in sixteenth-century England, as landlord and ruler. Henry decided to destroy the monastic system—once and for all and at one fell swoop. When Henry did a thing, he did not trifle with half measures. At St. Bartholomew's the King's Guards arrived, threw out the monks, burned down most of the church, stole everything in sight, and left the place in ruins. The identical scene was played out at Glastonbury, in Northumberland, Kent, Surrey, Yorkshire—all over England. It was a revolution: and aside from a few abbots (who were hanged) and a solitary uprising in the North, no one raised a finger to defend the churches or monasteries, hospitals or almshouses. Henry had gauged the temper of his fellow countrymen with remarkable precision. The Church, once the heart and soul of medieval England, was finished as a power in the kingdom. The monks, corrupted by riches, were detested by their wretched tenants; the abbots, whose splendor had been greater than that of the Tudors, were reduced overnight to refugees—amid the cheers of the populace. The Dissolution was something like a big-scale Fall of the Bastille.

There is a tendency among modern curators of the ruins to regard Henry VIII as a wicked vandal, burning down beautiful things and galloping away with gold plate and other loot that didn't belong to him. Henry was no delicate violet, full of sensitivity and good works. But history cannot be arranged for the benefit of art lovers four hundred years in the future. It is sad that so many lovely churches were lost in the Dissolution, but the England we know was born in the Tudor Revolution, and born overnight. There was nothing evolutionary about Henry's policy of a strong central government. The English are often said to be great compromisers; but when it comes to something big, like the medieval Church, or the divine right of kings, you can hardly describe their response as compromise. The modern traveler should think twice before getting wistful on the topic of Henry VIII's ruins.

Whether you are for or against Dissolution, the ruins, such as St. Bartholomew's, exist. At St. Bartholomew's the whole nave is lost, and for a long time the Lady Chapel was used as a fringe factory. Interesting point—people making fringes in a Lady Chapel! There was a blacksmith's forge in the north transept. The whole ruin fairly hummed with industry until 1863. At this point, the Victorians restored St. Bartholomew's.

Most modern English artists and architects (including the distinguished illustrator of this volume, who is both) fly into a temper about Victorian vandalism. Some architects think the Victorians were worse than Henry VIII when it came to making away with altar screens, Lady Chapels and the like. At St. Bartholomew's, the restorers decided that the Lady Chapel ruins were in too sad a state to do anything with, so they built a handsome new Lady Chapel in the "Gothic" style. The choir ending at St. Bartholomew's is not medieval. It was put up in 1886.

But neither Henry VIII nor the Victorian architects have managed wholly to make away with the glories of St. Bartholomew's. Prior Bolton's is one of the loveliest oriel windows in England, and the Norman columns, piers, and round arches in the lower part of the choir are ancient and beautiful. The cloister has been expertly and lovingly restored by modern architects whose respect for the past is only matched by their incredible skill in present-day techniques of preserving ancient Gothic stonework.

You can spend a whole morning poking about St. Bartholomew's, but the good tourist's motto has to be Onward Ever

Onward, especially in London. So leave the church by the Close, interesting because (*a*) Hogarth was born here in 1697, (*b*) Milton hid in the Close at the Restoration, 1660, and finally, (*c*) Benjamin Franklin lived here a hundred years later, when he was working in the print shop then located in the Lady Chapel; Washington Irving had rooms here as well.

I mention the Close in such detail to give a rough idea of the City. Every block in the City is hallowed, not once but six times over. Stone throwers can stand in the middle of any City side alley and aim for a dozen X Marks the Spots—Saxon, Roman, medieval, Miltonic, Georgian, Dickensian—take your choice. The General Post Office, behind St. Bartholomew's Hospital, has a bit of Roman wall in its basement—they will let you in to see it if you ask. Two blocks up on Aldersgate Street is the Charterhouse, which the Nazis reduced to a few walls. It has been carefully restored-rebuilt, however, and looks much the same as it did in 1939, only cleaner and newer. The history of the Charterhouse begins in the fourteenth century and trots briskly across time and tragedy to Thackeray, who calls it the "Greyfriars" in *The Newcomes*. During the Tudor period, the Charterhouse was jinxed. After the Dissolution (the Charterhouse was a monastery) Lord North remodeled the Little Cloister into a mansion. This was a frequent practice: Henry VIII, never a man to let things go to waste, gave or sold (mostly sold) monkish building lots to current favorites, and all over England people still happily inhabit manor houses made over from monastery remnants.

In the case of the Charterhouse, Lord North did not long hang on to the spoils. The Duke of Northumberland moved in —temporarily. He had a son, and a daughter-in-law, Lady Jane Grey. The duke went to the block along with his poppets. The next owner of the Charterhouse, the Duke of Norfolk, made extensive alterations. The paint was hardly dry on the new banqueting hall before this duke also made a miscalculation; he plotted to put Mary, Queen of Scots on Elizabeth Tudor's English throne. A mistake. Exit the Duke of Norfolk. Enter Thomas Howard, afterward Earl of Suffolk. He had better luck with the property, entertained James I before that chilly monarch was crowned King, and lived to sell the place to Thomas Sutton in 1611 for £13,000. Sutton was an Elizabethan merchant-adventurer, a self-made man. After years of racketing about on the Spanish Main, gambling on cargoes of slaves, Indians, tobacco, stolen Spanish gold, he came home to turn respectable. Like many another sudden millionaire, Sutton spent his fortune on good works. He founded a public school at the Charterhouse, and a hospital for aged men. It amuses me to reflect that Sutton's poor brethren had to be respectable—honest but impecunious retired Army officers, tottering clergymen, and the like were (and are to this day) eligible for berths at the Hospital. Retired rascals, former freebooters, bankrupt adventurers, and confidence men need not apply!

Sutton did not live to see his school and hospital flourish. He died six months after he bought the Charterhouse, but he left his fortune to his foundation, and the school (one of England's most famous) still endures to celebrate founder's day with

CITY PUB

solemn pomp. The school has long since moved to the country, but the hospital carried on at the original site of the Charterhouse. Today the thirty-two pensioners share their modern quarters with chartered accountants, solicitors, and the like.

The Charterhouse calls for a bit of lunch, after which, the Guildhall. The Guildhall was very nearly destroyed by the Nazis, but the Hall of the Corporation of the City of London, like St. Paul's, survived the Nazis, and for the same reason. The firemen of the Corporation determined to save the Guildhall no matter what else went (and nearly everything in the immediate neighborhood did go). Two direct hits knocked out the art gallery; but while the bombs exploded right and left, the firemen stood their ground in the ancient hall. The Lord Mayor still holds his state banquet in the Guildhall every November under the seventeenth-century roof. The Nazi bombings were not the first disaster the Guildhall survived; in the 1666 Great Fire the roof and assorted medieval fittings went up in smoke.

The Guildhall is medieval London. The guides will tell you that to this day the City has its own fire department, sewer system, and gas lights. London policemen wear a red-and-white wristlet within City boundaries to signify their "independence," and there are a dozen other traditions that recall medieval origins. It is typical of Englishmen, and Londoners in particular, to retain the picturesque aspects of the past while briskly inventing new forms to suit modern requirements. Do not be too beguiled by the Guildhall; or at least reflect that London was the first metropolis to organize an efficient, democratic, and adaptable form of city government. The Guildhall is quaint; but the enormous London County Hall, across the Thames from Westminster, is the headquarters of the municipal authority which administers the civic affairs of London's many millions.

The Guildhall has a splendid library housed in a handsome Tudor hall, but the afternoon wears on; we have still to walk from the Guildhall down Cheapside to the Mansion House, the Stock Exchange, and the Bank of England.

I do not know why so many tourists (including myself) solemnly trot around the outside of the Bank of England, peering at its handsome but unremarkable modern façade.

There is nothing to see—yet the place is eerie and sacred in a back-handed way. The Old Lady of Threadneedle Street was the first joint-stock bank (1694), and is still the biggest bank in the world. It is the banker for the Government of England, and it combines the functions of the American Treasury and the several Federal Reserve banks. "All that money!" people say in hushed tones as they gawk at the blank stone walls.

The Mansion House is livelier; it is the official residence of the Lord Mayor; regard the Renaissance façade built in 1739 by George Dance the Elder.

The square half-mile around the Mansion House is one of my favorite haunts in the City. Keats was born at 85 Moorgate Street; Daniel Defoe died in Ropemaker Street; the Honourable Artillery Company (in which Pepys, Wren, and Milton served) has its headquarters on City Road.

Just off City Road is what the English call a "Nonconformist" (Methodist, Quaker, Presbyterian, Congregational, and so on) cemetery. Bunhill Fields is moving for an American heart. After an afternoon spent in admiring the Guildhall, the Mansion House, and the Bank of England, it is refreshing to be reminded that not every Englishman conformed. The English have produced rebels, fighters, eccentrics, and divine madmen from Wat Tyler to the Chartists, from Lilburne the Leveller to George Washington. Westminster Abbey houses the monuments of so many great Englishmen that I confess I failed to notice who was missing—until I wandered into Bunhill Fields one dark and melancholy afternoon in December. I discovered that, when they call the roll at Westminster, Alfred Lord Tennyson may answer from his cozy nook in the Poets' Corner—but not William Blake. He lies in the defiant acres at Bunhill Fields, along with John Bunyan and Daniel Defoe and many another Englishman who hurled fire and fury on constituted authority. By no means all of London's early Nonconformists are buried here; a good many of them lie under weathered stone markers in the churchyards of Litchfield, Connecticut; or Boston, Massachusetts.

Bunhill Fields brings out the George Washington, not to say Sam Adams, streak in me. I expect every American is a touch schizophrenic about the Mother Country; after nine solid days admiring Sir Christopher Wren and Tudor architecture, I have a spell of remembering John Paul Jones, Ben Franklin, Tom Paine, and other serious Nonconformists. "Bah!" I say to myself as I regard the Bank of England, "When in the course of human events. . . ."

Thus, tramping truculently on from Bunhill Fields, you can see George Fox's grave in the Friends' Cemetery, and John Wesley's house at 47 City Road. Rebels both, and as you circle back to the Bank you may reflect with some pride that America inherited a rich share of English passion and reckless devotion to principle.

At the crossroads where King William Street runs into Gracechurch Street, Eastcheap, and Cannon Street, there stood, so local historians believe, a pub called Boar's Head Tavern. The immortal Falstaff and his Prince Hal were patrons of the Boar's Head—and Americans may be reminded that Shakespeare was no rebel, but a solid Tudor man, with a coat of arms besides. It would be a mistake to think we inherited only John Bunyan and Daniel Defoe. There are more poets buried in the Abbey than in Bunhill Fields.

The Monument, Wren's fluted Doric column on Fish Street Hill, is 202 feet high, a memorial to the Great Fire—which is supposed to have broken out exactly 202 feet away. This last nugget of information may be safely tucked away with Mother O'Leary's cow. An authentic item about the Monument was the inscription it bore from 1681 to 1831, blaming the Fire on the "Papists." Pope replied with his blistering lines:

> Where London's column, pointing at the skies,
> Like a tall bully, lifts the head, and lies.

I do not know how eager you will be for a famous view of London. My learned friend, the city alpinist, having climbed St. Paul's, tackled the Monument. He "strongly advises" visitors to ascend the 311 steps which wind around and around the interior.

"Every 100 steps or so there are markers which say encouraging things, like 'halfway,' and still more usefully, window seats where the aging and the obese can pant before resuming their climb."

The view from this particular top, my friend reported, is "splendid—not as high, it must be conceded, as St. Paul's Golden

Gallery, but compensated for by an unexcelled chance to see St. Paul's free from the interruptions of office buildings. For those unafflicted by vertigo, there is another impressive sight, the view to the bottom, through the winding interior stairwell."

A third high place, the new Post Office Tower, got a thumbs-down rating from the climber. In the first place, there was nothing to climb, just boring old elevators. The Post Office Tower is thirty-six stories high, about par for a medium-grade Cleveland or St. Louis bank. The view is wider but duller than from the human-scale Monument. "Besides, I do not believe St. Paul's was built to be looked *down* upon. Man does not live by elevators and revolving restaurants alone."

The Temple and the Wars of the Roses

THE Monument concludes the first day of our City tour. I skipped a number of interesting items because I do not think human strength is up to more. But, if you have an extra afternoon in London, you can take the Underground to Cannon Street station, and strike out from there to College Hill; Sir Richard Whittington, thrice Lord Mayor of London, lived in College Hill, and died there, 1423. The true history of Dick Whittington is more interesting than any nonsense about cats. He was a fifteenth-century success story, and probably the first English millionaire to become the stuff of folk legend.

The second morning of the City tour—the Temple. Except for the Tower, no other place in the English capital is so hallowed by history, tradition, and fame. For six hundred years barristers, lawyers, judges (and their hangers-on) populated the four famous Inns—Lincoln's Inn, Inner Temple, Middle Temple, and Gray's Inn. Before legal London settled into the Inns, the Temple was headquarters for the Order of Knights Templar, which, recalling *Ivanhoe*, I can never remember without feeling my hackles rise. The Templars were dissolved (good riddance!) in 1312, and a little later the Knights Hospitallers let the Temple on a fairly long lease to "certain professors of the common law."

The Inns of Court are complicated for Americans. Our nation started fresh in 1787, and our legal affairs are neat and clean-cut. Ambitious youths study at law schools attached to a university, after which they sit for the state bar examinations; the next step is an office and a client. Most American law is written, and decisions of the Supreme Court are indexed in large volumes, for the edification of the scholar. But in England . . .

The authors of this volume admit they are incompetent to write a treatise on English law. What follows is strictly for the layman. Roughly speaking, English law evolved from the thirteenth century and earlier to the present day. Most English law is not codified. Further, in England, there are no law schools, as we know them. Instead, the members of the four Inns of the Court "call" students to the English Bar. The candidates take rooms in the Temple or nearby, attach them-

BARRISTERS

selves to some practicing barrister, and gradually acquire what they hope will be enough knowledge to satisfy the fierce guardians of the Inns. Scholars must dine in the Common Hall of their Inn for a required number of evenings before they are eligible to take the Bar examinations.

The Temple is a law school after its peculiar fashion. The candidate admitted to the Bar in London settles down in chambers at the Temple. The great courts of London are within a short distance, and barristers may live, certainly they must practice law, in the Temple. The Inns are not only law schools, they are also Bar associations, legal libraries, offices, and clubs for London's barristers. In a sense, vague to the American but clear to a London barrister, the Inns act as both repositories and arbiters of law. The English judges are members of one of the four Inns, and their appearance at the Common Hall allows barristers the opportunity of study and argument. Some of the debates held on points of the law before our Supreme Court are heard at Temple over port in Commons.

The study of law has been going on at the Inns of the Temple—with one interruption—since 1338. The continuity of experience provides the Inns of Court, like the Tower, with an encrusted tradition. In the old days, the tourist could see the rooms where Oliver Goldsmith, Blackstone, or Cromwell lived; follow the trail of men as various as Dr. Johnson, Dickens, Thackeray, and Sun Yat-sen. The narrow lanes of the Temple area were haunted by the ghosts of Congreve, William Pitt, Disraeli, Gladstone, De Quincey, Francis Bacon, Burke, and Thomas Moore. (This list is picked at random; I could fill two complete pages with the names of the Temple great.)

The interruption, mentioned above, appeared, for a time, to be permanent. The Nazi bombers reduced the Temple—all those close-crowded medieval, Tudor, Jacobean, Georgian, Victorian structures—to rubble. For years after World War II, the Temple was a wasteland of broken stones, charred timbers, and sad memories.

But Englishmen are born under the sign of the Phoenix. First the big, important halls of the Inns, the Round Church (one of the four in England), and Wren's beautiful Gatehouse were restored. Then, year by year, as one decade flowed into another, the Inns and lodgings rose again, sometimes in new dress (Georgian, instead of "unfortunate Victorian") but all of them rehallowed with what could be saved from the past.

What you will see in the Temple is a memory, come to life again. The students still take their dinners in the Commons of the Inns, barristers still have their chambers where their firms put up brass plaques in 1820 or 1731 or 1911, and the roses still grow in the garden of Middle Temple, where Shakespeare says the Wars of the Roses began.

The time has come to take up the Lancaster-York affair. We have left poor Henry VI, foully murdered in the Tower, and not a word of why; and you will find Edward IV cozily installed at Windsor when you go there. You would not visit Grant's Tomb without a rough idea of the Battle of the Wilderness. I know the Wars of the Roses are not easy (it helps if you start to learn them, as English schoolboys do, at the age of nine)—but faint heart never figured out Windsor, the Temple, Westminster, Tewkesbury Abbey, or St. Albans.

The best way to begin the Wars of the Roses is with a date: 1450. I do not like to press dates on people, but this one is worth remembering. It is the key to the Wars of the Roses, and without it, you are lost. Fourteen hundred and fifty—forty-two years before Columbus, and nineteen years after Joan of Arc was burned at the stake. Gutenberg was working on his Bible; *Perpendicular* windows were being built in English cathedrals; in three years Constantinople would fall to the Turks.

In the year 1450 medieval England was dying.

The world of Westminster and Canterbury, the rigid, ordered caste system of Gothic England, was cracking at the seams. The reasons for the collapse of feudal society in England are numerous and subtle. Boiled down to a tourist's-eye view, I think 1450 can be explained as follows:

Item: land enclosures.

Any system of society, no matter how gorgeous (or solid) it may appear on the outside, rests on its least common denominator. Feudalism worked for hundreds of years in England because the poor serf was reasonably content with, or piously resigned to, his fate. He was tied by law to the land in semi-slavery (on pain of having his ears chopped off, his eyes put out, or some similar unpleasantness). But the serf had his strip of the common fields, his starveling cow in the common pasture, his place, however wretched, in the narrow world that was all he knew. If he ate little, worked like a beast, and died early, such was the Will of God. Life was short, and afterward came Heaven.

In the last half of the fourteenth century (about 1375) the price of raw wool went up in the Flemish cloth towns—Bruges and Ghent.

From time immemorial (for four hundred years or so) the noble lord of an English estate had lived off the backs of his faithful serfs. Medieval land tenure was not unlike share-cropping in Dixie. Every year the baron collected a fat percentage of the oats and barley his peasants harvested, the strong beer and cheese they made, the hides they tanned, the fish they caught and the honey they found in the woods. Under this system, the more serfs on the baron's land, the more labor power, the more oats and beer and fish, the more profit. The baron did not worry about soil erosion (wooden ploughs only scatched the surface of the earth), and overcrowding did not bother him. Plague or smallpox came with unpleasant regularity, and wiped out surplus serfs—and surplus barons, for that matter. The population of England was about 3,500,000 in 1450. The baron counted his wealth not so much in acres, as in able-bodied fieldhands: villeins, they were called.

Then the price of wool went up in Flanders.

Sheep are hungry and take up space. The noble lords of England at the turn of the fifteenth century were not deep thinkers. They did not get together and decide to smash the Gothic world they had inherited from their revered ancestors. Barons as a class were conservative sticklers for tradition against the new-fangled and revolutionary. The noble lords of England did not heroically pledge their lives, their fortunes, and their sacred honors to overthrow the feudal system. But, when wool rose in price, it occurred to some barons that it might be a good thing to raise a few sheep. Wool was a cash crop. A baron in Kent (forward-looking, on his toes) and an abbot in East Anglia (shrewd fellow) and one of the brainier earls in Devon, enclosed—fenced in—the common pasture on their lands, and started a sheepfold or two on the green English hills. The serfs could no longer keep their spindly cows on this land; the landowners could not sell wool in Flanders without some hardship.

There is nothing like a little money to whet the appetite for more. The barons of England had been collecting farm profits in oats and barley for four hundred years. One day a baron in Kent woke up to discover that his noble neighbor on the other side of the hill was rolling in new suits of armor and with plenty of big, red rubies sewed on his wife's dresses.

"Why don't you raise sheep?" the baron's lady asked bitterly. "I notice other men get ahead in the world."

Next fall the baron fenced in the common pasture. The serfs had the temerity to complain. They said the baron had no right to take the cow pasture for sheep. Whose land is it? the baron thundered; as a matter of fact, there was an old-fashioned, unprogressive statute on the lawbooks giving the serfs the legal right to common pasture and common fields. The baron paid no attention to such details. After all, if the abbot of the local monastery put his ploughed fields into sheep pasture, raising wool must be right in the eyes of the Church—and Heaven.

"It is God's will," the Baron said, as he took half the fields on his estate for his second flock of sheep. (One flock was good, two flocks were a lot better.)

For the first time since 1066, the wretched peasants seriously wondered about God's will. Some of the bolder spirits went so far as to ask the baron how the two hundred souls in the village were to live.

That reminded the baron. The serfs were right; the place was overcrowded. He was graciously pleased to release from their feudal duties twenty-nine villeins along with their wives and children, grand total, 123 villeins. "Go in peace!" said the baron. "You are free men, and your sons after you."

But the serfs were stubborn, stupid fellows, who could not seem to understand the idea of freedom. The baron was forced to give a practical demonstration. His knights-at-arms rode down from the castle, armed with whips and pikes. In less than an hour the 123 surplus serfs had quitted the place where their fathers were born, and set out to see the world. Actually, there were 119 who moved slowly up the dusty road; the other four were dead. But what could the baron do? A barley crop takes many men; a solitary shepherd can keep watch over a herd of sheep.

The medieval world came apart on the day the baron fenced in the village pasture. Land enclosures were only beginning in 1450. A hundred years later, after the Dissolution, enclosures shifted the English peasantry from the land to towns, to ship-yards, to mines, and primitive factories; the enclosures supplied seamen for the Elizabethan fleets, boatmen for the rivers, miners of coal and lead, apprentices in the printing trade—and the restless, dangerous mob of groundlings for Shake-speare's plays. With the passing of time, the enclosures freed the serf from feudal semi-slavery. It was a rough-and-ready process, and it took centuries before it was finished.

But in 1450 the change began. Thousands of hungry, des-perate men roamed the English countryside, crowded the narrow towns until they spilled over, begged and stole, and now and then fought back.

Wat Tyler's Rebellion was a forerunner for Jack Cade's Rebellion—1450. Jack Cade, with the aid of a fifth column in the city council, so ably organized and led his ragged, hungry peasant army that London itself fell to the rebels. The baron and his friends got a nasty scare; intelligent and well-paid treachery delivered Cade to the gallows, and the affair petered out. The barons could not understand what had come over English peasants. A generation before, a villein would not have dreamed of raising an eyebrow, let alone a pike, at a well-born nobleman!

A society can die in more ways than one. Enclosures attacked the bedrock of medieval life—land tenure. But the Hundred Years' War also rocked Gothic England on its crumbling foundations. The endless forays across the Channel took endless men and endless money; win or lose (England mostly lost), the battles had to be paid for. Taxes made the already restless serfs groan and groan again. The soldiers, back from France, armed and ready for anything, refused to return to the village and eke out a starvation living in the baron's castle or sheepfolds. Some historians believe that the armed bands, roaming the English roads, were the real cause of the Wars of the Roses; if they did not actually make the wars, they certainly helped them along. These armed veterans explain one of the mysteries of the struggles between Lancaster and York; no sooner was one side defeated in battle and fleeing for its life than the losers turned about and with fresh troops reversed the decision. From 1450 for a whole generation there were idle soldiers available, ready to join anybody's army for a bread allowance and a chance to loot.

Gothic England was dying. One must also remember that modern England was being born. In the rigid world of 1250 the feudal system of decentralized local government operated well enough. The barons forced King John to sign the Magna Carta in 1215, and this guaranteed them (in effect) home rule. Each and every baron was lord of his own domain; taxation (if any) was indirect.

But in 1450 trade was booming. Wool was exported in one direction, cloth in another. Venetian ships crowded the Pool of London; bankers lent money on foreign deals in the City; and in the Temple, barristers wrote Flemish contracts. But affairs were in a bad way outside London. The restless, shifting, increasingly landless population must be kept under control. It was all very well for the baron to turn his peasants out; then what? The growing towns clamored for protection against the marauding veterans, unruly apprentices, and throngs of cut-purses. The Crown itself needed funds in coin—more and still more. The feudal system of indirect taxes could not meet the new demand for cash.

What England needed was a strong, efficient, central government.

It took thirty years to get one. The Wars of the Roses were a struggle for power between two gangs of old-fashioned feudal nobles; the prize was absolute monarchy, winner take all. When the last battle of the Wars of the Roses was finished, feudal England was dead, the power of the barons was forever broken. On the throne of a united nation sat Britain's first modern ruler—Henry Tudor, the Seventh.

I suppose thirty years of uproar and bloodletting are little enough to pay for progress. Yet thirty years do make the Wars of the Roses fairly complicated. With the general background partially under control, we can review the cast of characters and the battles once over lightly.

The Wars of the Roses officially started at the first battle of St. Albans in 1455. (St. Albans is a suburb of London, on our schedule for this week.) Shakespeare portrays both sides picking roses in the Temple garden, which must have been in June, 1455. But trouble had been brewing for years before the fighting broke out. The Wars of the Roses had a prologue in the murder of Richard II, 1400. There was no epilogue. The Tudors did not care for epilogues.

The first thing to get in order about the Wars of the Roses is the color scheme.

LANCASTER .... RED Rose
YORK .... WHITE Rose

The Lancastrians and the Yorkists both begin with Edward III (died 1377), who had too many children for their own good—twelve, in fact. Some of them died young, but a good many grew up to make trouble. The girls married all over the place—Portugal, Scotland, and up hill and down dale in England. Years and years later, Henry VIII, Edward's sturdiest descendant, hunted down his fifth and sixth cousins on the female side and hauled them off to the Tower, with the usual results. He worried about the Portuguese branch of the family —he was always writing letters inviting them over to London for a long visit. Somehow or other, they never came. Perhaps they did not think the English climate would agree with them.

Of Edward III's twelve children, three were of first importance for the Wars of the Roses:

1. Edward, the Black Prince, the King's eldest son, and a credit to the whole family. Edward was the *beau idéal* of medieval legend, a gallant warrior and the hero of feudal Europe. He died young, leaving an eleven-year-old son, Richard.

2. John of Gaunt, Duke of Lancaster, a wily character, who considered himself nimble and alert. What he did to England does not bear thinking of—one catastrophe after another. He had children, among them a boy named Henry (Lancaster, of course), called Bolingbroke, and another son, John Beaufort.

3. Edmund, Duke of York, who did nothing of significance,

except get into family rows. His son was Richard, Earl of Cambridge.

So much for the preliminary line-up. It is now 1377; exit Edward III, the progenitor of the clan, leaving his grandson, aged eleven, King Richard II.

An eleven-year-old king means open season for uncles. Edward III's sons (the boy Richard's uncles) detested each other from the cradle up. One wonders about Edward III's family life. Uncle John (Duke of Lancaster) announced himself as little Richard's right-hand uncle. Uncle Edmund (Duke of York) was left out in the cold, making for more bad blood later on.

Time passed. King Richard's voice changed. A bishop was busy running the worst series of military campaigns of the whole Hundred Years' War, which is saying a lot. By the time King Richard came of age the Royal Privy Purse was empty, the Kingdom was bankrupt, the peasants were rebelling, the French had the English armies on the run, and everything was terrible. This probably served Richard II right. He did not have an attractive character. He was what is called "weak" in the history books.

All this time the price of wool was rising in Ghent, the Pool of London began to be crowded with foreign ships, the first cracks were showing in feudal society—but Richard paid no attention. He wasted time in family brawls. He picked a quarrel with Uncle John's son Henry, and banished him abroad. The moment Uncle John died (unseasonably) in bed, Richard stole the lion's share of the Lancaster estate, leaving a few driblets for the younger son John Beaufort (keep him in mind, his name reappears four generations later). The King cut his cousin Henry out of the will altogether—a mistake: Henry was a strong character. Richard II, a poor ruler, allowed the barons to get out of hand, and they revolted. But, whatever else may be said of Richard, he had a cultivated taste in achitecture (Westminster Hall) and in civil servants (Chaucer).

This brings us to 1399. A revolt broke out in Ireland, and Richard rushed to quell it. The moment he left London, Cousin Henry arrived from France to organize the barons, who were fed up with the crown levies, and the general and unseemly disorder. When Richard came home from Ireland (mistake number two, he should have run for it), he found his cousin Henry fully prepared—down to leg irons in Richard's measurements at the Tower. A paper must be signed; Richard went to Westminster Hall to have his abdication witnessed in the presence of the barons. Fatal error number three. Henry might have hesitated before killing a legal king, but when Richard gave up —Henry could proceed with impunity. Even so, Henry hesitated: he had Richard dragged off to Pontefract Castle, and he spent his leisure chewing over the problem of murder for almost a year. Finally, Henry screwed up his courage and ordered poor Richard to be liquidated. Exit King Richard II, thirty-four years old.

Meanwhile (1399) Henry Lancaster, son of Uncle John of Gaunt, had himself crowned Henry IV. This was the Lancasters' start as Kings of England. Not a pretty story. But it made a fine play (*Richard II*, by William Shakespeare).

Henry IV had his troubles, after Richard was disposed of. "Usurper," people said behind his back. Henry tried to buy off his critics with extra lands for new sheepfolds, but the barons would not stay bought—they changed sides so often that Henry IV's reign takes on from this perspective across the centuries the look of historical musical chairs. The Welsh under Owen Glendower revolted; the Percys (Northumberland and his son, Harry Hotspur) revolted; other noble chieftains revolted; something bloody was going on throughout all of Henry's reign. Concurrently, feudal England was disintegrating on the new sheepfarms. But Henry IV was too busy plotting and counterplotting to take notice of the true state of his realm. His son, Prince Hal, was, according to Shakespeare's mythology, hanging out in low pubs with a reprobate knight named Falstaff; in actual fact, he was intriguing in his father's Privy Council, making trouble. Feudal fathers and sons seldom seemed to like each other—perhaps because it was not the custom to bring the boys up at home. Prince Hal was raised by Uncle Beaufort. Henry IV was definitely afraid of young Hal; maybe he thought the lad was a chip off the old block; in any case, he banished young Harry from London and made signs of disinheriting him. Before he got around to drastic measures, he fell ill. Worn out from usurping, he died early (1413).

The next Lancaster King was Prince Hal, Henry V. Henry V has become so much the creation of that common scribbling fellow named Shakespeare that it is hard to distinguish, even in history books, where real life left off and art began. Presumably, Henry V was a reasonably popular king (no important revolt flared up during his reign) and certainly he had an uncommon lot of brains, for a Lancaster. He won some battles in France (Agincourt, among them, the last time the English won an important engagement across the Channel in the Hundred Years' War). You may remember Henry V (or Shakespeare) saying, at Harfleur:

> Once more unto the breach, dear friends, once more;
> Or close the wall up with our English dead.

I was brought up on *Henry V*:

> You must not dare, for shame, to talk of mercy;
> For your own reasons turn into your bosoms,
> As dogs upon their masters, worrying you.
> See you, my princes and my noble peers,
> These English monsters! My Lord of Cambridge here.

These English mon—sterr-r-r-rs! My Lord of Cambridge was the son of Edmund, Duke of York. We will come back to Edmund later. But now it gives me a pang to announce that Henry V, like his father, died prematurely (1422).

Lancaster Number Three, Henry VI, came to the throne in diapers. He was exactly a year old when his father died, and the vultures started gathering around his cradle before Henry V was cold in his grave.

I cannot make up my mind whether Henry VI was feeble-minded, neurotic, or merely dim-witted. The gang of thieves who brought him up led him a dog's life even in the romper period. His mother—Harry of England's Sweet Kate, the one whose tomb we saw in Westminster Abbey—went off to Wales and married again, a Welshman named Jasper Tudor. It is not recorded if Kate felt a pang at leaving her baby behind to the tender care of the Somerset-Lancaster crowd. Feudal queens were rarely permitted even a quick look at their offspring; high-born babies were pieces in a chess game played for blood and for keeps. This particular baby was the King of England, and the French princess was not encouraged to hang about in London and exert an Influence. She went off to Wales and had other children, little Tudors.

Henry VI had a wretched life from beginning to end. He was bullied unmercifully throughout his childhood; the moment it became clear that he was not bright (even for a Lancaster) the plotting grew more enthusiastic. Two characters, Suffolk and Somerset (Dukes, both of them), more or less ran the show. The usual monotonous run of bad luck (or bad management) plagued the English armies in France. Young Henry VI was also ostensibly King of France (by inheritance from his mother), but nothing came of this claim. A peasant maid, Jeanne d'Arc, an obvious witch, raised an army of clodhoppers against the English regulars, and Henry VI's forces by no means prevailed. By the time the English managed to capture the witch, Jeanne, and to deal with her in the approved manner, the French Dauphin was crowned King of France, and the game was over for Henry VI so far as France went. In England things were not much better. The sheep situation was coming to a climax; roads (if you could call them that) were infested with bloodthirsty ex-soldiers; Richard Neville (the King-maker), Earl of Warwick, quarreled with Somerset and Suffolk and switched sides to oppose the King; more noblemen up-country in Northumberland revolted; the monasteries grew more corrupt by the hour; the serfs muttered in their nasty hovels; feudalism was dying; in the City of London, merchants grumbled that what the country needed was strong, central government; and—this above all—the Opposition was closing in.

What Opposition?

Never think that for all those years while the Lancastrians were cocks of the London walk, kinging it in royal ermine, the Yorkists were taking it lying down. Uncle Edmund, Duke of York—the brother of Uncle John, Duke of Lancaster—did not live long enough to enjoy power. Exit Uncle Edmund. Next York man up was his son, Richard, "My Lord of Cambridge."

The rest of Henry V's remarks to his cousin Cambridge were in
the same vein as the monster bit (see above) and concluded:

> . . . . Get you therefore hence,
> Poor miserable wretches, to your death;
> The taste whereof, God of his mercy gave you
> Patience to endure, and true repentance
> Of all your dear offences! Bear them hence.

> *(Exeunt Cambridge, Scroop, and Grey, guarded.)*

That disposed of the second generation. Next we come to
Cambridge's son (third generation), a leading character indeed: Richard, Duke of York.

I do not want to overstress genealogical tables, but these
Lancastrians and Yorkists were sticklers for blue blood. They
kept what amounted to a studbook on Edward III; many a
vicious battle in the Wars of the Roses was fought on the
sensational issue of which side had the more bona fide, one
hundred-percent royal genes. Let me try to identify Richard,
Duke of York. He was the eldest son and heir of the late
lamented monster, Richard, Earl of Cambridge. His mother
was the daughter of Edward III's second son. This made
Richard the great-grandson of Edward III twice over, via the
second as well as the fourth of King Edward's male offspring.

Contrast Richard, Duke of York's qualifications with those
of King Henry VI. Henry's mother was French; she was not
related to Edward III, she merely married into the Lancaster
family—which made Henry a great-great-grandson and only
once at that. Moreover, Henry VI's grandfather, Henry IV, had
usurped the Crown. What right did Henry VI have to sport
the purple mantle when Richard, better qualified in every
sense, was available for the job?

On this question of qualifications: Richard appears to have
been normally endowed with brains—a mental giant compared
to his unfortunate cousin, Henry VI. Henry was delicate physically as well, and the betting at Windsor Castle was against
the King's surviving to have issue of his own. Richard, the
two-way great-grandson, began agitating the question of succession before Henry VI, the one-way great-great-grandson,
showed the first trace of a beard. Hardly tactful, because

Somerset and Suffolk, the Lancastrian bosses, who ran the Kingdom in the name of Henry VI, took alarm and decided to marry Henry off—pronto, before all was lost.

Henry VI was no bargain, even in the rough-and-ready fifteenth century. Kings were willing to hand over their nine-year-old daughters to some fifty-year-old royal degenerate, with a province or two thrown in to bind the deal; but when it came to Henry VI the most detached drew the line. The royal papas were not squeamish; but gossip spread fast. Henry VI was feeble-minded; that could be condoned. More important, what about cousin Richard, breathing down Henry's neck? No king liked to waste a princess. What if the bride should turn out to be a widow before the Lancasters could unpack the dowry? The various courts at Paris, Madrid, and elsewhere considered Henry VI a notably poor risk.

Somerset and Suffolk took alarm. The King was twenty-three years old, and he showed no improvement by the day. They must find him a Queen and arrange some issue at once, or their own prospects would seriously deteriorate. In the Yorkist camp, Warwick, the fresh recruit to the opposition, rubbed his hands, and Richard took on the grave, sententious air of a man who expected to be king any day.

Enter Margaret of Anjou, the leading figure of the Wars of the Roses, aged fifteen years. Suffolk found her in the French provinces. She was not exactly what the Lancastrian crowd had expected by way of Queen, but they were no longer choosy. She did not have much dowry, but she seemed intelligent, and she looked healthy. In 1445, without much pomp, Henry VI shuffled off to Westminster and was married to the remarkable Margaret of Anjou.

Margaret was a child prodigy. At sixteen, one year a bride, far away from home, surrounded by strangers in a strange land, she energetically worked with Somerset and Suffolk to shore up her wretched husband's sinking fortunes. She knew—fifteenth-century queens were not mealy-mouthed—that the most important item on her agenda was to produce a healthy male child, in fact, any kind of child, the sooner the better. Alas, even Margaret could not work miracles. One year, two years, then three and four years passed; it was clear that Henry VI was not likely, after all, to have issue. Richard bore up pretty well under this tragic news, and bided his time in France, as became a man twice great-grandson of Edward III.

Fourteen fifty. Land enclosures. Battles lost in France. Sheep. Trouble.

Suffolk decided to make a quick trip across the Channel, but the Yorkists caught up with him at Dover, there was a skirmish, the Duke was "impeached," and the Lancastrians had one less supporter. A month later Jack Cade marched on London, and as if peasants rioting around Westminster were not enough, Richard bustled back from France, raised an army, and finding the road clear (Somerset was up-country, raising an army of his own), surrounded Margaret. (Henry VI was surrounded as well but no one paid attention to him.) Margaret kept her nerve. She promised Richard that Henry VI would acknowledge him his heir. Richard went home.

The next two years were spent fighting back and forth over the question of whether Richard was heir to the kingdom or not. It was an important point, because Henry VI appeared to be cracking up altogether: he was working up to the first of those periodic fits of insanity which marked the rest of his dismal career. Richard expected to move into Windsor Castle as Regent. And then, as the King definitely lost his mind, Margaret triumphantly bore him a son, Edward (1453).

Consternation in the Yorkist camp.

Cousin Richard pulled himself together after the glad tidings, and reconsidered the situation. He was still twice great-grandson of Edward III; but without doubt the new baby, Edward, Prince of Wales, had muddied Yorkist chances. What to do? Richard announced that he would serve as "Protector" to Prince Edward; the Prince's mother, Margaret, fought tooth and nail against the proposal of the lion "protecting" the newborn rabbit, but Somerset was asleep at the switch and Richard arrived at Windsor, to give the baby Prince the full benefit of his loving care. Oddly enough, Prince Edward survived his first twelve months, perhaps because the Queen stood guard over him twenty-four hours around the clock, and at this point (1454) Henry VI recovered. That is, his insane spell ended and he resumed his normal state of being, sad, frightened, and dim-witted. The moment he was out of irons (what they did in those days even to insane kings is not pretty to contemplate)

Margaret had Richard fired as Protector—and this was the match to the fuse.

Richard could wait no longer. Prince Edward was a healthy, precocious baby, not in the least like his father; if permitted,

WARS OF THE ROSES—ROUND ONE

the Prince would grow up to inherit the throne. Moreover, the Prince's strong-minded mother, and her ally, Somerset, would "influence" Henry VI while he was more or less lucid, or act as Regents while he was insane. Richard saw his life wasted, himself excluded from power rightfully his.

From Margaret's point of view, the situation was clear. She had no concern with the past, with ancient wrongs, with usurpers long dead, with Edward III, or anything else. She was Queen of England, wife of the anointed King, and mother of the heir to the English throne, Edward, Prince of Wales. Richard, Duke of York, was a traitor to his King (or showed the signs of becoming one) and a mortal danger to the Prince. This last item weighed most heavily on Margaret's mind. At twenty-five she had experienced little joy as Henry's wife, but she was a passionate mother, ready to defend her Prince with life itself. "My lovely Edward," she called him, years later.

The issue was joined. 1455. The Pool of London was crowded with ships; merchants grumbled about the roads on their way to York or Chester; serfs died of hunger in the country hills; an old order was passing, a new was getting born; the Kingdom cried out for a strong, central government—

In the Temple, Lancaster chose a red rose and York chose a white rose.

At the Battle of St. Albans, in the summer of 1455, Margaret and Somerset (the King was out of his mind again) met the challenge of Richard and Warwick. The Wars of the Roses had begun.

Round one: to the Yorkists. Somerset was killed; Margaret, alone, had to accept Richard as Regent for her temporarily insane husband and Protector for her baby son.

Time out—1455 to 1459. The King "recovered." Margaret secretly rounded up the Lancastrian barons, raised one of those flash Wars of the Roses armies, and in 1459 attacked.

Round two: to the Lancastrians and Margaret. The Yorkists, Richard, Warwick, the whole kit and caboodle, ran for it, and arrived in France, panting.

But Warwick, the brains of the Yorkist crowd, sneaked back from France, hired some old soldiers he found floating around England, rallied the Yorkist barons, entered London, and in 1460 fought the Battle of Northampton.

Round three: to the Yorkists. Warwick captured Henry VI, who always seemed to be left hanging around unprotected, and advanced on London. Margaret, with her seven-year-old son, Edward, escaped across the Scottish border, in the nick of time.

The dirty work done, Richard entered the capital, all set to be crowned King. But Warwick hesitated. Henry VI, although holed up in the Tower on bread and water, was, after all, King. The Yorkists had made quite a point of what happened to Richard II. Why not let Henry VI fade away—naturally? Richard could be Regent, and heir to the throne. Surely Henry VI could not last forever.

Richard was disappointed, but reasonable. Henry VI's bread ration was cut, and the Yorkists waited uneasily for the "inevitable." It was given out that the King was poorly.

Up in Scotland, the Queen of England marched for the border, at the head of a wild band of Scottish brigands. The bagpipes swirled. Even Margaret was afraid of her new allies. The nights were hideous with the noise of the clansmen raiding chicken coops, cattle pastures, and young ladies' bowers. Down from Scotland came the Lancastrians.

At the Battle of Wakefield (1460) Richard met Margaret for the last time. Richard was killed; his last glimpse on this earth was of Yorkists fleeing across the countryside with Margaret and her Scottish terrors smartly on their heels. It is a bit late, but I must admit at this point that the author's sympathies are with the Red Roses. I cannot help admiring Margaret.

Round four: to the Lancastrians.

Round five, the second Battle of St. Albans: also to the Lancastrians.

A pause for announcements. Richard, Duke of York, was dead, but like his revered ancestor, Edward III, he left plenty of issue, none of whom came to a good end. Among his sons were Edward, the eldest and new Duke of York, titular head of the White Rose contingent, and another Richard, a hunchback. Edward was young and immature in 1460 (he was eighteen); Warwick took over the job of right-hand cousin, and the Wars of the Roses proceeded on schedule.

Margaret left St. Albans victorious. She rescued the King (his emotions are not recorded), but hesitated about letting her wild Scottish partisans into London. They were capable of burning the capital and stealing everything in sight, including the women. By hesitating Margaret lost. The Yorkists came up from the rear, and chased the Lancastrians to the Scottish border after a bloody battle.

Round six: to the Yorkists. This time Warwick brought his young protégé, Edward, to London, and had him crowned Edward IV. Warwick was taking no more chances on Henry VI's health. For twenty years the Yorkists had been expecting the frail, feeble-minded King to die; and for twenty years Henry VI had persisted in surviving insanity, capture, the Tower, and Yorkist "protection." Warwick decided to wait no longer—thus earning himself the title of "Kingmaker."

While Edward was trying on his shiny new crown in London, poor old Henry was traveling across the Scottish border, low in his mind and discouraged. Margaret was furious—but full of energy. She went right back to raising more troops, and in 1464 she tried again, at Hexham.

Round seven: to the Yorkists. This was a "final" defeat.

Warwick mopped the Northumberland hills with Margaret's Scottish allies, and gave the Red Roses such a trouncing that Europe thought the Wars were over, and that Edward was definitely King. Warwick not only defeated Margaret on the field of battle, he cashed in on his victory by forcing Scotland to a truce (England and Scotland were perpetually at war) and by collecting the living corpse called Henry VI as his trophy. Margaret and the Prince of Wales escaped to France, again by the skin of their teeth. Henry VI was reinstalled in the Tower, where he was made no cozier than before. Still, Warwick did not actually have him strangled. Who knew when an extra King would come in handy?

Time out again: 1464 to 1469. True love reared its head.

Warwick, drunk with success, every inch the Kingmaker, and never doubting for a moment that he had young Edward IV securely in his pocket, looked around for a brilliant foreign marriage for the King to secure the Yorkists solidly on the throne. Other kings, in France, Spain, and Austria, were critical of Edward IV. Warwick said Edward was the King of England, but—who was that in the Tower in chains, slobbering over his daily dole of stale bread? Warwick decided that a first-class foreign bride (definitely not from Anjou) would do a lot for Edward's future, and after much delicate haggling, he finally managed to line up the sister-in-law of Louis XI of France, definitely a catch.

Imagine Warwick's surprise, when he got back to London, to discover that Edward IV had already secretly married a little nobody, an English parvenu named Elizabeth Woodville. And for what? For love! Warwick was disgusted. He rapidly grew more disgusted, because Elizabeth Woodville had a horde of poor relations who descended on London in droves. Warwick, proud Warwick the Kingmaker, found himself elbowed aside at Court. The King let him know, politely, that the Woodvilles did not like him.

Warwick could take a hint. A month later he was in France calling on his ancient enemy, Margaret—almost forty now. Her beauty was gone. She was haggard and poor. But she had a son. Warwick thoughtfully regarded Edward, Prince of Wales, aged fourteen, a beautiful, gifted, remarkable boy. Warwick nodded. The Prince would do nicely.

In 1470 Warwick and Margaret, strange allies, returned to England, raised one of those sudden Rose armies, marched on London, rescued Henry VI all over again, dragged him off to Westminster, put him on the throne, and showed him to the barons. This time Henry VI was flanked by his shining young son, Prince Edward, the hope of England. Or at least of the House of Lancaster.

Round eight: to the Lancastrians.

Edward IV, trailing brothers, including hunchbacked Richard, and Woodvilles, hared off to Holland, where he intrigued for foreign support. He raised an army and set sail for Dover.

In 1471 Edward IV retook London. Remarkable as it may seem, Margaret and Warwick, in their haste to get Prince Edward to safety, forgot all about Henry VI. The King slipped their minds, and he was captured again, this time for keeps.

With Henry VI snug in the same old Tower cell, Edward IV galloped after the Lancastrians, and met them at the Battle of Barnet.

Warwick was killed; how odd of Warwick, to have died under a standard bearing the Red rose!

Six weeks later at Tewkesbury, Margaret was captured. They took her into the Abbey to see the bloodied body of her son, her "lovely Edward." The boy had also been captured, but the Yorkists were tired of Lancastrians; they stabbed Prince Edward as he pleaded for mercy at the high altar of the Abbey. In London the Royal Strangler found Henry VI in his dark cell, praying on his old, bony knees.

Round nine: to the Yorkists.

The rest of the Wars of the Roses you probably remember from high school. Edward IV died, unlike most of his relatives, in bed (1483). He left two young sons, Edward V, aged twelve, and his brother Richard, Duke of York, aged ten.

Edward IV also had brothers—but the death rate among these brothers was spectacular. Except for the hunchback Richard. Only Edward IV's issue stood between Richard and the Crown, and Richard dealt with the inconvenience of his nephews. He took care of the matter by locking the two little boys in the Tower.

Strange as it seems after thirty years of bloodletting, the murder of the Princes in the Tower turned out to be one murder too many. All England was horrified. Perhaps the merchants in the City were at long last fed up. Was there never to be peace, an end to the battles and murders and plots? What the country needed was a strong central government, and no more nonsense about roses. Richard III was bad for business; a few more years of murdering everybody in sight, and trade would fall off.

Do great men shape history, or does history produce great men? A little of both, no doubt.

Remember the Beauforts, back in Uncle John of Gaunt's day—John Beaufort, younger son of the Lancastrian faction? His brother Henry IV had usurped the crown. The first John Beaufort had gone along quietly, and presently he had a son, another John Beaufort. The second Beaufort produced a daughter, Margaret, before he was killed in the family brawl. No one paid much attention to Margaret. There were a lot of Yorkists and Lancastrians to fight it out on the old line. Margaret grew up, unmurdered and unmarried by any of her lethal cousins; though her mother grew nervous as the death rate rose among the Lancaster and York section of the family. She hustled Margaret down to Wales, and married her off to a Welshman, Edmund Tudor, whose grandmother had been Henry V's "Sweet Kate," his "fair Katherine and most fair. . . ." It's nice to think things turned out right for Katherine. Still, she must have been sad about Henry VI. On the other hand, she was a notably intelligent, learned—perhaps, so far as we can read the obscure records, even gifted Princess. She is very much part of that genetic explosion which produced *genus Tudor*. And so was that Margaret Lancaster, who married Katherine's grandson Edmund, off in Wales. This Margaret (Lancaster) soon had a son, called Henry Tudor, an uncommonly bright, strong, healthy baby.

One morning a messenger galloped up to the Tudors' castle in Wales with the news that the House of Lancaster was no more.

Edward III's descendants by this time knew the stud book by heart. Margaret did not have to think more than a split second. Her baby, hardly out of swaddling clothes, was (aside from some remote characters over in Portugal) the last twig on Edward III's family tree—except for the Yorkists. It took

Margaret ten minutes to get her baby out of hand-embroidered small clothes and into rags; little Henry was hidden in a serf's hut. Margaret was just in time. The King (Edward IV) sent several barons for Henry that same afternoon; they wanted to take Henry to Court as befitted a royal child.

Margaret sent back her most grateful thanks. Unfortunately little Henry was sickly; he had been farmed out to a wet nurse. She would send him along to Court when he was older.

For the next ten years the Tudors and the Yorkists played hunt-the-thimble with young Henry. The canny streak which was such a marked characteristic of Tudors, young and old, seems to have been inherited from Margaret. The Yorkists were forever enticing Margaret Tudor—Come Into My Parlor. Margaret did not say no (she did not dare), but she never said yes. Henry was sick, he was going blind, he had smallpox, he had rickets, he was feeble-minded, he was not feeble-minded—and so on. There came a day when the Yorkists would not take further no's; they wanted Henry, in person.

Margaret bade her son a brave farewell, and watched him set out, disguised in rags, for the dangerous journey across England to the Channel ports. Henry was fifteen years old, and for guard and guide he had a single friend. On the other hand, he was a Tudor. Five months after her boy left Wales, Margaret had a message: safe in France.

History makes the hero; sometimes the hero helps make history.

England desperately needed peace. The nation was sick of war and murder, roses and horror; England was through with Lancastrians and Yorkists, and the wicked Richard III.

Henry Tudor turned out to be one of England's most astute and efficient monarchs; but in 1484 what counted most was Henry's stainless youth, and his name: Tudor. He was no bloody Lancaster, no accursed York. In France he eagerly agreed to marry Elizabeth, Edward IV's eldest surviving child, thus uniting Edward III's descendants in the male line. The barons were satisfied with Henry; the merchants in London approved.

Henry Tudor (having characteristically arranged the details in advance) landed on the shores of his native land, advanced to Bosworth, and killed Richard III. "The white rose of

England turned red on Bosworth Field." Henry located Elizabeth, married her, and together they went hand in hand to
Westminster, where he was crowned King of a united England.

That was 1485, the end of the Wars of Roses, the finish of
medieval England, and the beginning of modern times.

The Wars of the Roses are not quite finished. Every summer
the Lancashire cricket team, red roses pinned proudly on
players' jackets, battles to the last innings against the Yorkshire
white roses. The match is a feature of the cricket season, rather
like the Yale-Harvard game. I mean to go next summer, and join
the Old Etonians in a round of mad applause for Lancashire.
I plan on wearing not one measly red rose, but carrying a
whole bunch to show my solidarity with Margaret of Anjou.
Up the Lancastrians! Prince Edward Forever! (You are supposed to cheer for Henry VI, but poor Henry does not strike
me as inspiring.) However, we can all join in on: Down with
Richard Crookback! Enter King Henry VII, the Tudor.

Museums: Soane and Keats

HISTORY is a hungry business, and after all this medieval clang
and bang in the Temple, we need a short pause for refreshments
before we make a staggering leap across centuries, up Fleet
Street to Dr. Johnson's house.

Dr. Johnson's house is at 17 Gough Square off Fleet Street.
The neighborhood is thick with literary history, and you can
spend an hour or two happily poking about from one small
back court to the next, reading the plaques which will tell you
exactly where Coleridge delivered his lectures on Shakespeare,
or Goldsmith wrote *The Vicar of Wakefield*. Dr. Johnson lived
all over this part of London, at the Temple, in Bolt Court, in
Wine Office Court, and in Gough Square, where the museum
authorities have collected together the official batch of Johnson
relics.

Dr. Johnson's house is delightful. I know many littérateurs are scornful of official museums, and I suppose there is something preposterous in trying to pin down the elusive, slippery, usually bad-tempered, and formidable spirits of literary heroes to anything so irrelevant as the roofs they lived under, the chairs they sat on, or the indignant letters they wrote to creditors. All the same, there is (for me) a kind of fascination in peering at Shakespeare's bed, or a Brontë washbasin. I cannot resist Wordsworth's birthplace or Shandy Hall, the residence of Laurence Sterne. Of all the literary shrines in England, two of the best are in London: the Keats Museum (which we will see tomorrow) and Dr. Johnson's house.

The Great Lexicographer's establishment in Gough Square may interest tourists who scoff at literary shrines. It is a beautiful eighteenth-century town house in the purest Georgian style, exquisitely furnished, down to the smallest candle snuffer, with 1750 period pieces. Architects, antique dealers, furniture makers, interior decorators, set designers from Hollywood, and young ladies studying art at finishing schools haunt the place, apparently unmoved by any interest in dictionaries or a man named Boswell. You can probably strike a nice balance between the eighteenth-century atmosphere and the first edition of the famous *Dictionary*, in the attic where it was written.

I fear the sturdy tourist will find himself subtly corrupted by Dr. Johnson's house; I always am. I linger to look up odd words in the *Dictionary* or to peer at the curios in the handsome Georgian cabinets. But there is no rest for the traveler. The Soane Museum in Lincoln's Inn Fields is not far on foot, but a taxi is permitted to the faint-hearted.

Lincoln's Inn Fields, one of London's largest and most imposing squares, comes after Dr. Johnson's house. You have seen a Georgian interior—Lincoln's Inn Fields is a stately eighteenth-century exterior. Until the seventeenth century, the Fields were a favorite dueling ground; between fights, footpads and unsavory citizens made the place headquarters for their wicked activities. Perhaps because the barristers at Lincoln's Inn protested against such indecorous behavior across the alley, or (more likely) because London real-estate values began to rise, the Fields were enclosed in gardens, plane trees were planted, and Inigo Jones (so architects think) designed the first of the handsome mansions on the square, Numbers 59 and 60. Numbers 57 and 58 are an eighteenth-century imitation of the original Inigo Jones design.

Lincoln's Inn Fields was a "good address" before and after Dr. Johnson's day. Among the more famous tenants on the square were Milton (who moved a lot), Alfred Lord Tennyson, Nell Gwyn, and Mr. Tulkinghorn of *Bleak House.* You might say that mortals may come and go, but Mr. Tulkinghorn will live in Lincoln's Inn Fields forever. (Sententious, but it comes from the heart.)

Some other immortals can be located on the square. Number 13 is the Soane Museum. I know people in London who acknowledge the worth of the British Museum, the National Gallery, the Tate, and the Wallace Collection, but who would rather spend an afternoon at Number 13 Lincoln's Inn Fields than any other place in England. I would not dream of choosing sides; I make comparisons with gingerly caution. I only remark that the Soane Museum is wonderful.

The Soane Museum is small and perfect; splendid for the end of a long day touring the City. Sir John Soane (d. 1837) obtained a private Act of Parliament directing that none of his treasures were to be moved, added to, or disturbed in any way— so what you see at Number 13 Lincoln's Inn Fields is the stately home and private collection of a cultivated Regency gentleman, who had the good taste to collect the works of William Hogarth. Here he is, at the Soane Museum, in a very different mood from the paintings at St. Bartholomew's Hospital—satirical, savage, fascinating. The Soane Museum has Hogarth's great "Rake's Progress," (eight scenes) and the "Election" (four). "Rake's Progress" is a mirror for the eighteenth century that looks so charming, so stately, so gracious in Dr. Johnson's house. The other famous Soane item turns up in history books. Sir John had catholic tastes. He liked Watteau and Turner; he also liked Egyptian curios. One of the most notable coffins, sarcophagus I ought to call it, is located in the basement of Sir John's London house: Seti I, King of Egypt in 1370 B.C., the revered father of Rameses the Great.

Everybody is happy at the Soane Museum. Historians (as

well as art critics) brood over Hogarth, archaeologists lick
their chops as they head for Seti the First, and museum curators
make for Canaletto's masterpiece, entitled (as usual) "View of
The Grand Canal, Venice." There are other Canalettos in London, but this Soane Museum canvas is reputedly top-notch.
Personally, I could breathe if I never saw another Canaletto,
but if you are a Canaletto fan, you will concentrate on the
Soane Museum triumph. With or without Canaletto, Number
13 Lincoln's Inn Fields is one of the most exciting places in
London to finish off two days in the City.

Next morning (your tenth in London) take the Hampstead
bus to the end of the line. I know the Underground is quicker,
but the forty minutes you spend bumping gently uphill to the
Heath will show you the great, gray London of the people.
Most visitors spend their time in London concentrating (quite
properly) on places like Lincoln's Inn Fields, St. Paul's, and
Dr. Johnson's house. As a result they think of England's capital
as a collection of stately squares and glorious architecture. But
London is dull and enormous as well as beautiful; drab, dirty,
and weary as well as lovely. The trip uphill to Hampstead
will make an accurate backdrop, a more exact setting, for the
Keats Museum—and give you a notion of London's immense
size.

Hampstead is rich in character, charming with Georgian and
Regency houses, gay when the holiday crowds swarm on the
Heath. If the ordinary American visitor had a few months, not
a few weeks or a few days, in London, I should be the first to
agree with the lady at the dinner party; a good solid three days
tramping through the back streets of Hampstead would be little
enough to explore the main items of the pleasant village (for
Hampstead is a village apart) overlooking the Heath's rolling
green hills. Our approach, I fear, will have to be brisk.

When you get off the bus at Hampstead, walk directly up the
hill to the Heath. Richard and I are veterans of Easter Bank

Holiday on Hampstead Heath; it was superb. I counted seven
one-man bands on a single block, and the children ate cockles
and rode on roundabouts until they were dizzy. There were half
a million (at least) Londoners on hand to eat spun sugar candy;

"PENNY A PITCH"

everybody (except Richard, who felt sheepish) wore paper
hats and listened to the carnival men's rich Cockney spiels.

Holidays are special on the Heath; between times, the hurdy-
gurdies and roundabouts vanish and the Heath is empty. It is
hard to remember that Hampstead Heath is a city park, set
close to miles of dirty streets and endless houses. It looks serene,
rolling, open country. The hills rise and gently fall as far as the
eye can see. The grass is green, the trees beautiful—and on the
other side of the horizon is London!

Leigh Hunt and Shelley and Hazlitt walked on Hampstead
Heath. Then, as now, Hampstead was a village favored by London writers who fled from the distracting city crowds to seek
sweet solitude, and each other. The side streets leading from
the Heath are nearly as famous as back alleys in the City. Constable and Galsworthy and Romney—dozens of painters and
writers lived in Flask Walk or Well Walk, Church Row or
Heath Street.

The Keats Museum is in Keats Grove.

In the year 1818, John Keats, already fatally ill with tubercu-
losis, came here to live with his friend Brown. The pretty Re-

gency house was, in those days, divided into half; a motherly widow lived next to Keats and Brown. Her name was Mrs. Brawne, and she had a daughter, Fanny.

The Keats Museum is instructive. The exhibits are cleverly arranged, the letters and diaries fascinating. The series of Hogarth engravings which Brown spent the winter of Keats's illness trying (without success) to copy, hang on the wall of the study, along with the blistering comments Keats made in his diary.

But the museum in Hampstead is more than instructive; it is haunting. The passionate, tragic ghost walks Wentworth Place in broad daylight. His voice (faintly tinged with the Cockney that betrayed him as no gentleman) echoes through the room where he learned, with such anguish of spirit, that he was to die. His red hair almost blazes in the sunlight under the great old tree in the garden; the memory of his beloved is like a perfume, faintly on the air.

Keats is the classic hero of English-speaking adolescence (which does not make him a less great poet). If you are one of the many, many Americans who spent your youth hearing in the secret reaches of your soul, "Bright star, would I were steadfast as thou art," the Keats Museum will be a voyage to your own as well as to the poet's past. The ghost that walks on Hampstead Heath is not only John Keats—but Everyman, aged sixteen. Youth dies of time and experience, as well as of consumption. The Keats Museum is sad, but for me the most moving experience in London.

Pall Mall, the National Gallery, Richmond, and Kew

AFTER lunch: Pall Mall and St. James's, by way of brisk contrast. There is nothing like a real loop-the-loop to suggest the variety, the rich complexity of London itself. Keats was no gentleman; in his entire lifetime he was never invited into the sacred reaches of a Pall Mall club. I fear that in 1818 or 1820 the noble lords who grandly paced the elegant pavements of Pall Mall would have considered Keats a cad, a low bounder. Thackeray, on the other hand, was a leading member of the Athenaeum Club—but that was a good deal later, and besides, Thackeray spoke the King's English, and did not write heart-breaking poems about love.

I fear I sound a bounder myself about Pall Mall. Yet I love this part of London. The Georgian and Regency streets around St. James's Square are as fine as anything in England; one feels soothed, walking in a world of dignity and understatement, power refined by taste. For nearly two hundred years the rulers of what was then the world inhabited the nearby clubs, drove along these streets in beautiful carriages, gambled until day-light with thousands of pounds—sterling. Nowadays Pall Mall is a little dusty, maybe haunted, itself. The jokes about the old gentlemen looking out the windows of a London club are not very funny in the modern world of crisis. The rulers no longer sit at cards under a blaze of candlelight; English gentlemen who still dine at the clubs along Pall Mall have a nervous air, and the laws of the Kingdom are made at Westminster, not over port in St. James's Square.

The best way to explore this area is to start at St. James's Square, and branch off from the square onto Charles II Street, Duke of York Street, and so on. St. James's Square was laid out in the Restoration and was the first fashionable "West End" address. Alas, some of the stately seventeenth-century houses have been replaced by business offices, but duchesses and dukes and Prime Ministers lived in St. James's Square, and it is still a comely relic of eighteenth- and nineteenth-century London. King Street leads you from the square to St. James's Street; turn left for St. James's Palace and the Mall, then walk toward Trafalgar Square along one of London's stateliest avenues, past Marlborough House to Admiralty Arch, at which point you make an abrupt switch, head right into Whitehall, the seat of the British Government, or at least the home of the British Civil Service.

Downing Street is off Whitehall. With any luck you may see

ST. JAMES'S SQUARE

the TV cameras assembled at Number 10 for one of those modern rituals without which, apparently, no twentieth-century government, in any country, càn function. I am amused by travelers and anthropologists solemnly reporting savage rites in the South Sea Islands, or voodoo in Haiti; nobody seems to regard with the same detached interest our own tribal magic— the virtue attached to recording by camera the images of our leaders in some crucial moment of history, such as the welcoming by the British Prime Minister of six visiting chieftains from Iraq. The English reserve their pomp and circumstance for the Queen and the Royal Family; our own President, who must combine the jobs of official greeter, national hero, and working head of an enormous and complex government, is necessarily surrounded by a good deal more protocol than the English Prime Minister. Most American tourists are surprised by the unpretentious air of Number 10 Downing Street, and fascinated by the casual appearances of English Government leaders. The TV cameramen add a touch of pageantry to what is otherwise classic English understatement in the grand manner.

You will want to walk all the way down Whitehall, gay with flower boxes, past the Horse Guards (lovely, they are!), Inigo Jones's Banqueting Hall (where Charles I was executed), and the Cenotaph; if you have the strength, you can double back on Victoria Embankment to Northumberland Avenue; otherwise return to Trafalgar Square and the National Gallery.

I feel guilty, putting the National Gallery so late on your London schedule. Many critics think it the best and most important collection of paintings in the world. The Louvre is bigger, but its size makes the gallery difficult for tourists, and among its vast acres of exhibits are some (at least) that might be retired to a decent obscurity. The National Gallery is smaller than the Metropolitan in New York or the Louvre; but every great school of painting is represented, each by a series of masterpieces. Selection rather than size has made the National Gallery unique among the world's collections.

In this book, Richard and I cannot attempt a discussion of the National Gallery treasures. If you are a passionate admirer of Botticelli, Michelangelo, or Raphael, Bellini, Titian or Leonardo, the gallery catalogue will be all the guide you need. Perhaps before you left America, you had never seen a Tintoretto, a Velásquez, a Rembrandt, a Turner, or a Holbein? And Degas, Toulouse-Lautrec, and El Greco are only names without personal content? In that case, go to the National Gallery, buy a catalogue, and march through the various rooms. Every art requires a certain discipline; only the Philistine knows what he likes before he has acquired the ABC, the idea, of the idiom. If painting is unknown to you, the National Gallery may provide you with the most important souvenir you can bring home from Europe—a new dimension of experience. Every art critic began by looking at a picture, and feeling that authentic flash of awakening, that exquisite second of recognition which was the prelude to a new world. If you do come to the National Gallery to acquire your first experience of easel painting, you will be fortunate. I cannot imagine an easier or more sublime introduction to "art."

It is high time, on your eleventh day in London, for the Changing of the Guard at Buckingham Palace. I confess I think the Changing of the Guard is a crashing bore. The British Army is decorative and fascinating—I went to a tattoo (military show) at Chester, which was splendid—especially the Horse Guards, who, mounted on matched black steeds, waltzed slowly past the grandstand, helmets gleaming, standards flying, in perfect three-four time. But the Buckingham Palace performance is second-rate, in my opinion. This is heresy, but you cannot see what is going on, for the most part. The music is all right, but the traffic drowns out all but the noisiest tootling, and I cringe when I hear the drums rolling. No doubt there is some mystic, historical reason for all the marching up and down the soldiers do, but I must say, as a modern piece of stage managing, it strikes me as nonsense.

The Changing of the Guard does not take more than three-quarters of an hour—which leaves plenty of time for your expedition to Richmond and Kew.

Richmond is a handsome old town on the banks of the Thames. It is now part of metropolitan London, but it has a particular history of its own. The streets from the station leading up to the Quadrant have a sleepy air under the summer's sun. On Richmond Green are the ruins of the ancient Richmond Palace, where lived Edward III (remember, the one with

twelve children?). Henry VII rebuilt the palace, Queen Elizabeth died there, George II lived in one of its wings, and now
there is not much left, except a romantic patina of the past.

From the Palace, walk up Richmond Hill to the Terrace
Gardens, where you will find the "celebrated" view of the
Thames Valley, recommended by guidebooks and Thackeray.
It is lovely, the river and green hills and sailboats far away; and
Richmond Park, opposite, is beautifully kept, artfully designed,
with many delightful picnic spots. If you care deeply (I am a
fanatic) about *Vanity Fair*, Richmond Park will recall Thackeray's best scenes. This was the backdrop for London society
at the turn of the nineteenth century.

Kew is altogether different. Kindly, fatherly George III
(otherwise known as That Tyrant) moved to Kew Gardens to

GEORGE III AND FAMILY

get away from the pomp of Hampton Court. He operated a
semi-public royal nursery in the gardens (people were admitted on Sundays to peer at the little Princes and Princesses
parading among the rose gardens) and started the botanical
collections, now the finest in England.

It gives me a shock to hear the casual English view of George
III. Evidently more modern Londoners have been raised on
Fanny Burney than on Edmund Burke. George III was not
exactly the dear good-natured, homely, bumbling character
the guides describe at Kew. Even as a paterfamilias, I fear
George III was a flop. It is a delightful picture, the whole Royal

Family out walking of a Sunday in the rose gardens while loyal subjects cheered from a discreet distance. But look how the Royal Princes turned out! George III may have spent his spare time collecting rare water lilies, but during business hours he was busy corrupting the English Parliament, buying rotten boroughs for those unsavory rascals called the "King's Men," and exasperating certain overseas subjects, notably George Washington, Benjamin Franklin, Sam Adams, and many, many others. From a strictly English point of view, George III was the most butter-fingered King in British history since Ethelred the Unready—a disaster in every sense of the word. He may have been quaint at Kew, but he was pig-headed at Westminster. As a tyrant he was a one-hundred-percent failure; as a papa he produced a spectacular brood of wastrels; as a King he almost wrecked the monarchy. Only as a Hanoverian was he run of the mill.

All the same, the botany at Kew Gardens is fine. Lovely orchids—and a tea garden too, in case you get exhausted.

I read this over and discover I sound surly about Kew Gardens. Our whole family adores Kew; we go out on Sunday afternoons to see the roses, and watch the goldfish in the big pond. After all, George III may not have been much of a king, but he hired splendid gardeners; no wonder Londoners remember him with tolerance. On a smiling, sunshiny afternoon at Kew, it is hard to recall George III's infinite sins—he collected such fine water lilies!

Windsor and Eton

FOR YOUR twelfth day in London—Windsor and Eton. You can take the train or go by the Green Line coaches to Windsor. It takes about an hour and a quarter on the bus, an hour on the train, so I am afraid you had better be up with the birds to get an early start.

Windsor Castle, from a distance, is a fairy-story picture, incredible, magic, indelible. It is everything you imagined England would be—the delightful green of the park, the rich grass, the fragrant flower-beds, and rising on the hill in the distance, the frowning gray turrets of the Norman Castle.

The Castle itself is full of variety. I am sure you will instantly recognize the *Norman* stonework and the *Early English* additions (William the Conqueror built it, Henry III and Edward III extended it, the wretched Henry VI was born here), although you may be surprised by George IV's alterations, not to mention Queen Victoria's cozy interiors. St. George's Chapel is in late *Perpendicular*—you will know it because it is a variant of the Henry VII Chapel at Westminster. Knights of the Garter are installed here, and in the chapel choir are their stalls and banners. In the north choir aisle is the tomb of Edward IV, our Yorkist friend. Many other royalty are buried in St. George's Chapel, among them poor old Henry VI and his cousin Henry VIII. Charles I is here with George III, Edward VII, and George V.

Henry III built what is now called the Albert Memorial Chapel, off St. George's Chapel; it was partly rebuilt by Henry VII, who originally intended it to house his tomb. The unfinished chapel was presented by Henry VIII to Cardinal Wolsey, who fitted up something first-class by way of a last resting place in the chapel—for himself. Cardinals propose, but Tudors dispose. The Cardinal did not even get into the lower regions of St. George's Chapel, and his tomb was thoroughly taken apart during the Reformation. I do not know if Henry VIII made a try for this handsome annex. Some three hundred years later Victoria, his great-niece to the tenth power, took over the chapel and made it a memorial for her beloved Albert.

Between St. George's Chapel and its annex is a small passageway which leads into the part of Windsor I like best—old courtyards, called the Dean's Cloister and the Canon's Cloister. Just beyond is Winchester Tower, where Chaucer probably lived when he was Master of Works at Windsor.

The grand tour of the state apartments at Windsor is *de rigueur* for tourists. The furniture is pretty ugly, and the general effect does not come up to Chatsworth or Blenheim or Versailles. All the same, there are some fine paintings—Rubens,

Rembrandt, Titian, and so on. St. George's Hall is handsome but synthetic; it has been restored beyond the point where Master of Works Chaucer would recognize it.

After the state apartments comes the . . . Doll's House. I am told everybody loves the Doll's House.

I hope you will take the 220 steps to the top of the Round Tower; from the battlements of Windsor Castle, spread out before you, is the curving silver Thames far below the frowning cliff, and on every side, the green garden of England. Approaching the Castle from the bustling tourist town of Windsor, one loses its meaning in space; from the Round Tower you can feel in your bones how the Castle, commanding the river, dominated the heart of the ancient kingdom. William the Conqueror had a sharp eye for a strategic situation. He built the Tower of London exactly at the Pool—the port—of his capital; at Lincoln, his Castle frowned over the Midlands; and Windsor was the key, the bastion, for the twelve richest counties in England. He who held Windsor, in medieval times, held London and the kingdom.

I never go panting to the top of the Round Tower without feeling the spell of England's past. Chaucer stood on these stones, wise, sardonic, amused by life, and watched Richard II and his train of creaky, armored knights come riding across the hills from London. Henry V's proud banner flew from this tower on that happy day when the Queen, French Katherine, bore His Majesty a son in the royal apartments below. Not so many years later, Margaret of Anjou, weak from childbed, anxiously dragged herself up these steep stone steps to study much of the same landscape the traveler sees today. Those richly armored knights on the horizon . . . Margaret watched passionately as the standards floated in the sunlight. Was it Somerset, come to rescue her? But across the soft valley Margaret saw the white rose embroidered on the banners. Richard, Duke of York, rode furiously at the head of his barons, galloping on to Windsor to "protect" Margaret's new-born Prince of Wales. . . .

Centuries of time have moved around this tower at Windsor. Black-draped horses bore Edward IV's coffin up the steep hill; the funeral train of Henry VIII came slowly across this same gentle country; the sable flags flew from these battlements

for the Prince Consort Albert, while below in the chapel the
Queen of England wept for her husband.

Incidentally, Albert is not buried in the Memorial Chapel,
but lies beside his Queen at Frogmore Mausoleum, in Windsor
Home Park. The mausoleum is seldom open to the public.

"QU'EST-CE QUE C'EST, CE TOAD-IN-THE-HOLE?"

On the lunch situation: Windsor is a tourist town. The
French have the theory that history takes a lot out of the
traveler and that tourists are apt to remember what they eat
in scenic locations. Across the Channel there is a good deal of
putting the best foot forward at Versailles cafés; and restaurants in Chartres are so good some tourists go all the way from
Paris to gallop through the cathedral at a brisk trot (*pour
gagner un bon appétit*), after which they retire to a five-course
luncheon, red and white wine, champagne with the fruit. But
at Windsor the emphasis is on high thinking and plain—even

atrocious—living. The Castle is wonderful, but most of the restaurants, especially those catering to the tourist bus trade, are—well, terrible. From time to time some enterprising soul opens a decent restaurant, but such establishments have a way, after a season, of collapsing into the general scene, going native. Still, you might collect an address or two and try your luck. The odds are against you, however. I have heard sharp disputes break out, among American tourists, on the relative horrors of eating at Warwick or Windsor, but little good can come of these distinctions.

Let us face it. Tourist food in England (a separate category from the ordinary fare) is grim. The last time I lunched at Warwick, I heard a Belgian at the next table ask the waitress, *"Tiens, mademoiselle, qu'est-ce que c'est, ce* toad-in-the-hole?"

"Ha," I said, strictly to myself, "he'll find out."

He did, too.

"Horreur!" he kept shouting, but nobody paid any attention.

But then, as I think of it, Belgians would probably cry *horreur* at American establishments featuring signs, "Welcome Tourist Buses," greasy hamburgers, or that interesting delicacy deep-fried shrimp special, sometimes unfrozen, more often, not quite.

Who are we Americans to talk about *English* tourist food?

Eton is less than a mile from Windsor Castle; you can walk (across the bridge, up the main street) or take a bus or taxi.

I think it is rather odd that Eton, the best-known of what the English call their "public schools," was founded (1440) by Henry VI. He seems the last man to have been interested in education. However, there it is—Henry VI, Founder of Eton— and a statue of the lamented (and lamentable) last king of the House of Lancaster stands in the school yard to prove it. A delegation of Eton boys goes up to the Tower of London every year on Henry's birthday and places a red, red rose on the very spot where the founder perished, strangled by the White Rose gang.

There are plenty of other ancient traditions practiced in the school. The guides at Eton formerly belonged to the lush, chatty, legend-has-it section of tourist spielers, and they used to lay on heavily with the quaintness, especially for American visitors. I have not been back to inquire whether they were included in the big Windsor reform wave. *The Times* announced that Windsor guides were to be cruelly strait-jacketed by a mere eight centuries or so of strictly history. No more legends, not even the one about Anne Boleyn languishing in the Curfew Tower dungeon! The Eton guides will be sadly handicapped without their store of moss-grown fables, although the true story of England's great public school will interest travelers (such as myself) who grow restive under the deluge of vintage jokes (*circa* 1907) and colorful bits about the whipping block. On this question of using physical violence against children, I have never thought the striking of a small boy with a heavy bull whip was especially funny. A question of taste.

Once past guides and whipping blocks, Eton is fascinating. The courtyards are stately: the mellow brick has a patina in the summer sun; and if you come before end of term you will see the young scholars, decorative in broad white collars or dusty tail coats.

The Chapel at Eton is *Perpendicular* again, with a number of curious tombs, and a series of wall paintings discovered in the 1920's. These frescoes are fifteenth century, and will suggest what English churches and cathedrals looked like before the Roundheads smashed the glowing stained glass in the windows and plastered over the showy wall panels.

Of all the sights at Eton, the one I find most touching is the frieze at the entrance to the school yard. Here are written the names of 1,175 Old Etonians—FOR KING AND COUNTRY, IN MEMORIAM, 1914–1919.

The last two days of a London fortnight are difficult to plot out in advance. Obviously you will have to cancel your airplane tickets, cut yourself into sections, or, barring such drastic steps, make some kind of a choice among the various riches. For one thing, you must see some more London museums—the Tate, the Wallace Collection, the Victoria and Albert Museum, at the minimum. You have hardly had time to go shopping. Bond Street, Regent Street, the antique shops, the old-silver emporiums are bedrock for the London visitor. These items you can perhaps "work in" (to use the jargon of the wild-eyed last-minute tourist). However, the following sights require solid mornings, or whole, complete days, and frankly each one is a double-must. Perhaps you have by this time developed a preference for Norman architecture, or a passion for Christopher Wren, in which case you can make your selection with intelligent calm. Otherwise, the pin method (close your eyes and jab at the page) will serve as well.

Greenwich

Greenwich Hospital is (except for one wing) the work of Christopher Wren. I think you should see it first from the river boat. The harmonious white columns rise from the Thames in one of Wren's stateliest compositions. When you land on the pier, you can walk through the grounds, and across the road to Inigo Jones's Queen's House, which is English Renaissance at its pure and beautiful beginning. The National Maritime Museum nearby may sound dull—it is one of those museums that you wander into for a quick look, compelled by that nagging sense of duty which haunts all tourists, and leave five hours later, totally bemused. The museum reveals the history of the English Navy: ship models, uniforms, battle plans, souvenirs, admirals' gold braid and orders of the day. You will be vividly reminded that England is a maritime nation, and a nation of maritime painters as well. The naval scenes at Greenwich are fascinating, almost as hypnotic as the mementos of Nelson, of which my favorite is his grog jug, located cheek by jowl with his Bible. With his Bible, and his grog jug, and his diamond plume for his gold-braided hat (not to mention Lady Hamilton's autograph), Nelson went into the battle ready for anything, especially Victory.

Before you leave Greenwich, you should climb the hill to the park, where there is an impressive view of the river and the great city of London, and the ruins of the old observatory. This is zero meridian of longitude, you will remember, and the home of the classic phrase "Five (or six, or whatever) o'clock, Greenwich Mean Time."

On your way back to Charing Cross by train, you may have time to stop at Deptford, where, in the Church of St. Nicholas, Christopher Marlowe is buried. There is not much to see (Deptford itself is dreary) except a memorial to Marlowe—yet poor Kit was killed here, in a drunken brawl, before his genius had time fully to flower. Richard and I made the pilgrimage, solemnly, to Marlowe's stone tablet and got lost and had a dismal, irritating time getting home; for several weeks we denounced Deptford, violently, and then one day I heard myself saying (smugly) to some old London hand: "What! You haven't been to see where Marlowe is buried? Well!"

St. Albans

St. Albans is not far from London on a Green Line bus. I would not recommend St. Albans because of the two Wars of the Roses battles; the battles, unfortunately, do not show. But the Cathedral is a remarkable *Norman* church, built on the site of a Roman settlement of great antiquity. Modern architects and scholars sniff at St. Albans because the Victorians let themselves go on a big "restoration" job in the interior of the church, 1856–1877. All the same, I think St. Albans is interesting, if not as grand or beautiful as some of the other more famous English cathedrals. The thirteenth-century paintings on the massive *Norman* piers in the nave are curious and the altar screen (*Perpendicular*) is splendid. St. Albans will be a good introduction for Canterbury or Durham or Winchester; it illustrates the wonderful English method of combining *Early English* with *Norman,* and *Perpendicular* with *Decorated.* The Victorian vandalism we can overlook—there is no sense in being so choosy. Besides, the *Norman* tower is unique: if you look closely, you will see that it is made of Roman bricks, no doubt quarried out of the Roman-British ruins the Normans found on the site.

St. Albans will give you a chance to practice the Foolproof System for Churches, and after a happy morning poking around the nave, and sitting on the ancient tombstones in the tree-shaded cathedral yard, you will want to walk down from the abbey gatehouse (1380) to the little River Ver. I like best this part of St. Albans. It is not too hard to imagine Margaret of Anjou leading her wild Scotsmen into battle across this small stream, or Richard, Duke of York, laying about him with broadsword and creaking armor while overhead floated the banner of the White Rose. The Fighting Cocks Inn stands at the bridge of the River Ver—and claims to be the oldest inhabited dwelling place in England. Mine host says the inn was formerly a boathouse for Offa's Saxon monastery, which probably occupied the site of the cathedral. Historians politely call the "claims" of the Fighting Cocks Inn "rash" and say it was surely rebuilt, pretty thoroughly, in 1600. Of course, 1600 is only yesterday for English historians, but an innkeeper in the United States would hardly be downhearted with a certified patent for his establishment dated 1600. Anyway, the Fighting Cocks Inn does not claim to be Roman (perhaps the management is fainthearted?) —which seems odd, for Offa and his Saxons were mere newcomers to St. Albans.

Verulamium (beyond the Ver bridge) was the most important city, long, long ago, in Roman Britain. You can inspect the theatre, a fine mosaic pavement, and other interesting reconstructions. If you have a pleasant day for the journey to St. Albans and Verulamium, you can stand on the bank of the little river, and suddenly feel yourself touched, saddened, by the great passage of time—Romans, and Saxons, and Normans, and Lancastrians rode across this stream, galloped up that hill, and disappeared into the centuries.

England Is Easy for Americans

RICHARD and I have arranged this second part of our book in a series of seven journeys out of London. Obviously, these journeys (each one of which might take a week) can be combined, cut short, or expanded, as your time, money, and taste suggest. We hope you will be able to read through Part II, and then, armed with a good map of England, plan your own trip—because travel is as personal as love. One man's wife is another's *bête noire*; Durham will be magic for the first traveler, but not for the second.

How to make these journeys in England? We are in favor of almost any means of travel, from rowboat to pogo stick to Rolls-Royce, except the Guided Autobus Tour, surely the most pernicious invention of modern man short of the singing commercial. A smart crack over the back of the neck with a heavy blunt instrument can produce (and much more cheaply) the same sensation as a day in the company of thirty-six fellow victims, seeing Stratford, Warwick, Kenilworth, Broadway, and Tewkesbury Abbey—tomorrow Chester and the Lake District.

Across such hideous scenes I draw a veil. If your money and time are limited, make a leisurely circuit of Canterbury, Oxford, and the Cotswolds; you will have pleasure, and learn a good deal about England. Ten days spent furiously jouncing across hill and dale from London to Scotland to Cornwall and back will produce nothing but an involuntary twitch at the mere sight of a megaphone, and a sort of delirium, compounded of Wordsworth, *Ivanhoe* and Mary, Queen of Scots. England is beautiful—so beautiful—and fascinating; but not on the receiving end of a guided tour.

If the how to travel in England should not be by guided tour, what then? Many Americans end up behind the megaphone because they are not sure how to manage trains, or where to stay, or what to see. A guided tour is simple; all problems are officially under control.

England, we remark firmly at this point, is easy for Americans. Train service is good, fares (third-class) are relatively reasonable; ticket agents speak your native tongue; and timetables are not in French or Hungarian. Pluck up courage, and plot your own strategy. Your travel bureau in the United States can make hotel reservations and buy train tickets in advance, if you like; or, once in London, you can make your own arrangements. The best way to get around (short of a Rolls-Royce, with chauffeur, but then it is always nice to be a millionaire, both at home and abroad), the most practical method of operations for the average tourist is by express trains for long distances, plus local bus for hamlets. The most remote villages in Northumberland, let alone the famous showplaces in crowded Kent, are connected with mainline trains by bus. Across England, you see buses wending their way from Stonehenge to Salisbury, or from Battle to Bodiam Castle. There is hardly a Yorkshire moor so lonely that a bus does not pass it twice a day.

An example of our suggested method of operations, for Journey Number Three: Take the London express to Bath. The train will startle you, a mere American, by its speed. English trains zip through the countryside. Once in Bath, make your headquarters at your chosen hotel, and after inspecting England's lovely Georgian city, go around to the bus station and peer at the schedules posted on the bulletin board. The bus for Wells makes a leisurely, delightful journey across the

Somerset hills; from Wells you can either take a circular train that night back to Bath, or go on by bus to Glastonbury. Travel light if you stay overnight at one place or another; but you can easily get back to Bath each evening for dinner. The time you spend chugging through the Somerset villages will show you a charming corner of England which many tourists miss.

Each of our seven proposed journeys can be comfortably made by express train from London, hotel at some convenient headquarters, local buses from there on. Should you have a little extra money to spend, car rentals flourish all over England. A pleasant way of inspecting the more remote corners without utterly bankrupting your privy purse is to take the fast train from London to, say, York, spend two or three days seeing the Minster, the museums, the walls, and the immediate suburbs of the old city, and then hire one of the little drive-yourself English cars for a two- or three-day round trip on the moors. This system of train-plus-U-Drive-It would work well for Durham and the Border Country, the Cotswolds, and Yorkshire. Kent is so well served by local buses, so crowded, its towns so close, a car is almost a waste, unless you are very rich; the same for Oxford and Cambridge, Bath and Wells.

Driving in England on the major expressways which connect big cities is the same as driving on ditto in the United States— no fun, but plenty of carbon monoxide, and not a few perils. Once away from these triumphs of cement mixers and road engineering, however, the narrow country lanes and winding market-town roads are pleasant. These British back roads are not designed for high speeds. They are full of narrow turns, blind corners, unprotected crossings, and steep, old-fashioned grades. You are not supposed to drive fast, but then the only reason you have rented a car is to see the scenery.

Two fundamental points, however: beware the bicycle menace, in the summers especially, AND KEEP LEFT.

Another fundamental point: hotel prices. In this naughty world, you generally get what you pay for, in England as anywhere else. Hotel accommodation costs about what its equivalent would cost at home; a beautiful room, handsomely furnished and with a private bath, plus breakfast served in bed, attractive hotel lounges, lovely scenery, costs a lot of money,

THE BICYCLE MENACE

in England or the United States. A room at an English pub is cheap, but so is a boarding house at home. Perhaps English hotels are a shade less expensive than American ones, yet if you smoke cigarettes and have an occasional cocktail before dinner, your daily travel budget will add up to about what it would be in Indiana or California or Maryland. Big cities are more expensive than villages. London is fiendishly hard on the purse; the visitor to New York City also goes home bankrupt. If, in planning your trip, you use American prices for your British budget, you should arrive at a fairly accurate idea of costs. But do not forget: use American holiday prices to calculate an English vacation. Some Americans arrive in England and expect a meal at the Savoy Grill to cost the same as a debauch at Jack's One Arm Eaterie.

I begin to sound like Scrooge—all this talk about mere money. No matter whether you travel by shank's pony or Mercedes, lodge at the Youth Hostel or in a converted castle (indoor plumbing!), England awaits you. No other country in the world has so much to show you, in distances so small, and in time so short.

Choose one or all of our Seven Journeys from London. Combine them, expand them, delete them, take ten days, or a month, or a week—wherever you go, whatever you see, you will remember always.

Canterbury, Kent, Sussex, and Surrey, the Southeast

WHEN I was a fat, strong-minded little girl in East Cleveland, Ohio, there was a picture on the wall above our dining-room buffet. The picture had once graced the Benwether Brothers Fancy Meats and Reliable Poultry calendar for 1923, but my Aunt Kate hated to waste things. Besides, she considered the picture educational. So (in January, 1924) she cut off the part about the reliable poultry, found a frame of golden oak in the attic (left over from a photograph of Uncle Pat, who died in circumstances of which the less said the better), and hung the finished product to the left of the new electric percolator—where my sister Eileen and I studied it, over cornflakes or chocolate cake, during most of our childhood.

The picture was interesting. In the center was a quaint white-plaster cottage, lavishly punctuated by black Tudor beams, and thatched (until the picture began to fade along about 1927) in thick, butter-yellow straw. In the foreground there was a

winding road, a gurgling brook, a low red-brick wall, a white
wooden gate, and a garden riotous with pink roses. To the left
of the cottage was a spreading oak tree. In the background,
sharp against a sunny sky and a solitary, fleecy white cloud,
were three church towers. Underneath (slightly frayed, where
the scissors had slipped) was one word, in large Gothic type:

England

The road to Canterbury winds up and down over low hills.
One day, I looked idly out the bus window. Suddenly I came
to attention. I jerked Richard's coat sleeve. "Oh, look!" I cried,
in a voice shaken by emotion. "Look, darling! *England!*"

My husband, like most men, is keenly aware of fellow customers on a public conveyance. He muttered irritably, "Not so
loud. What'd you think it was, Lapland?"

*"No! No! You don't understand, it was over the dining-room
buffet for years...."*

But the bus had passed my thatched white cottage, mounted
a final hill, and below us was Canterbury.

"Chaucer!" my husband said, rather too loud himself.

I recount this excitable approach to Kent because it will
probably happen to you. Canterbury and the three south-
eastern English counties—Kent, Sussex, and Surrey—are, for
Americans brought up on calendars or Chaucer, the classic
England of our dreams. East Anglia is flat, fascinating, and
strange; the Border Country is wild; the Cotswolds and the
golden stone villages of the Shakespeare country are a surprise. But Kent is the picture on the calendar, Sussex is the
illustration from the sixth-grade geography book, Surrey is the
travel poster. Thatched Tudor cottages (complete with pink
roses) line the winding roads of Kent, Dover, and Sandwich,
the timbered villages of Littlebourne, Wickhambreaux, and
Ash, Barfreston with its Norman church—these are pages from
the *National Geographic*. Sussex has the story-book castle of
Bodiam; the dreamy, crumbling turrets stand in the middle of
a lily-covered moat. The steep streets of Rye, lined with
beamed Tudor inns and Georgian mansions, are so picturesque
as to seem unreal. Across the flat valley, Winchelsea, a seaport
deserted long ago by the sea, is silent and perfect. On the Sussex
coast, Bosham's ancient Saxon church overlooks a blue inlet

where sailboats ride at anchor; and in the Kent hills at Seven-oaks, Knole, the greatest Tudor palace of them all, rises grace-fully from a sweep of wholly incredible lawn.

Kent, Sussex, and Surrey—the flowers are so bright, the fields so rich, the lawns so thick and soft; the villages are kept like museums; on every horizon is the tower of an ancient church.

Southern England! Even before Caesar, daring traders and settlers crossed the Channel and landed at one of these Cinque Ports. Pevensey's stones, worn gentle now by time, were once the walls of a bristling Roman fortress. The legions left, the fort crumbled, the winter seas beat savagely against the empty watch towers. Centuries passed. On a stormy day in autumn, ships fought their way into Pevensey harbor; that night William the Conqueror pitched his tent against the ruined walls. In the morning his fleet was gone, battered to pieces against the rocky shore; like Cortez, Duke William turned his back on the sea and marched ten miles inland to Battle. There, on what was then a lonely moor, the Conqueror met Harold, King of the Saxons: October 14, 1066.

Kent, Sussex, and Surrey—these ancient hills saw the begin-ning of British history. This is England.

I admit my heart leaped that day in June when I saw the Benwether Brothers' calendar from the window of the Canter-bury bus. Few things in life turn out to be as one learned them, aged eight, in East Cleveland, Ohio. No reasonable adult sup-poses life will show him, in full color, the thatched cottage and the pink roses of his childhood. The southern counties of En-gland are a bonus. Richard and I have traveled into every part of this island, but after all the towns and varied landscapes, when I think of England I see, in my inner vision, that Tudor farmhouse, the winding road, and the three church towers against the sky. But now I see Kent—not the 1923 calendar.

The first and most important sight to visit in southern En-gland and, after London, in the whole of the British Isles, is Canterbury Cathedral.

Canterbury is one of the greatest Gothic masterpieces left to the modern world; it is as significant in the record of western civilization as Chartres or Notre Dame de Paris. The Cathedral is the seat of the Archbishop of Canterbury, the Primate of All

CANTERBURY CATHEDRAL

England; Canterbury occupies in the Church of England the same position as does St. Peter's for the Roman Catholics. Since A.D. 597, when the earliest Saxon building on this spot was consecrated by St. Augustine, Canterbury has been the first church of the kingdom—first in point of grandeur, riches, power, and influence. Moreover, Canterbury is encrusted with legend, hallowed by myth. It was the tragic scene of the most haunting murder story outside the Bible itself. Its ancient chronicles link our modern world with the distant past. Finally, as Shakespeare is the Tower's poet, Canterbury has Chaucer.

Canterbury requires at least an overnight stay. The town itself was cruelly bombed in a "Baedeker Raid," but the Cathedral—like St. Paul's—was saved, and most of the medieval and Tudor buildings within and without the old city walls have been patched together again, restored or rebuilt. The Cathedral stands in a close, with cloisters, gardens, strange passages, monastery ruins, the King's School (this was the school in *Of Human Bondage*), and many other buildings curious or antique. All this takes time: Canterbury is one of the few places in England where hotel reservations during the summer season must be secured weeks, even months, in advance. You can leave other arrangements to be made in London, if you like, but have your travel bureau in the United States book your room for Canterbury. People slept a hundred to a dormitory in Chaucer's day, and the situation has not improved.

If this bad news comes too late, do not despair. Richard and I, ever the optimists, ignored the spoil-sport wiseacres, and turned up at Canterbury without a hotel reservation. We figured it could not be that crowded. We spent a wonderful afternoon at the Cathedral, and about twilight decided to hunt out the hovel. No hovels. No tents. No nothing. Even the Youth Hostel (supposing that Richard could disguise himself as a lad of twenty-four, with me posing as his mother)—even the Youth Hostel was jam-packed. The *père aubergiste* told us with some hauteur that reservations closed a year in advance for the entire season.

As we were drearily deciding to take the train back to London and sodden defeat, a policeman came along and suggested Ash or Littlebourne or one of those places. We caught the nine-o'clock bus up the Dover Road and spent the night in a pleasant Georgian country house, made over into an inn. The plumbing was new, and we turned out to be not ten minutes from Barfreston, which we had marked down on our schedule, "church supposed to be as good as Iffley, Oxford." It is too. Ill-wind department. We explored a corner of Kent during the morning and were back in Canterbury for lunch. All the same, it would be safer to make a hotel reservation about February for your trip to Canterbury in July.

The history of the Cathedral is so absorbing that I had better get the technical details out of the way before we take up characters like St. Alphege, Thirkill the Tall, Thomas of London, Wat Tyler, Archbishop Sudbury, and so on. (Archbishop Sudbury is buried at Canterbury, though not all of him. It seems he . . . but no, I am wandering!)

Canterbury Cathedral is the most important *English* Gothic masterpiece. I emphasize the word *English* because Canterbury is characteristic of what is sometimes called Island Gothic. Now, English or Island Gothic is different from French, Spanish, Italian, German, or Austrian medieval building. The Continental styles seem to have set an all but inflexible pattern on some modern minds. Confronted by Canterbury (or Lincoln, or Wells, or York) there are critics who have called English Gothic peculiar rather than original, and confused instead of richly various. What gall, in my opinion! However, the wind has been veering. Some French art authorities have lately "discovered" that *Perpendicular* was a unique contribution, and an Italian critic rocked scholarly circles with the argument that since symmetry was not the essence of Gothic (on the contrary), how can one sneer at English churches for being less symmetrical than Continental examples? The English themselves, whose modesty in such matters is an obsession, spent whole generations going around with a feeling of inferiority; recently they have been edified to hear from local art moguls that the homeland has at least as many medieval masterpieces to the square mile as any foreign rival.

I stress such points in advance, because I think comparisons should be instructive, not invidious. Canterbury is different from Chartres; Island Gothic is original, not second-rate.

How original? Why is Canterbury different from Notre Dame or Rheims?

French Gothic flowered in great city churches. Until modern times, Chartres had butcher shops and bakeries jammed between its flying buttresses. The space around Notre Dame was only cleared in the nineteenth century. It is a rare Continental church that does not have a gentleman's retiring room located directly to the left of the north porch, or handily backed up against the apse.

English Gothic was usually built behind monastery walls. Yet in Chaucer's day the Cathedral Close at Canterbury was as cluttered as the approaches to medieval Chartres. The monks built hospitals, breweries, dormitories, baker's shops, and cut-rate souvenir stalls all over the place. The Dissolution brought a big change. Once the rubble left by Henry VIII's wrecking crews was cleared away, the Tudor clergy resorted to grass seed. Today the English cathedral is surrounded by lawns, framed by ponds and gardens, and manicured clumps of trees. Wells stands in a tranquil, sunny close; at Ely you may eat your picnic lunch in a meadow overlooking the famous eight-sided tower; at York the lawns sweep up to the flying buttresses of the chapter house.

The approach to Canterbury is classic. The Cathedral towers can be seen at a distance; but as you come into Mercury Lane, Tudor-beamed houses hide the close. You reach a cobbled courtyard, and the massive Christ Church gate. You walk through a narrow, dark passage, damp with the smell of stone five hundred years old, twenty feet thick. A short, twisting alleyway; and suddenly . . .

A blaze of sunlight, a great sweep of lawn and open space.

Canterbury Cathedral rises, tremendous, glorious, and alone.

I do not suppose Henry VIII intended the effect, but he certainly improved the view. For sheer drama, nothing medieval can surpass this introduction to Canterbury.

What I am going to say next about English Gothic should be understood relatively, against the background of medieval building philosophy. If it is kept in mind that Gothic was never symmetrical or deliberately "composed," English churches display an amazing variety of style compared to the "High Gothic" of Notre Dame or Chartres. The expert can write (has written) books about the development of architecture inside Notre Dame; for the traveler's eye, the first over-all effect at Paris is one of soaring arches, rose windows, decorated pillars, vaulted roofs, multiple aisles, the corona of chapels.

Now walk into the nave at Canterbury. The carved columns rise unbroken, ribbed until they develop into the graceful spreading fan vaults of the elaborate stone roof. The great windows in the aisles of the nave are only slightly pointed; Canterbury, from the west, is flooded by light—the walls of the nave are glass, punctuated by slender stone supports. This nave, you can see at once, is sophisticated, finished, harmonious; you recognize the *Perpendicular* that developed into St. George's Chapel at Windsor and the Henry VII Chapel at Westminster.

Canterbury is built on three levels. The nave ends in a flight of broad, shallow stone steps beyond the transept crossing. Raised above the lower aisles is a magnificent screen, pierced by an archway, deeply recessed in the massive stone. A second flight of steps, narrow and steep, leads upward again, to the choir.

After the airy nave, you will notice the subdued light of the choir in shadow, mysterious and strange. In the dim half-light you will need a moment before you are conscious of the thick, round, plain pillars, with their rather clumsy, solid, square capitals, naïvely carved; and the narrow, pointed windows set deep into massive walls; and the triforium, with its *Norman* design of spaced shafts, though its *Early English* arches are steeply pointed.

The Canterbury choir is *Transitional*—perhaps you have not seen anything quite like it before. It was built (1180) exactly a hundred years after the Chapel of St. John in the Tower; but more than a hundred years before the transepts at Westminster. You can feel the *Norman* weight, but the pointed arches, the roof vaulting, are a prelude to the *Early English* of Westminster.

Canterbury's *Transitional* choir was the beginning of Gothic in England. Here is the medieval world, new and innocent, a little awkward, yet engaging. Here is the work, clumsy and fresh, of architects who were slightly scared and very excited at the daring they displayed in vaulting a stone roof and pointing a round arch and sinking a tall glass window into a solid wall. Here is the twelfth-century mind, on the threshold of the

Magna Carta. The workmen who hauled stones for these pillars would have been startled, not surprised, to meet a unicorn on the way home for dinner, or to find a bona fide dragon belching fire down by the cabbage patch. Even scholarly Canterbury monks worried lest some enemy or joker would cast a spell on them, and the various formulas for exorcising devils from sick men and using charms to ward off leprosy were hotly debated in clerical circles. The architects who decided on pointed windows for the Canterbury choir were confident that St. Augustine, St. Alphege, the new St. Thomas, would take a direct interest in the finished product. Heaven was much in the thoughts of the men who built the *Transitional* triforium. The earth might be flat and the sun might revolve around it; man was born serf or king, according to God's will: but more important was it that the human life span was merely a brief interlude, and the Last Judgment and Eternity the great realities.

The men who finished the vaulting on the roof of the nave might well have lived to see a printing press; in 1421, even hod carriers discounted unicorns and laughed at old-fashioned dragons. Canterbury monks were too busy arguing local politics to take interest in casting out devils—that sort of thing belonged to the simple-minded past. The architects who put up the ribbed nave pillars and great glass walls, with such easy assurance, spent their spare time debating theology and praying to saints.

At Canterbury Cathedral, the choir (1180) was the beginning of English Gothic; and the nave (1421) was almost the end. Indeed, Bell Harry, the central tower, was one of the last (1503) great medieval projects in Britain. Twenty years later, Cardinal Wolsey was finishing Hampton Court.

Perpendicular and *Transitional* are two of the styles at Canterbury, the most important and the most striking. But the variety of other styles is amazing. Roman stone has been found in the masonry, some of the foundations are *Saxon*, and the crypt is *Norman*. The stone screen before the choir is *Decorated* (1304), the chapter house is late *Perpendicular* (as is the vaulting in the cloisters), the quadrangle at King's School is largely *Georgian*. On the west front, the right-hand tower was built in 1452, but the left-hand tower is a famous case of vandalism.

Until the early nineteenth century, the left-hand tower, as at Chartres, did not match the right. Symmetry was a fixation with the generation before Ruskin; people felt Canterbury was barbarous in general, but the odd towers were especially horrid. In 1832, at great expense, and considerable danger to the whole fabric, the *Norman* tower was laboriously demolished and a *Perpendicular* one, to match the right-hand masterpiece, was erected in its place. Fifty years later everybody at Canterbury was deeply pained to hear that the unmatching towers of Chartres were beautiful and unique. Who would have thought it!

The case of the demolished tower brings us back to our comparison between French and English Gothic. Although there were considerable developments of style in both Notre Dame and Chartres, no French cathedral displays the characteristic Island Gothic contrasts of *Early English, Decorated, Norman,* and *Perpendicular* work, found side by side not just in Canterbury, but in every large English medieval church except Salisbury. Notre Dame does not have a nave all sunlight and a choir all shadow; Chartres does not leap from the clumsy capitals of *Transitional* to the ornate and delicate fan vaulting of *Perpendicular. Island Gothic* is rich with a profusion of style; it lacks unity, but it is full of contrast and variety.

But why? Why were the French content with more or less one major style at Notre Dame, while the English had five, with variations, at Canterbury?

The answer is that the English were the most reckless, absorbed, passionate, and excitable builders of the medieval world; the most extravagant, too. The French were worn out after they finished Notre Dame, Chartres, and so on; besides, Notre Dame was obviously a success—why not let well enough alone? What you see in Paris today is about what you would have seen in 1350.

The English, on the other hand, could not let a cathedral alone. No sooner was a church completed than the next archbishop or prior or local set of wool merchants started itching to pull the whole place down and put up something a lot bigger and much better. Feeling ran high in clerical circles. If York had a new, elegant nave, the monks at Ely took to brooding; result: they outmatched their rivals by building the most grandiose central tower in England. The tower did not last long; it fell down after a few years and wrecked the whole Ely choir, plus one of the transepts. "Ah!" the Archbishop of York remarked. He sang a different tune when the Ely architects figured out the famous lantern tower over their remodeled crossing.

Master masons (the architects of the medieval world) were kidnaped back and forth all over England; up at Norwich the head mason was stolen while he was in the middle of building the new roof vaulting: a matter of earthly gold plus promises of happiness hereafter from the monks at Lincoln.

The operative phrase in the above sentence is earthly gold. French builders did not fool around with their finished products because they could not afford it. Cathedrals are expensive. The architects at Notre Dame (fortunately for us) did not tear out the rose windows and put in something new-fangled because they did not have the cash. Notre Dame was a secular cathedral, built with church taxes and the contributions the clergy could wangle out of kings, dukes, and so on. But English churches belonged to foundations of monks; and these monks were canny from the beginning. They did not encourage pious ladies to donate odd pieces of jewelry or even spot cash. If the countess or baroness or lady wanted to insure her immortal soul, why not leave the monastery a few acres of land in her will? That farm down by the river bend? The forest on the hilltop?

By 1300 the religious orders were the largest landowners in the kingdom and the most efficient. They worked their land with a sharp eye on profits. While barons were off to the Crusades or hacking at each other in local wars, the monks went on raising oats and barley and afterward wool. Some of the proceeds from the monastery estates (especially later on, when the monks grew corrupt) went into living quarters for the abbot and his friends; but in the early days the monks lived simply; the emphasis was on hair shirts, burlap gowns, and vegetable soup for dinner. Monastery wealth went into Gothic architecture. Monks who were blue with cold all winter (fires were a devil's luxury), who dined on cabbage water and rancid black bread, thought nothing of gilding choir stalls with solid gold leaf, or hiring two hundred hod carriers to build a new transept.

You may argue that the wealth of the English monasteries came out of the backs of the wretched serfs; and that every time the canons remodeled York or added a new chapter house to Wells, the peasants paid for it in sweat. Too true. But as nobody noticed this fact—not for a long time, anyway—the monks went along blithely taking down naves, putting up new ones, inventing *Perpendicular* windows, experimenting with towers, and creating the glory in stone that is *Island Gothic*.

To round out a period: I do not say that Canterbury is greater than Notre Dame. But taste should be catholic. French Gothic has unity, English Gothic has variety; both are wonderful. Chartres has the drama of soaring stone; Canterbury the contrast of light and shadow.

Because it was the richest foundation of monks (the fields of Kent are still lush and fertile) and the most powerful church in the kingdom (the Archbishop was Primate), Canterbury was the most continuously rebuilt, remodeled, enlarged, improved, and redecorated cathedral in England. When you buy a guide (remember the Foolproof System!) you will read that the cathedral was in splints and scaffolds from 1070 to 1503. For more than four hundred years some kind of building project was going on. If the monks were not taking down the nave, they were fiddling around with plans for a new chapter house or revaulting the cloisters. They had trouble with fire: the Cathedral burned down three times—once on purpose (Thirkill the Tall, a Viking), and twice by mistake. A sad blow. The monks moaned and beat their chests, after which they pulled themselves together and started arguing about pointed arches.

From one disaster, however, Canterbury never recovered—Richard Culmer, known to friends and enemies alike as "Blue Dick," who appears to have been quite the tin hero in seventeenth-century Kent. I am in favor of progress, Puritans, Cromwell, Lilburne, and Milton; but I must say my blood runs cold when I come to Richard "Blue Dick" Culmer. He was the man in charge of smashing up the stained glass at Canterbury; he had a job of it too. The windows were thought to be on a par with those of Chartres; several of the largest and earliest were evidently the work of the same master glazier, perhaps imported from France for a season or two. The later Yorkist series, Edward IV's gift, were said to be a splendor unrivaled in fifteenth-century glass. Canterbury in 1641 must have shimmered with magic color, as Chartres does today. In 1642, however, Blue Dick arrived at Canterbury with a long ladder and a sledge-hammer. The crowd followed him around, cheering.

Richard Culmer must be one of the most sickening characters in English history. Some writers say they do not understand him. I do. I spent half my adolescence battling to the death with an uncle who insisted that Robert W. Service was a better poet than Keats. It sounds funny now, but it was not so funny then. "How could a man find it in his heart to hate beauty?" a lady philosopher inquired eloquently, apropos of Dick the Blue. The answer to that is: easy. Plenty of people hate beauty, among them my uncle and the contractors who built the London suburbs; for that matter, a member of the United States Congress made interminable speeches denouncing Picasso and other modern artists—it seemed that abstractionism was un-American. Mr. Culmer felt stained glass was un-English, a menace to people's souls. Out, out, damned menace!

We had better veer around to St. Augustine, A.D. 597. I am a passionate admirer of St. Augustine, because he was obviously a nervous, high-strung man scared to death of missionary work. Heroes who never consider possible consequences are not true heroes, in my opinion, but dim-witted, insensitive brutes who win battles or walk planks because they do not have the imagi-nation to realize what is going to happen next. But St. Augus-tine was subject to night terrors and sincere second thoughts. Pope Gregory assigned to him and a squad of forty assistants the task of converting the wild Saxon heathens of England. St. Augustine set out from Rome; before long he was back again. He had run into some refugees who had made their way to Gaul from across the Channel. Augustine hated to say so, but he was afraid Pope Gregory had made a mistake; the Saxons, according to the men Augustine had talked to, were in no mood to be converted. They were just waiting for forty Christians—forty-one, with Augustine—to turn up in Kent. St. Augustine did not mind for himself (he would adore being turned into a holy martyr), but surely Pope Gregory did not want to waste the forty other missionaries, all in one fell swoop?

Pope Gregory advised St. Augustine to be calm. Everything

would be all right. The Queen of the Saxons, a lady named Bertha, was definitely a Christian; the situation was not half so black as St. Augustine painted it.

The expedition started out from Rome for the second time. Four months later St. Augustine was back again. Pope Gregory was annoyed. "It had been better not to begin a good work, than to draw back halfway!" he snapped.

St. Augustine took ship once more, and this time, however reluctantly, crossed the Channel and, with his heart in his mouth, landed on the Isle of Thanet. Now he was face to face with the Worst, and after all his hesitation, he behaved with such admirable courage, such calm and unruffled dignity, that he won over the wild Saxons (the Queen helped some, too) and he baptized King Ethelbert himself.

St. Augustine, to my mind, was a brave man. So, for that matter, were Canterbury's two other leading saints. Alphege, captured in 1012 by the Danes, refused to be ransomed with church treasure. The Danes put him in chains and dragged him along with their murdering, looting gang of thieves. For seven months they demanded the cathedral plate and jewels for Alphege's life; and for seven months Alphege said, "Never!" On the night before Easter, the Danes, annoyed by such stubbornness, used the greasy ox bones from their heathen feast table to beat the old man to death. He is said to have died without a cry.

Thomas Becket (Thomas of London, he called himself), Archbishop of Canterbury, had the same triumphant courage. But he was no simple, humble Saxon, nor was he beaten to death with casual ox bones by a murdering gang of barbarians.

The case of Thomas Becket has fascinated poets, story tellers, scholars, historians, for eight hundred years. He was an extraordinary human being, both in the manner of his life and in the haunting drama of his death. I have hesitated about adding even a footnote on Thomas Becket. T. S. Eliot wrote a play about St. Thomas; historians at Oxford and Cambridge hotly debate the tragedy which made Canterbury famous throughout the Middle Ages and which still brings thousands of visitors to stand, silent, before the stones where Thomas Becket fell murdered that night of Tuesday, December 29, 1170.

All English schoolboys learn by heart the facts of Thomas

Becket's story; the American must have at least an outline of the Canterbury drama before he can know what he sees in the Cathedral. Very briefly:

We have concentrated during our London fortnight on Henry VIII—and how the Tudors broke the power of the medieval Church to make a brave new England. That was (in round dates) 1540. To understand Thomas Becket, we need to wrench our minds backward across the centuries to 1170. Consider this: Henry VIII, when he smashed Thomas Becket's shrine, was as distant from the Canterbury tragedy in time as we are from the Tudors.

(Here is a rough timetable which will help, perhaps, in comprehending Canterbury and Becket:

Cromwell, the Puritans, Richard Culmer, 1642—*three* hundred years ago.

The Reformation, the Dissolution, Henry VIII, 1540—*four* hundred years ago.

The Wars of the Roses, the crackup of feudal England, 1455—*five* hundred years ago.

The great pilgrimages, the peak of Canterbury wealth, fame, and power, 1250–1350—*six, seven* hundred years ago.

The murder of Thomas Becket, 1170—*eight* hundred years ago.)

When Henry VIII carted off the gold plate and jewels from the shrine of St. Thomas, he was, in his crude way, making a new world.

But when Thomas Becket died, boldly defying the Crown of England, he was also building a bright new future.

I have written a good deal about the collapse of feudal society in England. At Canterbury we may watch it being born. What was old and finished in Tudor England was young and fresh in 1170. We are still so close to the revolution that destroyed the Gothic world, so much the children of the Renaissance, that we use the word "feudal" as an epithet. We say of a man so mentally backward that we consider him hardly fit for polite society: "Good heavens, his ideas are absolutely *feudal!*"

There was an hour in history when feudalism was young. In 1170 the long night of piggish barbarism which followed the collapse of the Roman Empire was ending. In the twelfth century the medieval Church was organizing Western society, and

Rome was the center of European progress. Thomas Becket was the hero, the significant figure in his life and death, of the struggle which resulted in Magna Carta (1215) and the power of the great Pope Innocent III.

I know this is not easy; I find it difficult to grasp the fact that systems of society are born in struggle, grow to power, then decay and die away; and that what is new and forward-looking in 1170 grows old and inefficient in 1540. Obviously it was not particularly ethical of Henry VIII to haul off the plate from the shrine of St. Thomas and to use it for his personal privy purse; yet the Reformation and the Dissolution were historically valid acts, because each destroyed institutions which in England had outlived their time.

In the same way, much of Thomas Becket's story is not exactly edifying; without doubt he was a traitor to the friend who had loved him, to the King who had held him dearer than a brother. Yet Thomas Becket died a martyr to the future; he was one of those moral heroes, like Cromwell or Abraham Lincoln, who in a moment of change rise to challenge the future and leave on history an enduring imprint.

Great men are usually aware of their genius. They may be modest (like Lincoln) or the opposite (like Henry VIII), but for the most part they share the same cool, matter-of-fact, almost artless assumption that what they do is done for the ages, what they think is thought for history, what they write or feel or say is written and felt and said for all time. The late Franklin D. Roosevelt arranged a museum for his state papers—he took a lively interest in the details. He assumed that scholars still in knee pants or unborn would need the Roosevelt documents for their future studies. He was right; the museum on the Hudson will be an invaluable source for historians in 2050, and probably 2550, as well. But only a great man can see himself with such detachment as a historical figure. Even Lincoln, personally humble, was well aware that he was playing a giant role in time.

Thomas Becket acted deliberately, with cool conviction, for history. From the moment he first appeared on the stage around 1150, he behaved with the self-confidence, the pride, and the dignity of a man whom time has marked out as a hero.

This is all the more extraordinary because, in the medieval world of caste, Thomas Becket had no family, no lands, no inheritance to bring him success; yet his life was a dazzling triumph from the beginning at London to the great end in his Cathedral in Canterbury.

Thomas Becket was born in London in 1118, of a Norman family. This last point was important to him; only two generations had passed since the Conquest, and Thomas Becket did not care to be mistaken for a Saxon. All the same, his family, however Norman, was impoverished; young Thomas had the choice of becoming a humble esquire to a rich knight-at-arms, or a City merchant. Both these normal methods of making a living he discarded without a second thought. Somehow he found a patron in that London of long ago, and persuaded various barons and monks to pay for his elaborate studies at home and in France. A lay scholar (he did not take orders until long afterward) was so rare a character in twelfth-century London as to attract respect and interest. Thomas Becket went to Court, and at the age of thirty-seven (1155) he was Lord Chancellor of the Realm, Keeper of the King's Seal, and the dearest, indeed the only, friend of young Henry II.

The character of Henry II is almost as interesting as that of the man who played Pythias to his Damon. Henry II was one of those ever-tragic figures—a man born long, long before his time. It is easy to see why Thomas and Henry were friends. Across the centuries, the King and his Lord Chancellor tower above the crowd of rough pygmies who surround them: two subtle, complicated, wise, and daring men, living in a crude, naïve, and brutal world. Thomas and Henry were studying the philosophy of law at a time when their contemporaries were hacking each other with battleaxes to settle real-estate disputes. It is not odd (although it proved to be sad) that the King trusted Thomas Becket. The two men worked together; they developed the policy of secular law. Side by side, King Henry and his Chancellor fought the growing power of the Church and the bishops. It was Thomas (the older) who first taught young Henry how the Crown must undermine the Church by limiting its power to punish and to tax. Henry II was an apt pupil and a gifted ruler; indeed, after William the Conqueror, Henry II was England's greatest medieval king, by far the most intelligent and able British monarch until Henry VII, all those hundreds of years later.

But Henry II was fighting the mainstream of history. He had the idea of a strong central government four hundred years before it became reality in England. Did Thomas Becket understand that the King was moving against the tide of time? Did he realize all along that the Crown was the losing side? Did he foresee from the beginning that Henry II's defeat was inevitable, even morally desirable? Did he walk softly, cautiously, and play the wily double-dealer year after year? Nobody knows. After eight hundred years, we have only bare facts: Thomas Becket was the astute Lord Chancellor who organized the Crown's attacks on the English Church; and he was the teacher, the comrade, the collaborator, the dearly beloved friend of Henry II.

These facts we know. We also know that in 1162 Henry II was jubilant. The Archbishop of Canterbury was dead, and the King had the right to nominate the new Primate of All England. Here was the opportunity Henry and his Lord Chancellor had worked for across a decade; now the Church could be fought from inside its own great fortress. The Primate of All England would no longer be the Crown's deadliest enemy—but instead, its chief ally.

On Sunday, June 3, 1162, Thomas Becket of London, Lord Chancellor of the Realm of England, Keeper of the King's Seal, was enthroned in his Cathedral as Archbishop of Canterbury.

One week later the Archbishop of Canterbury resigned as Lord Chancellor of the English Realm, and sent the seal back to King Henry.

The King wept. He raged. He wept again.

Poor Henry! Who can regard his suffering without pity? Nothing in life is harder to bear than the pain of treachery; nothing hurts so much. To have deeply loved and wholly trusted—and then to be betrayed. Anyone who has endured this torment must feel a great compassion for Henry Plantagenet, King of England.

Henry found, within the space of weeks, that he had not only lost his dearest friend, but he had made an implacable enemy as well in the Archbishop of Canterbury. This was natural enough. It is necessary to hate those whom you have wronged. Thomas Becket moved swiftly against the King who had made him prince of the Church. Thomas knew every secret plan in the royal archives; he knew every ideal, every hope, every scheme of his old comrade. He knew the rusted links in the royal armor, the calked holes in the ship he intended to sink. Henry fought back weakly; he seemed alternately dazed by sorrow and maddened by fury. Within two years Thomas Becket forced the issue of Crown control over the law courts. Henry replied by driving the Archbishop of Canterbury into exile, a nearly fatal mistake, for it cost Henry the organized opposition of Europe. He was in no position to fight the entire weight of the Church. How cleverly Thomas Becket had brought down on King Henry's head the hornet's nest of Papal outrage!

Late in 1170 Henry capitulated; he thought it was a compromise. The Archbishop of Canterbury, Primate of All England, returned to Sandwich on the Kentish coast. He was met by thousands of ecstatic serfs, who kissed his robes as he walked ashore from the landing boat.

Thomas Becket went to work the day after his triumphal return to the palace at Canterbury. He wrote the King (then in France) a short letter; the Church, the King must understand, did not compromise. Now that Thomas was safely back in England, it was time for Henry to know that the Pope had excommunicated the Archbishop of York—in fact, Thomas had brought the Papal Bull across the Channel in his luggage.

When Henry read these bitter words, he went insane with fury. Once again he had been betrayed, and this time the foundation of his power was destroyed. For the Archbishop of York had supported the King while the Archbishop of Canterbury was in exile. If the penalty of being the King's partisan was excommunication, the Crown could hope for nothing but the deadliest opposition from the whole clergy of England, beginning with the meanest clerk. The monarchy was lost, and the Church had triumphed. Even the vestiges, the trappings, of the Crown were gone. The King was humbled indeed when he could not protect an archbishop from the fatal Bull.

Who had done this thing? Who had twice betrayed the King of England? Thomas Becket, old friend, dear enemy; Thomas Becket, the man the King had trusted. Thomas did this thing to Henry, who had loved him as a brother.

The barons and lords of Henry's court stood, pale and afraid, watching the King read the letter from the Archbishop.

The King rose, and cried out in a fearful voice:

"*Fools and dastards* have I in my realm, who are faithless to their Lord; and none of them will avenge me on this—low—clerk!"

That night Reginald Fitz-Urse, William de Tracy, Hugh de Moreville, and Richard le Breton, knights of the King's household, crossed the Channel separately. The following afternoon they met at Henry's castle of Saltwood, near Hythe. Twenty-four hours later they sent the King's word to the barons of Kent.

It is interesting that in 1170 the barons of Kent obeyed their liege lord, King Henry, and rallied in considerable number to surround the palace of the Archbishop of Canterbury. Fifty years later the Church would have obliterated the very messengers who spread such blasphemy. Two hundred years would pass before anyone would again dare to attack a prince of the Church; and then it was Wat Tyler, a base-born serf. It cannot be said that Thomas Becket died in vain; the Crown's last chance at power went down when the Archbishop of Canterbury fell a martyr in his own Cathedral. Did Thomas Becket understand the issue he was to defend with his life? It seems that he did, very exactly.

The four knights rode furiously into Canterbury on the winter afternoon of Tuesday, December 29, 1170. The King's men spread out around the palace, the monastery gates, and the Cathedral walls. Fitz-Urse and the other three knights forced their way into the dining hall, pushing aside the trembling servants.

The Prince of the Church faced his enemies; he was not afraid—he was furiously angry.

Fitz-Urse had expected this low clerk to ask for mercy, to make the compromise that the King demanded. The Archbishop of Canterbury had only not to deliver the Papal Bull against Roger of York. That was all. A small thing and reasonable.

Thomas Becket would not hear Fitz-Urse to the end. In the great climax of his life, this low clerk was superb. Compromise! Thomas Becket's rage rang through the whole Palace. "Never! Never!" The Church did not compromise! The Archbishop would listen to no message from Henry Plantagenet—no message delivered with a sword.

Fitz-Urse rushed from the palace, his knights after him. In

the courtyard, the clank of their armor could be heard; the servants, weeping with fear, saw them unsheathe the great, ugly, two-handed swords.

"Sire! Sire!" the monks cried to their lord.

Thomas Becket slowly put on his cloak. It was growing dark; time for evensong in the Cathedral.

One of the brothers put his hand on the Archbishop's arm, and tried to drag him along the cloister avenue.

Thomas thrust the monk aside. "What means this, sirs? What is your fear?"

When the Archbishop of Canterbury walks to evensong the great cross of his office is carried before him. On this night it was missing.

The Archbishop waited, his face composed, while the desperate monks ran wildly across the cloisters, dragged the cross bearer from his hiding-place, forced him to take his place in the Archbishop's procession.

Outside, the noise of the armed crowd grew louder; there were cries and wild shouts, the clash of swords against chain mail.

The cross bearer, hands shaking, the cross wavering in the somber December twilight, started up the cloister walk. Behind him, unhurried, at his usual stately pace, came the low clerk, resplendent in gold-embroidered robes.

Inside the Cathedral under the flickering candlelight the monks had begun to sing the service. The church doors were flung open, and two boys, eyes bulging with terror, cried: "Save yourselves! The King's men!"

The Latin chant quavered to an uncertain halt. The monks scattered from the choir and ran wildly through the Cathedral; some hid in the crypt; others crept silently into the black shadows of the great pillars or remembered the Tower of Lanfranc and made their way up the steep stone steps in silence and darkness.

A few of the brothers found the courage to meet their lord and Archbishop at the cloister door. "Come in," they said, bravely enough, "and let us die together."

The Archbishop regarded them. When they wanted to bolt the Cathedral doors he waved them aside with an imperious gesture. "I will not have the Church of God made into a castle."

With these words, Thomas Becket mounted the steps to the choir.

Through the open door came the four knights, their naked swords shining in the candlelight, their visored helmets hideous.

Fitz-Urse cried, "Where is Thomas Becket, traitor to King and Realm?"

In the shadows there was silence. The monks fled into the blackness. Thomas Becket was left alone to face his enemies.

"Where is the Archbishop?"

"Here! No traitor, but a priest of God, and Archbishop."

No traitor! These were the words Thomas Becket sent to his King, to his friend.

"No traitor, but a priest of God, and Archbishop." It was Thomas Becket's epitaph and argument, his challenge to the future, the apology for his life, and the meaning of his death.

"No traitor . . . !"

The four knights ran up the steps to the choir. The Archbishop faced them. They tried to lay hands upon him, because they did not want to kill him by the holy altar. But this low clerk had strength. He fought back. He would die where he had lived his greatest triumph—in his Cathedral. One of the swords was lifted high, and brought down with fury.

The Archbishop of Canterbury committed his soul to God in a loud voice, so that the monks, cowering in their secret hiding places, heard his last prayer.

"In nomine patris . . ."

Four swords rose and fell.

". . . et filii. . . ."

The blood was black in the candlelight.

". . . et in spiritu sanctu. . . ."

From the dark Cathedral the monks whispered, the word rose like a sigh from the massive pillars: "Amen."

In the choir there was silence.

An Archbishop had been murdered; the monks buried the greatest English saint of the Middle Ages.

Henry heard of this deed many days later.

The problem of guilt is always interesting. On his deathbed

Henry repeated what he had said from the beginning: he had not intended the death of the Archbishop; Fitz-Urse was to have forced a compromise.

"I am innocent," Henry cried; but the world did not believe him and, in a curious way, Henry did not believe himself. If he had not commanded the deed, he had wished it. When Henry was told of the death of Thomas, he covered his face with his hands. "Friend," he cried. His grief was so terrible it was thought he would die. He lay for days in his private chambers, sometimes rigid and speechless, sometimes torn by storms of weeping. "*Ami! Ami!*" he sobbed hoarsely.

When at last he recovered, he was no longer young. The chroniclers of the Middle Ages, who wrote in symbols, recorded that Henry never smiled again. No doubt the King smiled; but he was cured of anguish and of love. After the springtime of his youth, he lived a long winter.

To me it seems curious that the four knights were never punished, if indeed it was a mistake they had made on that fatal night at Canterbury. Fitz-Urse and the others lived out their normal span; they went to the wars and the tournaments, they did penances, and they died.

It was the King of England who paid for the murder of Thomas Becket. He submitted to a spectacular penance at Canterbury—with all the colorful trappings, hair shirt, bleeding feet on the cobblestones, monks flogging his naked back by the altar, an all-night vigil at the martyrdom. But this was politics. Henry nearly lost his throne in the wave of rage which swept Europe at the news of the murder; hair shirts and vigils were exacted in return for his remaining vestiges of power. A few years later the new Archbishop of Canterbury organized the barons and forced Henry's son, King John, to sign Magna Carta. Feudalism was born the night that Thomas Becket fell under the King's swords.

Perhaps because I write novels, I find myself standing around Canterbury Cathedral and looking blankly enough at the stones which are supposed to mark the spot where Thomas died; I cannot forget the dark and tragic drama of two men, who still speak to each other across eight hundred years.

"Here!" Thomas Becket said. "No traitor, but a priest of God, and Archbishop!"

History is more than love, the hero said, and died to prove it. "Friend!" Henry answered.

Canterbury is the jewel of southern England. I hope you will have time, after you have examined the great Cathedral, to take a week's journey through Kent, Sussex, and Surrey. You will find listed in our chart a suggestion for a considerable tour of towns and castles and churches you should not miss. Of the many fascinating places, I like best the town of Sandwich and the villages of Kent; the miniature railroad at Hythe; the abandoned seaports of Rye and Winchelsea; Pevensey, because of William the Conqueror; the wonderful castle of Bodiam; Chichester and Bosham; and, finally, Knole.

Whether you have time for all these or for only a weekend, southern England will be the key to your journey in Britain. The thatched cottage, the story-book castle, the ancient seaport, the Cathedral of Canterbury—this is Kent, Sussex, and Surrey, England's beautiful heartland.

WHAT TO SEE IN THE SOUTHEAST

*** Extraordinary. Don't miss this—a *must*.
** Don't miss this if you can help it.
* See this if you have time.
No star: This is officially a sight; it may interest you, but there is no need to break your neck to see it.

* *Rochester.* A pleasant city, with a ruined castle, old houses, and a small but good Norman cathedral. The Dickens town *par excellence.*

* *Aylesford.* On the way to Maidstone. It is pleasant, with a fourteenth-century bridge, and a Norman tower to the church.

Maidstone. An interesting group of buildings along the river, of which one house was formerly the palace of the Archbishop of Canterbury.

*** *Canterbury.* The Cathedral is the most important in England. See text for history and description. In the town, see **the Weavers, St. Thomas's Hospital,* the ***West Gate.* ***St. Augustine's Abbey* has a memorable gate dating from the end of the thirteenth century.

** *Littlebourne, Wingham, Ash, Wickhambreaux, Sandwich, Barfreston, Eastry, Betteshanger, Knowlton,* and *Waldershare.* Charming towns and villages, not far from Canterbury, typical of the green and pleasant Kentish countryside.

* *Richborough Castle.* Near Sandwich, now a ruin, a relic of Roman times.

* *Dover.* An important port and garrison town, has a fine castle, more striking from a distance than close up.
   Hythe. One of the Cinque Ports, has an *Early English* church. But the traveler should try to take the **miniature railway from Hythe across the marshes to New Romney; lots of fun. Then on to:

* *Rye.* Picturesque, if somewhat overrun by tourists, and:

** *Winchelsea.* A splendid town, with fine houses laid out in checkerboard fashion.

*** *Bodiam Castle.* A good late pile, fine moat with water lilies and a romantic setting. This is everything a castle should be, directly out of a fairy story, highly recommended.

* *Battle.* Site of the historic engagement between Harold and William the Conqueror—the location of the battle which is always called the Battle of Hastings. Not much to see, but the feeling is eerie.

* *Herstmonceaux Castle.* A brick mansion, fortified, built in 1450. The gardens are superb.

** *Pevensey Castle.* Roman walls, Saxon forts, Norman gates. Here William the Conqueror landed on the English coast, and here he camped before he marched on Harold. Very exciting place.

* *Alfriston.* A small but pretty town, with a fine *Perpendicular* church, known as the Cathedral of the Downs.

* *Brighton.* A famous seaside resort, with some good Regency terraces, not very interesting for the tourist. The atmosphere is staid, not in the least like Coney Island. However:

** *The Downs,* from Brighton to Bramber and Steyning, are wild and exciting.

* *Arundel.* Has a Castle rebuilt from the foundations up in the nineteenth century.

* *Boxgrove.* Has a good *Early English* church and some fine romantic priory ruins.
* *Chichester.* A pleasant town with a small Cathedral, not one of the best, but worth seeing if you pass this way. St. Mary's Hospital is fine.
** *Bosham.* A tiny village on a little bay, an enchanted spot. The church is drowsy, with an ancient Saxon tower. A little daughter of King Canute is buried here.
Guildford. Renowned for its High Street and old clock. Frankly, industrial and disappointing.
*** *Knole.* Outside Sevenoaks. One of the greatest show places in England, absolutely *de rigueur* for the tourist. This is the palace of endless rooms. Check admission days before making the journey. A pleasant day's trip from London.
* *Tunbridge Wells.* A fashionable Georgian spa; it has fine environs, and a promenade in the center of town called the Pantiles, quaint and evocative.
Chiddingstone. This is always described as charming. A favorite picnic haunt, especially for Youth Hostellers.
* *Penshurst Place and environs.* Some of the fine homes of England, lush country, pleasant driving and weekending.

Winchester, Salisbury, New Forest, Devon and Cornwall, the Southwest

ENGLAND is a relatively small island, roughly the area of New York State. Yet, even excluding Scotland and Wales, the variety as well as the beauty of the scenery, the sharp contrasts that the traveler finds after no more than an hour's train ride are amazing, especially for Americans accustomed to the slower changes as one travels through our vast country. I remember when Richard and I and the three children drove from San

Francisco to New York City. We spent three whole days speeding along at an average of sixty miles an hour across the high plateau of Nevada and Wyoming. I see the endless miles still: on and on and on, one hour, one day, very much like the next. The Middle West began at Omaha; and for days we drove through rolling farmland, until at last we drew near to the great industrial areas.

The drive from my favorite village in Sussex, Bosham (pronounced Bozzum), to Lyndhurst does not take sixty minutes. Bosham is graced by an ancient Saxon church and a succession of dignified Georgian houses. Whereas Lyndhurst—! To describe the contrast between Bosham and Lyndhurst, I need to explain that Bosham, like most of Sussex and Kent, is civilized, cultivated, manicured. Every blade of grass has been brushed neatly into order—for the last five hundred years or so. Knole, the great showplace of Kent, has been a mecca for landscape gardeners and poets since the sixteenth century.

Lyndhurst is full of cowhands, branding irons and Boy Scouts. One of the most astonishing—and engaging—sights anywhere is the main street of Lyndhurst on a sunny afternoon in summer. The pavements are filled with youngsters in shorts, pullover T-shirts, and hobnailed boots. Bicycles are parked by the dozens at every ice-cream shop. Old-fashioned wooden hotels, rather like an Edwardian resort town in the Poconos, line the main street. Tourist buses and little English cars, heaped with holiday luggage, crowd the road. In the midst of all this hustle and bustle and summertime holiday making are a large number of wild horses strolling around Lyndhurst as though they owned the place—for that matter, they do. I am told by nature lovers that there is a sound logic behind the behavoir of the Lyndhurst horses. Reasonable or not, one of the drollest things I have ever seen was a wild horse window-shopping for a hat on the main street of Lyndhurst. It was a mother horse, and she was looking through the plate glass with an expression of such wearied disdain, such utter, cynical disgust, that I was surprised the management did not rush out to protest. There were five more mother and father horses, and an offspring about three days old and unsteady on its pins, waiting for the mail at the Lyndhurst post office. They looked annoyed, too; apparently the service of Her Majesty's

NEW FOREST PONIES

Royal Mails left much to be desired. At the traffic light I counted seven wild horses tying up westbound traffic. Buses honked, cyclists shouted, motorists blew the English beep-beep horns—the horses were quite unmoved. They stood around, calmly having a bit of a chat or nose rub, right in the line of fire. Finally a policeman came with a broom, and hit the leading member of this kaffee klatsch. The horse shrugged. Several more pawed back and forth; in their own good time, they moved off the road, around the corner, and settled down to make a tea on somebody's prize delphiniums.

The logic of all this is interesting. The New Forest is Crown land. It's New because William Rufus swept away numerous villages in the area, planted trees, and made the region into a royal hunting ground. All this happened a mere nine hundred years ago: thus *New* Forest. You will remember William II was murdered here; good riddance, everybody agreed at the time.

He may have been shot by William Tyrell; then again, one of the serfs Rufus drove off the land to starvation and death may have replied to tyranny. In any case, the Crown has held the New Forest through thick and thin, all these centuries; as a result, it is one of the largest open areas on the island, and traditionally the home of the wild horse and the summer hiker. The horses are not very wild; we would call New Forset an open range. Horse breeders have an annual roundup (called a drift), which is arranged by "verderers" (cowhands), and assisted by commoners and helpers (also cowhands, underprivileged). The horses are herded into barns for the winter, branded in the spring, and turned out to graze in prairie style. Cattle also use the New Forest range, and sometimes they too turn up in Lyndhurst, but only for a quick look. But the horses are driven out of the forest during heat waves by a vicious gnat which attacks the tender lining of their flaring nostrils. In 1915 some New Forest horse, no doubt a genius, discovered that by pressing his nose against the cool plate glass of the Lyndhurst shop windows (and especially the post office) he could escape torment. Ever since this Columbus found his way to Lyndhurst, the villagers have steeled themselves for the annual descent of the wild New Forest ponies. I suppose you can get used to anything in two generations or so; the postmen at Lyndhurst push the horses out of the doorway so that customers can come in to buy stamps. Delphinium fanciers rush into their gardens, flapping their aprons and bawling, "Shooo!" when wild horses come to call (as Betsy Trotwood did to the wild donkeys).

The New Forest is charming, with or without horses. Near Lyndhurst is Beaulieu (pronounced Bewley); on a sunlit summer day, it is a dreamy, picturesque sort of ruin. I am going to take up the whole problem of ruins when we get around to Yorkshire and Fountains Abbey; but Beaulieu, with its setting of lake and lawn, is in some ways as handsome a ruin as you will come across. If you do not have time to see Tintern or Rievaulx, etc., Beaulieu will do well as a sample. It is Cistercian, as some of the other more famous ones are; it was founded by King John, and the refectory, now used as the parish church, is serene.

Now for Winchester. Item A: King Arthur did not have his Round Table here. I sound like a spoilsport, but there it is—the

Winchester Round Table located in the hall of Winchester Castle was built about 1250. Since King Arthur operated (if he operated at all) not later than A.D. 500 or thereabouts, this particular Round Table is seven centuries off base.

However, Winchester is a fascinating town, full of authentic relics, if not of Launcelot. The Cathedral, the longest in England, is one of the important and interesting great piles, *Island Gothic*. The transepts are *Norman;* the nave is *Perpendicular*; the east end is mixed *Early English, Decorated*, and *Perpendicular*. Now that you are an expert on medieval styles, you will enjoy Winchester. Be sure to buy your guide as you enter; Winchester is tricky without a chart.

The Hospital of St. Cross is a heavily worked tourist sight to which I dragged myself somewhat reluctantly. The aged gentlemen of the foundation wear picturesque costumes. I am suspicious of Tudor bonnets on contemporary, if tottering, characters, but I was one hundred percent wrong about the Hospital of St. Cross. It is beautiful. The church is a haunting Norman, and the courtyard, with its old houses lining the lawn, is full of peace.

The bus from Winchester to Salisbury crosses the county line. Winchester is in Hampshire, Salisbury in Wiltshire. The two small cities are only eighteen miles apart. During the trip you approach the great downs—Salisbury Plain.

Salisbury Cathedral is the exception to the rule of English Gothic. Probably you will visit the Cathedral first, and discover the reason for it second, at Old Sarum, a mile or two farther on.

From the outside, Salisbury Cathedral is a glorious "view." It was built all at once, and in one single style—*Early English*—from 1220 to 1260. The city itself was built on a virgin site in the water meadows of the Avon; the Bishop laid out a handsomely shaped close for his new church. The walls and gates of the original foundation still stand, and you come to Salisbury first through the medieval market place, past the great thirteenth-century fortress towers, and—abruptly—you are standing in a sunlit space of ancient grass. Elizabethan and Georgian houses of pale, mellowed brick rim the enclosure; and in its center stands the Cathedral, crowned by the most glorious spire in English Christendom.

SALISBURY MARKET-PLACE

A breath-taking moment of an English journey—Salisbury, as you see it first, superb and majestic.

Inside, I find Salisbury disappointing. Architects are interested by the first square apse of English medieval building, and the first extended west façade and so on. But the Purbeck marble of the interior is black and dull, and somehow the expanse of *Early English* gives the Cathedral an empty look. We spent a whole afternoon at Winchester, and went back the next morning; but after forty minutes inside Salisbury we felt restless.

The town of Salisbury makes up for anticlimax inside the Cathedral. Laid out (1260) in regular "checkers," the streets run straight to the Avon water meadows. Many of the medieval, Tudor, and Georgian houses still stand, and Crane Street leads, by a footpath, to the landscape of river, meadow, and Cathedral spire which Constable made immortal in his great picture.

Old Sarum is two miles from Salisbury. You can take a taxi, and on your return the bus stop is within easy walking distance.

I think Old Sarum is as exciting as any place in England. In ancient days, perhaps as long ago as 1700 B.C., Stonehenge men had a camp on this cone-shaped hill overlooking meadows and river. Many centuries passed, and many more, and the Romans came to fortify the neighborhood. The whole Sarum-Salisbury area (with Winchester) was a thriving Roman community. For a matter of some four hundred years (it is easy to forget that the Romans were in Britain for centuries more than the whole history of our American Republic) Roman soldiers tramped in and out of Old Sarum, Roman chariots galloped in a two-lane traffic circle around the fort, a Roman brick factory flourished down by the river, Roman villas dotted the pleasant countryside. Then one day the legions marched away from the hilltop fort. The Britons watched uneasily as the Eagles floated for the last time over Sarum, and were gone, forever.

Ten years. Twenty years. Life went on, not quite as it had before, but well enough. Trade lessened. Here and there an abandoned villa stood empty; and each spring there were fewer fields put to the plough, fewer boys to chant their Latin verbs in the schoolhouse. Over all the countryside settled a curious pause, a moment of dread waiting. The elegant British ladies, still smart in their draped Roman gowns, went to pray in the Christian church.

On the hilltop, men who were more accustomed to writing bills of lading and reading the latest poetry from Rome than to handling a pike or a shield, mounted a half-hearted guard in the Roman towers. A few acid-tongued wiseacres complained because the Sarum fort was falling out of repair; the drawbridges did not work very well, the water mains had cracked in a winter freeze and were not put back in order. People shrugged. No sense in being hysterical. Probably the so-called barbarian menace was much exaggerated. To be sure, the news was not good from Kent, and worse from Sussex. Still, these Saxons were merely looters—they would never come inland. Perhaps it was possible to make a deal? Perhaps hire one of their childish "kings" to "protect" the province?

Thirty years. Forty years. Forty-one, forty-two years.

News came from Winchester. To arms! To arms!

The Britons fought at Winchester (about A.D. 500). This battle may be the origin of the folk memory we label "King Arthur." If so, the facts were not as glorious as the legends they breed; the Britons were crushed by the savage hordes. They fled across Salisbury Plain to the fortress on the hill.

Old Sarum was their last stand in south England. The women and children huddled inside the already half-decayed Roman walls; the men, starved, hopeless, waited beyond the useless moats for the inevitable end.

A week . . . two weeks.

A priest chanted the Christian litany. An old man leaned against the brick wall and read Horace to pass the time.

The Saxons did not use the neat, straight Roman roads. They poured across the plain into the river meadow, an inchoate, screaming mass. The Britons could see their naked bodies, streaming sweat, brightly painted.

The old man closed his book, and stood up, to die.

It was several centuries before anyone else read a book in that neighborhood. Old Sarum stood empty for a time—the Saxons were afraid of brick buildings, walls, towers, and ruined water mains. But the fort was a natural defense point. Around

800, some earls and others, rude characters, moved over to the Sarum hilltop, and built earthen walls on top of the crumbling Roman towers. Two centuries more, and there was a considerable wooden palisade at Old Sarum; the cohorts of the Noble Harold took refuge here after the disaster near Pevensey. They kept nervously watching the horizon; nor did they have long to wait. William was at Winchester (he made it his co-capital of England), and sent a squad or two of knights, battering rams, and the like, to clean up Old Sarum.

The Normans occupied Old Sarum from 1066 to 1220. In their usual determined manner, they built a large stone castle, a large stone church, and other improvements. What builders those Normans were! Everywhere you go in England you run across their work.

After various bloody ups and downs, Old Sarum became the local cathedral and monastery. For some obscure reason, the monks were on exceedingly bad terms with the barons of the region. This was before Thomas Becket, and Church dignitaries were militant in the Old Sarum district. The castle, with its secular lord, changed hands constantly, and the abbot, defending his adjacent church, was more often in chain mail than in priestly robes. The monks stood one siege after another; and this brings us around to an important technical point. The Romans had an elaborate water system at Old Sarum; it is not known for certain, but they may have pumped water to the fort from the river, or perhaps they had a connected series of deep underground wells. They realized that water was required for a fortress, and they had the technical skill to make Old Sarum a feasible defense site.

The Normans learned the need for water—the hard way. Every time the monks stood a siege, the well went dry. They had either to surrender or to fight their way out of the trap. One abbot after another sought a solution to the water problem. But not only Horace had been lost on that day when the Britons perished in the Saxon attack; an immense store of Roman know-how disappeared in the collapse. The Normans had no idea how to lift water more than thirty or forty feet. The abbots of Old Sarum could not figure out how to supply the fortress with water for any considerable period of siege. Finally, exasperated at losing a local brawl, one incumbent made a bold decision: abandon Old Sarum altogether and move downhill to the Avon.

That is how Salisbury was founded on unbroken ground; and how the Cathedral came to be built all at once from its foundations up.

And Old Sarum? Old Sarum was left to die. A few townsmen stayed in their houses clustered near the empty castle; little by little, generation after generation, the men of Old Sarum moved downhill to the more comfortable town of New Sarum—Salisbury. An odd fact: Old Sarum was one of the most famous of the rotten boroughs swept away in the nineteenth-century electoral reform. Up to 1832 Old Sarum had a total population of fifty-seven, and returned two members to Parliament (William Pitt, the Elder, was the most celebrated). In 1832, at long last, the rotten borough was abolished, after which the population declined rapidly.

Today Old Sarum has a daytime population of one—the custodian; he goes down the hill at night, and abandons the ancient stones to their ghosts.

After Old Sarum, Stonehenge and Avebury should be next on your schedule. Stonehenge is the most famous, and Avebury the most important, megalithic monument in England. Archaeologists have studied these immense stone circles for generations; each succeeding school has a definitive—and new—explanation. Stonehenge was once supposed to be the haunt of Druids and the scene of horrid human sacrifices along the lines of Aztec orgies. Nowadays archaeologists scoff at the Druid theory; and the latest information has it that not a single white-robed maiden got sacrificed in the whole of Salisbury Plain. Stonehenge was a sort of immense calendar, frequented by sun worshipers from the Mediterranean—backward Egyptian-type men.

Richard was disappointed that there were no Druids at Stonehenge, but I think it is sufficiently eerie even without human sacrifice. The place is somewhat overrun by sightseeing buses; and wax paper from picnic baskets is wafted across the stone pillars. All the same, it is enough to make some people wish they had not wasted their lives writing books or manu-facturing washing machines. It must be exciting to be an archaeologist. For instance: how did a pack of Mediterranean sun worshipers end up in Wiltshire, England? I know the Channel used to be part of the European Continent, and the Thames was a tributary of the Rhine; but whatever led Medi-terraneans to leave sunny Italy or cozy Greece, and trek all that way up to the breezy Rhine? I do not see why they did not stay at home and enjoy themselves. But perhaps *tourisme* started early in the history of *Homo sapiens*? After all, what are we doing at Stonehenge? Maybe the Mediterranean sun worshipers came to look and decide they might as well put up a calendar to see what year it was.

Scenery is important in Devon; also in Cornwall. Richard and I are puzzled about what to say of Devon and Cornwall for American tourists. If you spend six months or so in England, you will want to have several weekends or a vacation in the scenic villages, or along the dramatic coast of Cornwall. But America has a lot of scenery, too, such as the Grand Canyon, the Maine and California sea coasts, the great mountains and so on. Frankly, I would not come three thousand miles to spend a week out of a month's journey looking at English scenery, no matter how superb (and it is superb, no doubt of that). Moreover, Devon and Cornwall are traditional vacation haunts of the English themselves; Cornwall is crowded to the gun-

TEA-TIME IN DEVON

wales every July and August, and all the picturesque Devon villages are jammed with exceedingly unpicturesque refugees from London, soaking up the sun in bikinis, and crowding the self-conscious Olde Tea Shoppes until the queue forms on the right.

Warning! There is a village called Clovelly in Devon which I consider an outright trap, except for mountain goats. It is celebrated—tourist buses deliver you to the top of an awful height. You walk down a perpendicular cobbled alley, down, down, down to the sounding sea. It is medium quaint. Fishermen's houses are huddled against the cliff; geraniums grow in flower boxes; postcards for sale at every shoppe. After you get down to the beach, you turn around, and walk back up to the top of the cliff. It is about a mile straight uphill as the elevator goes—why should you complain? What fun! Ah, delightful little fishing villages of Devon! Ah, Clovelly! I will never, no never, forget your dear red roofs, or your wee cobblestoned streets!

Permit me to be blunt. Unless you are definitely in your prime, about twenty years old, clear-eyed, and in football training, do not fool around with trips to fishing villages until you make absolutely sure they will let you ride one of those sure-footed donkeys, or, failing that, some more mundane transportation, such as an automobile, back up the hill to safety. The perpendicular alleys of Clovelly were littered, the last time I saw them, with stout tourist ladies (like myself) seated in the middle of the cobblestones, giving low groans of pain. One of the most gruesome mornings of my entire life was billed on the advertising boards: SEE QUAINT OLD-WORLD FISHING VILLAGES OF DEVON AND CORNWALL. Never again! I have seen my last fishing village (except one in Yorkshire, where the inhabitants are civilized and let you drive down—and up—the hill).

Exeter, if you do come so far west on one or another of your English journeys, was once a city of superb medieval and Tudor streets and Cathedral. The Nazis reduced Exeter to ruins, which have been pieced together again, sometimes to a fine effect, sometimes only medium. A good deal of modern architecture, not particularly striking, has been fitted into the gaps between reconstructions. Still, the Cathedral is fascinating, and St. Nicholas Priory worth exploring.

WHAT TO SEE IN THE SOUTHWEST

*** *Winchester*. Capital of England under Alfred and Canute, co-capital under William the Conqueror. The Cathedral, longest in England, is a mixture of all the great medieval styles. The charming close leads to:

** *Winchester College,* one of England's great "public schools." Near the West Gate of the town, in the remains of Winchester Castle, is a thirteenth-century hall containing what obviously could not be King Arthur's Round Table. Fun to see, anyway. On the main road to Southampton, about a mile from the center of town, is the lovely ****Hospital of St. Cross*. Be sure to visit this; the church is wonderful and so are the ancient pensioners.

* *Romsey*. Has a fine Norman abbey church, left over from a nunnery founded in Saxon times.

Southampton. Great English port.

Portsmouth. Important English naval base.

Isle of Wight. Nice scenery with pleasant seaside resorts, but hardly worth the traveler's time, unless you are making a very leisurely journey through England.

** *The New Forest. Lyndhurst* makes a good center for this ancient Royal Preserve; it is also the summer headquarters for the New Forest "wild" horses.

** *Beaulieu* (pronounced Bewley) *Abbey*. First-class ruins, wonderful setting by a little lake. In many ways Beaulieu is quite as good as the more famous Yorkshire relics, highly recommended for all ruin fanciers.

* *Corfe Castle*. A thirteenth-century ruin, blown up in 1645 by the Roundheads after Lady Bankes had gallantly defended it during six weeks' siege. A Saxon boy king (Edward) was murdered by his wicked stepmother Elfrida at Corfe. People brought up on Dickens's *Child's History of England* will shed a tear for Edward.

* *Dorchester*. Rather nice little town. It has a Roman amphitheatre, and was the scene of the Bloody Assize of 1685 (the Monmouth Rebellion affair). However, the big item about Dorchester is Thomas Hardy, many of whose novels are about the town or the nearby countryside.

*** *Salisbury.* The Cathedral (described in the text) has the most beautiful spire in England. The town is filled with handsome old houses.

*** *Old Sarum.* A mile out of Salisbury. Interesting ruins, Roman, Saxon, and Norman.

*** *Stonehenge.* On Salisbury Plain, by far the best known of England's prehistoric ruins. Scholars guess the date at 1700 B.C., and call it "megalithic."

*** *Avebury.* Another twenty-five miles on from Stonehenge, has bigger and better megalithic relics than Stonehenge. If you care about prehistory, Avebury is more important than Stonehenge.

* *Exeter.* Sadly bombed, but all the same is worth seeing. (See text.)

Dartmoor. Grim moorland, famous from detective stories.

Plymouth. One of England's oldest seaports, associated with Drake, Hawkins, Raleigh, and Captain Cook. From this port a ship named the *Mayflower* sailed in 1620.

Penzance. A dull town, and no pirates whatsoever about. It is called the capital of the "Cornish Riviera," which will strike the tourist as an unfortunate label.

Land's End. Lots of scenery, orange peel, crowds. You can look right across the Atlantic from here.

St. Ives. This has even more scenic joys, plus an artists' colony, and a modern seaside resort.

Tintagel. Excessively famous, and patronized by sightseeing buses. "See the Most Picturesque Village in England." Scenic.

Clovelly. Very quaint, especially for goats or alpine climbers. You should use ropes and ice axes for the descent from the cliff to the fishing village by the sea. An elevator would be nice, coming up.

From Clovelly along the coast to *Ilfracombe* and *Porlock* is wild and beautiful scenery, not unlike the California Carmel coast. However, the main road is far inland, and you must walk or have a private car to see the steep cliffs and blue inlets.

* *Dunster.* Just off the main road, two miles from Minehead. Its main street is medieval, and the whole village rewarding, including the castle.

Bath, Wells, Glastonbury, and Gloucester

They arrived at Bath. Catherine was all eager delight; her eyes were here, there, everywhere, as they approached its fine and striking environs, and afterwards drove through those streets which conducted them to the hotel. She was come to be happy, and she felt happy already.

They were soon settled in comfortable lodgings in Pulteney Street.

THESE sentences are from Chapter Two of Jane Austen's *Northanger Abbey*; I put them down because I hope that, like Catherine Morland, you will come to Bath to be happy.

Bath lies in a saucer of West Country hills. It is a small elegant city, built all of one stone, curiously colored, a soft gold melting into a luminous, pearly gray. Its style is a harmonious development from early to late Georgian. Aside from London itself, no other city is so important in English drama and literature: the streets of Bath are haunted by ghosts as disparate as Mr. Pickwick, Mr. Elliot of *Persuasion,* and the immortal Mrs. Malaprop. In real life, Bath was the center of English society and fashion from 1720 or thereabouts until after Waterloo. Its architecture mirrored its history. Bath was the only city of the eighteenth century built in one style of one lovely stone, small enough to be cupped in one graceful rounded valley, and inspired by a single mood—elegance. The Circus and Queen Square designed by John Wood the Elder; the Royal Crescent by his son, John Wood the Younger; the Pulteney Bridge of Robert Adam—these masterpieces appear in every textbook of architecture. But, more than for any individual work of art, Bath is remarkable for its composition, its harmonious whole.

The history of this health resort begins in A.D. 54, when the Romans built their first pools, pump rooms, steam rooms, villas, libraries, and theatres over the hot springs which still make Bath a medical center and a geological curiosity. Only a few of the Roman buildings at Bath have been entirely uncovered; they rival the style and interest of Pompeii. I was amused by the ingenious central heating system used by the

Romans at Bath; you can see how they piped hot water under mosaic pavements to heat the ornate swimming pools and massage rooms. The modern city is built on Roman foundations; it is commonplace for repairmen working on gas mains or electric conduits to dig up a statue here, some ancient's best silver platter from behind a wall, and so on. Indeed, Bath is a city of layers. Beneath the well-preserved Roman elegancies are prehistoric tools and ancient altars—apparently England's earliest inhabitants were fascinated by the hot springs, and used the bubbling mineral waters for various cures as long ago as Stonehenge. After the Roman layer comes an early, and then a later, Saxon sprinkling of relics. Bath must have been one of the first Roman sites the savage Saxons gingerly occupied; and the Normans moved right into Bath immediately after the Conquest: perhaps Norman spies had the place all marked out in advance. Medieval building was considerable; it is the first layer under the Georgian foundations.

Bath Abbey, built in 1499, is still the center of this predominantly eighteenth-century city. The Abbey is almost entirely *Perpendicular*, a little ornate but beautiful, and not incongruous in relation to the later and elegant Pump and Assembly Rooms.

There is one way to see Bath, and that is to walk. You will probably come from London by express train; as soon as you are settled in your "lodgings" (which I hope are comfortable, like Catherine Morland's—we did not have much luck), buy a map of the city. The houses once occupied by Jane Austen and General Wolfe and so on are neatly marked by plaques. I do not know a city in England so well arranged for the walking visitor. A good plan is to start roughly at the center of the city with the Abbey, the Pump Room, and the Roman baths, and tramp out diagonal slices on your street map, like cuts from a pie. On our second day we took buses from the Abbey to the end of the line, and walked downhill past the various parks and terraces. There is no vista which is not lovely, but the Royal Crescent is incomparable Georgian, and from its round courtyard the city leads gracefully downhill to parks and main streets, Guildhall and Assembly Rooms.

As I read back over what I have written, I reflect on the maddening, irrelevant accidents of travel. Before I came to England there were two places I especially wanted to see—besides London, of course. The first was Bath, and the second was Canterbury. Richard and I went off to Canterbury, as I reported, on one of those heavenly days of an English June; the sun was golden, the air smelled of roses, and we were in a fine holiday mood before we caught our first glimpse of the Canterbury towers. But I could not wait for summer to see Bath. Jane Austen is my favorite author. So far as I was concerned, Bath was sacred; long before I crossed the English Channel I had read every book about Bath I could put hands on, I had studied photographs of the Royal Crescent and the Circus until I was sure I could recognize them in my dreams. As the train drew near, I was in a wild state of impatience.

At which point it began to rain. Since it was February, there was no good reason why it should not have rained; but I had rather planned on first seeing Bath touched by its famous golden sunset glow.

Three days later it was still raining, which baffled Richard and me. We could not understand why it did not snow. It felt cold enough for glaciers. I have never in my life been so continuously, wretchedly cold as in Bath. Our hotel smelled of cabbage, and although Georgian on the outside, looked within like Nicholas Nickleby's boarding school—mustard-colored paint new in 1919 and bilious chocolate woodwork. The management cleverly resisted any and all attempts by their clientele to get warm. There was an electric fire in our bedroom; one put a shilling in, and presto—warmth! This was the theory. In practice, after feeding four shillings into the slot and not getting even a back draft, we called the bellboy (by hallooing down the unused elevator shaft) and discovered (by his hallooing upward) that the electric fire was temporarily out of order. The hotel planned to have it repaired in two or three years. We had a private bathroom, too. (There was no end to luxury at this establishment.) However, we could not see any vestiges of a heating system in the bathroom. Challenged on this point, the room clerk expressed surprise. Heat in a bathroom? Why?

"What?" Richard said.

The room clerk and my husband regarded each other across a vast chasm of different customs and cultures; both of them were utterly appalled.

"The hot water," the room clerk finally said in the words of one syllable. "You put on the hot water, it runs through the pipes, and heats up the room."

The food at our hotel was about (although not quite) up to the standard of the heating arrangements. In the evening we could gather around a jolly coal fire in the lounge—two lumps of coal, which the porter ceremoniously knocked apart at 9 P.M. to save for the morrow's teatime. I thought I might shame the opposition by appearing for dinner in my fur coat, scarf, gloves, and lined galoshes, but I was outmatched by another lady guest who wore a knitted aviator's helmet and a blanket wrapped around her knees. She was in Bath for the "cure"— rheumatism, she told me.

"It must be great around here, for rheumatism," I said sardonically. I thought I was sardonic.

"Oh, it is," she advised me earnestly. "The mud packs are wonderful."

Richard and I walked dutifully up and down the streets of Bath. We saw all the famous buildings (between the worst downpours) and sloshed our way to 13 Queen Square and 4 Sydney Place (Jane Austen); we had morning coffee in the Pump Room (drearily, in overcoats) and examined the Roman ruins (fascinated, as I remarked, by the vestiges of the central heating system); and we stood around in the damp, admiring the Royal Crescent. But it is no use pretending we captured the world of Beau Nash and Miss Morland. We could see with our own eyes that Bath was the most elegant city in England; after three days we no longer cared. When Richard asked for the hotel bill (sneezing), the manager himself appeared to say, "But you had a reservation for a week."

Richard allowed his teeth to chatter freely. "My wife can't stand the cold."

"Cold?" The manager had to laugh. "This is a mild winter. You should have been here last year."

In the summer we went back to Bath, on our way to Wells; the city glowed golden in the sunset, as advertised, and the people strolled around the Royal Crescent, evidently enjoying themselves. Undoubtedly Bath is the most beautiful city in England. But in my mind it is indelibly associated with wearing two pairs of Richard's socks and my fur coat to bed.

That is the reason I began this report with Catherine Morland. Our experience was an accident. I mention it to explain the possibly wintry tone that blows through even my account of the Adam bridge, and to warn you off February visits to the residences of my beloved Jane Austen.

From Bath to Wells is a short journey by bus over the Somerset hills. The scenery is beguiling, the villages have a soft and drowsy air. You will stop in the ancient market place of a small medieval town—Wells.

I have tried not to use too many superlatives in this book, or to argue personal preferences which may find no echo in the more matter-of-fact reader. But I cannot resist saying that after London, and perhaps Canterbury, Wells is one place in England most dear to my heart.

The world is not with Wells—nor ever has been, very much. Somerset drowsed away the passing centuries of history. It is curious how exactly, how physically, one can feel these long, soft centuries of peace. The Monmouth Rebellion operated in these parts (1685); there was a good deal of unpleasantness during the Cromwellian wars (1646); and the Reformation brought Wells a new dean, also Cromwell, Thomas, in 1537. But these events were interruptions in the pattern of passing time. Somerset was far away from the wild Border Country, where the Scotch fought the English; far away from Windsor Castle and London, York and Lincoln, Kent and Sussex, where the Conqueror landed, and far from where the Wars of the Roses were decided, and feudalism made its last stands in frowning Gothic castles. Wells was never larger than it is today, a smiling little market town of seven thousand souls. Bath was on the main road to Bristol and the sea; Glastonbury was rich with accumulated monastic wealth. But Wells was a secular Cathedral; its vicars and canons were not monks; its chapter was more interested in architecture than in politics. The Cathedral lands were adequate for the support and building of what critics consider one of England's greatest Gothic masterpieces. Yet Wells was not so powerful or so wealthy as to attract the eagle-eyed interest of kings or archbishops. For long centuries the Bishop of Bath and Wells used the appointment as a stepping stone. He seldom bothered to appear in Wells after the ceremony of his installation—he was off to London, intriguing for promotion to Canterbury or York. Meanwhile the dean of Wells chapter and his vicars remained at home, experimenting with flying buttresses or *Perpendicular* windows.

Backwaters in time or geography (or both, as in the case of Wells) have many advantages. Since Wells had never been altered from the early secular foundation to the customary Norman arrangement of monastery, monks, and abbot, the lovely close was left almost untouched by the Reformation. The bishop's palace was partly wrecked, and one or two dining halls and kitchens were torn down, but for the most part the chapter buildings were left at Wells. The Cathedral lost some glass, a few of its tombs and ornaments, but its richness survived Cromwell as its close survived Henry VIII.

The Cathedral and buildings are approached by a great gate in the market place.

I despise writers who begin a paragraph unctuously, "Words cannot tell . . ."—after which follow a large number of words telling, or anyway purporting to tell.

But I have had a good deal of trouble with Wells. If I were only a poet, Wells would be easier. What I want to say is that as you go through the gate and first see the Cathedral, the lawns, the Palace, the lake, the silver river, the meadows, the Chain Gate, the Vicar's Close, the scene is beautiful—gloriously, triumphantly beautiful. But alas, the word "beautiful" is overworked; it sounds empty. It is like the boy who cried "Wolf." We rub the word thin on a beautiful dress, a beautiful day, a beautiful bride; and then, for Wells, the word is bankrupt. So are all the other words: alluring, enchanting, bewitching, ravishing, magical, lovely. None of them has a sharp enough edge for what you will see at Wells as you leave the market place and go into the close. Perhaps, after all, I must fall back on the dictionary:

Wells has beauty, "that quality which gratifies the eye or ear, or which delights the intellect or moral sense by its grace or fitness to the end in view."

To this I will add that when I first saw Wells I was shocked; it was so perfect and so sudden. It made my knees feeble. Nobody ever says anything adequate at such a moment of intensity. I stutter when I get excited; as Richard and I walked into the close, I said (when I had breath to say it), "Oh, d-d-d-darling, l-l-look!"

"Yes," Richard said.

Only a great poet or a great painter could say anything more.

I am trying to take Wells in order, because what happens first is this scene of beauty; it keeps happening. Indeed, it gains in depth. The landscape from the Cathedral roofs is a combination of natural glory (grass, river, meadows, flowers, hills, and blue sky) with some of the greatest triumphs of man in form and composition (the Cathedral towers, the Bishop's Palace, the contour of Vicar's Close and Chain Gate). Usually landscapes are either natural in feeling or works of art; this view at Wells is an extraordinary symphony of the human and the natural.

Wells is a union of the sensuous and the curious. As you approach the west façade, you are first stunned by its glory, and then fascinated to discover its history: it is the first twin-towered façade in England. As you will see by walking around it, the west front is a mask, concealing a narrow nave, an ingenious scheme to give the Cathedral grandeur far beyond its modest interior size. The chapter must have learned (1206) of Chartres and its enormous nave; there was not enough money at Wells to make a nave of such dimensions. But why not a glorious façade, with great towers to give proportion and rich statues to adorn its height and breadth?

The nave gives the same sensation of sudden beauty, followed by an excited, "Why?"

There is no other nave like this. The style is handsome *Early English*—pointed arches, rising stone stems to the triforium. But, as you stand at the west doors, your eye travels first across the now-familiar medieval sharpness and the upward thrust of the pillars to the transept crossing, a great stone curving figure eight. This sounds, in print, queer rather than lovely; in life it is superb.

But why? You will discover that the three famous figure eights at the Wells crossing are ingenious engineering schemes. It seems that Wells put up a grand central tower in 1321; the tower, like the one at Ely, was the pride of the chapter and the crown of the newly finished church. So far so good. In 1338 the chapter was called together for an extremely dismal meeting. The tower was going—fast. A slight miscalculation had been made with the piers. Nor was the tower the worst of it; there was no way to take it down, and when the tower went (in the first big wind) the choir, the transepts and part of the nave were going with it.

The vicars wept. Their beautiful, brand-new Cathedral was doomed.

Fourteenth-century builders seem to have been emotional about their work. The old records report that the sound of bitter lamentation rose from the chapter meeting.

At this point enter the hero, name unknown; but the evidence of his genius you may see at Wells today. The Dean and the vicars must have been dubious at first when inverted arches were proposed to prop up the tower. Who had ever heard of figure eights in stone? How would it look? The local engineer pressed his point, sketching the arches on the back of an old slate. See? You take the stresses of the tower on all four arches ... like this. . . .

"M'mmmm," the Dean must have said.

What did the chapter have to lose? The tower was going anyway. Medieval builders, as I said farther back, were wonderfully reckless—try anything once.

"New-fangled," some people carped, when the arches were hurriedly wedged into place.

"If you ask me, the arches won't last a lifetime."

The inverted arches at Wells have endured for six hundred years, and the last time the inspectors were down from London, it was announced that there appears to be no reason why the arrangement should not last another six centuries.

So the central tower proved to be a big success; everything the medieval builders turned to in the Cathedral came out well. The Cathedral even escaped that sinister item entitled Victorian vandalism, and the repairs done in modern times are lovingly accurate. As a small, but unimportant item for visitors, if it is still available, the official book about Wells (by Richard M. Malden, B.D., Dean of the Chapter), sold at a modest price, is the best of its kind I found on our English journey, a model of popular writing; accurate, intelligent, thorough. It does not condescend, it explains; it is illustrated with splendid photographs, and is both a guide, a history book, and a souvenir. Loudly recommended.

Every detail of Wells is worth examining. Armed with your copy of *The Story of Wells Cathedral* you can try the Fool-proof System on Chapter House, Chain Gate, Vicar's Close, and Bishop's Palace. In the north transept is a curious old clock, one of the earliest in England; I think the clock rather exasperates the vergers—it is popular with the Boy Scout and Youth Hostel set, who bike over from the Cheddar caves to see the little men come out and bong each other with fourteenth-century sledge-hammers.

"Sh-h-h-h-h," the vergers hiss furiously as the boys and girls tramp down the nave, headed for the clock.

My sympathies are strongly with the vergers. Clocks are all very well, and this one is amusing, but Wells deserves, as you enter it, a moment of awe-struck silence. It is so—well, it is so beautiful.

After Wells, you can go to Cheddar, or directly on to Glaston-bury. Tastes vary, in *tourisme,* but allowing for a fairly wide-spread range, I cannot think of any reason why an American should join the English Boy Scouts at Cheddar. The feature of Cheddar is caves, and frankly these are eighth-rate. Besides, there are more good caves in the U.S.A. than in the whole of Europe. If you must spend your time glooming about in the dark, why not do it at home? Cheddar has the usual cave top-side atmosphere. Sightseeing buses, cheap souvenirs, and ice-cream stalls. You will not like it. Don't go.

Glastonbury is famous, *too* famous. Some towns acquire a professional tourist patina, disconcerting to the traveler from afar. I do not know why it is that Wells, which has at least as many visitors, manages to present a calm, peaceful, untroubled face to its guests, while Glastonbury, a few miles along the road, is all a-hustle and a-bustle behind its clicking turnstiles. The Glastonbury ruins, the center of the tourist trade, are effi-ciently fenced in; guides rush their sightseeing lambs around at the end of a megaphone; you can buy paperweights shaped like the Abbot's Kitchen, or pamphlets entitled: *Did Christ Come to Somerset?*

HIKERS

This businesslike atmosphere is the more noticeable because the whole point of a ruin is its poetry. England is crowded with unruined Gothic churches. It seems fairly certain that Wells must always have been more interesting than Glastonbury, even in 1400. Now, Glastonbury is largely rubble, and there is no comparison. But the fashion for ruins started in England with the romantic poets—and there is much to be said for Rievaulx Abbey up in Yorkshire. There crumbling walls, the ancient relics of a dead past, molder in a lonely valley. Silence and sunlight bathe these "forgotten" stones.

Rievaulx Abbey is enchanting, especially in the twilight of a drowsy summer's day. We ran across a quite uncelebrated ruin in Sussex, too. The natives shrugged and gave us a stare when we asked which way to Boxgrove Church (on the road to Chichester). We finally found our way across country lanes by sighting on the spire; and once in the lonely, forgotten churchyard of the Benedictine priory, we were very pleased. It is a fine, desolate, silent place, full of poetry, wild roses, and peace. There is an extremely good ruin at Minster Lovell outside Oxford. In the August evenings boys and girls from the village "walk out" over the green lawns, and sit, talking softly, on the stones.

I mention these other ruins to indicate that I am not opposed to ruins in general; but I must say I found Glastonbury pretty loud and organized. You may be interested in the relics of what was once one of England's richest monasteries, and if your time is limited and you will not have a chance at Yorkshire or Sussex ruins, by all means see Glastonbury. The effect, however, is not Byronic.

Gloucester is in the opposite direction from Bath; if you make your headquarters at Bath, you can take buses to Wells and Glastonbury, then to Gloucester and back to London. Or Gloucester might come at the end of a journey to Oxford and the Cotswolds.

Gloucester is famous for its Cathedral. The town is pleasant enough but not exciting. If you have by this time developed a passion for medieval architecture, you will not want to miss the Cathedral, in many ways as interesting as any in England. It has a tremendous east window filled with fourteenth-century glass. Gloucester is Norman recased in *Perpendicular*. Usually, when medieval churches were remodeled, the new walls would be put up inside or outside the old; when the job was completed, the old walls were torn down. But at Gloucester, perhaps they ran out of money or had second thoughts about the roof caving in without the massive *Norman* piers, the eleventh-century walls were allowed to stand after the *Perpendicular* screen was finished. Today Gloucester is Exhibit A in the history of medieval style; it is like a museum with cross-section models, but in full-scale stone.

The cloisters at Gloucester are labeled by critics "unsurpassed" and "unrivaled," a "gem" and so on. I feel dubious and hostile when people make remarks like "unsurpassed," but as a matter of fact, the Gloucester cloisters are wonderful.

Gloucester has two "first-class" (what I call first-class) tombs. My standards for tombs are simple but severe: the party buried must be interesting, and the décor ditto. I have seen so many tombs that frankly I bounce around cathedrals, raking over the tombs with a quick eye. Tombs have to be AAAA to arouse more than a fleeting interest from me.

Gloucester has Robert Curthose, Duke of Normandy, eldest son of William the Conqueror. He lies in front of the altar, under a thirteenth-century oaken effigy. Robert was the simple-minded branch of the clan: Rufus (William II) was wicked, but crafty; Henry Beauclerc was cultured, for the period: he could read and write and furthermore was a sensible king, in favor of law and order and against grinding down the Saxons. The barons, fresh over from Normandy, regarded the conquered yokels as fair game. One of their playful *beau gestes* was to capture a fairly prosperous Saxon peasant or ex-earl, and send one of his eyes home to his wife, along with a demand for ransom. If that did not do the trick. . . . Henry I was opposed to this kind of sport. He argued that (*a*) it was un-Christian and unlovely and (*b*) it was bad for business. Saxons got so they would no longer put in a barley crop or harvest their hay. Why bother, when the Norman barons took everything in sight? Henry made strict rules about a Fair Deal for Saxons, and harried and handicaped his high-spirited Norman vassals in other ways as well. He kept insisting on law and order, and on justice instead of duels. Naturally, the Norman barons were against Henry Beauclerc. They felt he was an example of what happened when a man took up reading and writing.

In the middle of this controversy, Robert, the eldest son of the Conqueror, came home from the Crusades. While his brothers had been inheriting the family estate, administering kingdoms and dukedoms, wrestling with Church and barons, Robert had been joyously slaying the heathen in the Holy Land. As soon as he got home, Henry encouraged him to leave—right away.

"Huh?" Robert said to his nimble-witted brother. As Henry had anticipated, the barons rallied around and encouraged Robert to think of himself as King of England.

Robert was a more sympathetic type, the barons felt. He understood a good fight with broadswords or hatchets, and no dim notion of good government had ever flickered across his mind. Henry hated to do it—it broke his heart—but he rallied the Saxons and attacked brother Robert's army in Normandy. Robert was instantly captured, and the barons resigned themselves to another stretch of good, or reasonably good, government. Henry brought Robert Curthose home to England, and presently, for reasons not stated, Robert died. Henry gave him a big burial, and a fine, fancy tomb.

Poor old Robert! I have always wondered why they called him Curthose. Maybe his stockings kept slipping down, the way mine did in the sixth grade?

Edward II is buried to the left of Robert Curthose, in a tomb with a carved canopy. If you look him up in the chart at the back of this book, you will see that Edward II was one of the juiciest scandals of the Middle Ages. He came to a spectacular end, murdered by his wife, Queen Isabella, and a close personal friend of hers named Mortimer. Fancy my surprise to discover in the Gloucester guide that the local monks operated the tomb of Edward II as a pilgrimage site during the fourteenth century. In fact, they collected enough from the "shrine" to put up a lot of the *Perpendicular* trappings in the church. Considering the fact that in life Edward II was one of the most all-round unpopular kings in medieval history, it is odd to find the Gloucester monks were able to sell him, in death, to the neighborhood as a minor Edward the Confessor or Thomas Becket. A triumph for advertising, any way you look at it.

The affair of Edward II was considered deplorable by the elegant eighteenth-century inhabitants of Bath. Georgian England used to shudder when confronted with the medieval world. Gothic architecture, along with Gothic behavior, was too crude for the enlightened mind of Beau Nash and his circle. In fact, this journey through Bath to Wells and around to Gloucester is a zigzag through time as well as scenery—lovely, although not in February.

WHAT TO SEE IN BATH, WELLS, GLASTONBURY, AND GLOUCESTER

*** *Bath*. The beautiful eighteenth-century gray-and-golden city of England. (See text.)

*** *Wells*. One of the most beloved cathedrals, described in the text.

   Cheddar. Caves, not recommended.

 * *Glastonbury*. Famous ruins, as ruins go.

 * *Monmouth*. A pretty and interesting town. Henry V, who was sometimes called "Harry of Monmouth," was born

here, and there is a splendid gateway on the bridge over the Monnow River. Monmouth is situated at the point where the Monnow flows into the Wye, which brings us to:

** *Tintern Abbey.* About five miles beyond Monmouth in a water meadow on the banks of the now-tidal Wye. This is a first-class ruin in every way; it has a poem, a view, romance, and beautiful settings.

 * *Chepstow.* Also on the Wye, an old town, which has its walls and west gate, plus a good castle, on a rocky ledge overlooking the river. The spectacular Severn Road bridge is one of the largest in Europe. From Chepstow up the Wye to Ross is a beautiful patch of river scenery, lush and green and lovely. In the nineteenth century the Valley of the Wye was a favorite vacation haunt for poets. (Thus "Tintern Abbey," by Wordsworth.) Nowadays the Valley of the Wye is thick with tourist buses. It is worth seeing, though, if you have the time. Ross itself is a charming old market town. From Ross, you can go on to:

** *Gloucester.* A cathedral town, described in the text.

Oxford, the Cotswolds, Stratford-on-Avon, Warwick, Kenilworth, and Tewkesbury

OXFORD and Cambridge are the gateways to longer journeys: Oxford leads to the Cotswolds, and Cambridge to East Anglia. If your time is limited, you should make an overnight trip to Oxford, and the same for Cambridge. Fast trains from London take, in each case, less than two hours.

It is preposterous to grade England's glories like so many cans of tomatoes; a label "Grade AAA" cannot be attached to Wells or a sign "B plus" hung over Winchester. All the same, a tourist must have some categories. I shall sound didactic, but a visit to England however brief, must include: (1) London, (2)

Canterbury, and (3) the two great universities. After that, you can follow your own gleam. We have come across Americans who have seen Anne Hathaway's cottage and Wordsworth's home, but not Magdalen Tower or the Cambridge "backs." A mistake.

I admit Oxford and Cambridge are difficult. There is an immense amount to see; you can go on and on and on, from one college, chapel, and dining hall to another. It is confusing and exhausting, especially on a hot summer's day, to tramp the endless blocks from Magdalen to Christ Church to the Bodleian; or from King's College to Trinity. One can absorb just so much architecture at any one time, and acquire just so much legend and fact, after which the law of diminishing returns sets in with a bang. Many a traveler, beginning with the most earnest intentions, ends up dragging himself to one Oxford college after another in a kind of daze; afterward all he can remember is how long it took. Oxford and Cambridge overwhelm, rather than invite, the traveler.

I speak from bitter experience. The first time I saw Cambridge, we "did" eleven colleges, with half an hour off for lunch. The temperature was hovering around ninety, and by the time we tramped into the courtyard of College Number Eleven I was daydreaming of a hammock back home, a pitcher of ice water and something utterly dim-witted to read.

"The quadrangle," the porter said, "is considered a fine example of English Renaissance. Notice the pediment on your left, the design is attributed to Inigo Jones. If you will step into the chapel . . ."

"Uh!" I cried, shuffling my feet.

Our Aunt Adele, a wily, experienced hand with tourists, proposed an Oxford tour. She had a young American niece in tow, and suggested that Patrick, for the good of his twelve-year-old soul, and I, for the good of this book, might like to be her guests.

"Why, thanks," I said, with false cheeriness. "How nice for Pat."

I fell in love with Oxford. Richard and I have been back three times since and tackled Cambridge all over again, using the guaranteed Aunt Adele University Method, painless and exciting. We strongly recommend the A.A. Method to you, or some variation of it. Here are the fundamentals:

Acquire a rough idea of what you are seeing, the origins and meaning of English university life. (We take a stab at this, below.)

Concentrate on not more than four colleges, at most five, in a day; take taxicabs, or buses, even for a few blocks; allow plenty of time for morning coffee, a long lunch, and a leisurely tea.

Spend at least one of your afternoons in the "backs" along the Cam at Cambridge; at Oxford, sit in the gardens of Magdalen or St. John's.

Does this sound lazy and anti-tourist? I can assure you, from painful experience, that the English universities are hopeless in big doses. A solid month is not too long really to see Oxford; in two or three days you cannot hope even to glance at most of the treasures, and in no place in England, outside of London itself, is quantity so illusory, and quality of such importance.

The English university, like English law or government, was not born overnight; it developed across the centuries. Even today, Oxford and Cambridge are in the process of change; the Oxford of Matthew Arnold looked immutable (to him) but it is already dead. The ivied, cloistered world which produced Cardinal Newman now debates experimental physics. The gentlemen scholars of the 1900's are replaced by a hungry crew who advertise in the personal column of *The Times* for "any kind of work during the long vac." Crusty graduates of Oxford deplore today such signs of changing times, just as crusty graduates in 1650 and in 1450 made the welkin ring with drear complaints. But the strength and virtue of Oxford has always been its ability to shift more or less with the world around, to mirror, and sometimes to lead; it would be a mistake to think, as you look at the historic spires, that Oxford represents only the great past. The future is here, too.

The future has been in Oxford, from the beginning, which was probably in the late twelfth century. Nobody can be sure when the first medieval scholars appeared in the old walled town, nor why they came to Oxford instead of to London. It seems certain, however, that sometime during the reign of Henry II (perhaps just after Thomas Becket was murdered) the first group of ragged clerks arrived across the Channel from the medieval university at the Sorbonne in Paris. By 1200, Oxford was a corporate body; later the university was closed by the authorities during a big—and now obscure—row. Some scholars, infuriated by attacks on academic liberty, traveled across country to Cambridge, and when Oxford was, at length, allowed to reopen, many of its exiles stayed on the banks of the Cam to found its great rival in learning.

The medieval university was, by modern standards, a peculiar institution. Its scholars were young; they generally went up to Oxford at thirteen or fourteen, and stayed seven years to take a degree. They were in minor Church orders (thus the gowns and caps of today), which did not, however, produce an atmosphere of sweet reason or Christian resignation. Riots broke out constantly, between town and gown, or between one maestro and his gang of intellectual partisans, and another. Studies were neither uniform nor regular. A professor set up shop in a tavern, in a field, or at a convenient street corner. Scholars appeared to debate or listen. The language of learning, in England and abroad, was Latin, so students could shop around, from professor to professor, from country to country. Mathematics, logic, a smattering of "science" were the subjects taught, or more accurately debated, at Oxford in the beginning.

The building of the ancient "halls" (of which one still exists at Oxford) was the first university reform. The starving, ragged scholars were gathered up from streets and taverns, and installed under central roofs. The earliest colleges grew out of these medieval halls, a revolution in university life. The college system today is not too different from that of the fifteenth century. Students are—and were—gathered together behind college walls, comfortably lodged, required to dine together, and encouraged to pursue an orderly course of studies under the direction of a selected body of teachers. Great and rich men in the outside world endowed colleges, especially during the fifteenth and sixteenth centuries; the age of the undergraduates grew older. The first public schools, founded in the same period, prepared for entry into universities. Still later, tutors were introduced to provide supervision of students' work. Today, Oxford students may leave their colleges to attend lectures given for anyone in the university, but the emphasis is on a small group of students gathered for serious work under the direction of a college foundation.

Views of Oxford are debated by connoisseurs. Matthew Arnold made immortal the distant vista of spires, a panorama famous since the sixteenth century. However, a gas works is now located directly in front of some of England's stateliest architecture, spoiling the celebrated view. It seems perverse that the Nazis who destroyed so much of Bristol and Canterbury and elsewhere, could not have scored a hit on the Oxford gas works. Maybe, being earnest students of Baedeker, they missed it on purpose.

Close up, the gas tanks do not show—not much, anyway. The best way to start a visit to Oxford (this is the Tested Method) is with a general view, from the cupola of Wren's Sheldonian Theatre. Your opening look at Oxford, as you come panting upstairs to the theatre's octagonal tower, will be another of those stunning, shattering moments. You stand in the middle of a maze of towers, gates, domes, chapels; architecture revolves around you—Saxon, Tudor, Perpendicular, Renaissance, Norman, Victorian.

The Sheldonian Theatre is roughly at the center of the university. When you have come cautiously down the steps from the cupola, you will be in a handsome square; the Tower of the Five Orders on the Divinity School, across from you, is Jacobean with Wren overtones. (He was a great "restorer" too.) If you are on a leisurely three-day tour of Oxford, see the Divinity School; it has a handsome fan-vaulted hall and a lot of history. On September 30, 1555 (in the reign of Mary Tudor), Latimer and Ridley were ordered to appear here to answer for "sundry erroneous opinions." A cross in the pavement of Broad Street, in front of Balliol College, marks the spot where they were burned at the stake. The entrance to the Divinity School (it had its ups and downs) is usually called "The Pig Market." Henry VIII installed the pigs. He did not agree with various Oxford dons of the period.

Our first scheduled college is down a little alley from the Sheldonian. Ask anyone for New College (or a street map

THE SHELDONIAN THEATRE, OXFORD

would be practical). New College was founded June 30, 1379 (the buildings were dedicated in 1386), by William of Wykeham, Bishop of Winchester. You came across William's track at Winchester: he founded the public school there. Incidentally, that will solve a mystery you may have found puzzling. Old boys of Eton are Old Etonians but old boys of Winchester are Old Wykehamists.

New College is a considerable tourist project. You will want to see the cloisters, the chapel, the dining hall (through the Muniment Tower), the Garden Court, the lovely gardens, and finally try not to miss the college treasure. If it happens to be closed, inquire of the porter—it is possible he will show you the Treasure Room. At most of the colleges, the porters will be your guides. They are well-informed if you put an intelligent question or two (otherwise they are apt to shirk). Oxford college porters do not share the widespread American view that payment for time and trouble is demeaning.

I make a point of the New College treasure because I could not sleep nights puzzling over one of the objects—a beautiful Chinese celadon bowl mounted on a Tudor base, one of the first Chinese objects of art to appear in England. It was a present to Archbishop Warham, a fellow of New College, from Archduke Philip of Austria, who was visitng Henry VIII in 1506. Question: How did Philip get this bowl? Where did it come from? Who was touring China in 1500 and bringing back souvenirs to Austria? Or did Philip "pick it up," as travelers say, in Italy? Did Marco Polo bring it originally to Venice?

The treasure includes platters and silver bowls still used for state dinners, and Bishop Wykeham's jewelry. He must have glittered like a Christmas tree when he was dressed up for a big procession; I like his pendant especially. But, aside from the Chinese bowl, the other important relic is the unicorn horn presented by William Port in 1458. Unicorn horns were extremely scarce in fifteenth-century England, and no doubt New College took a justifiable pride in its possession. They would have done better to keep quiet about it. Imagine their consternation when one morning during Queen Elizabeth's reign there arrived a sealed parchment from the Earl of Leicester. Would of fellows of New College please send (by return messenger) the unicorn horn? The Earl understood it was an antidote for a certain type of poison, and without dwelling on sordid details, he felt the horn would be handy to have around. The request was urgent; would New College please rush the horn by fast horse express to London?

"Oh my!" the fellows of New College said. "How awkward! How very awkward!"

"I mean to say, the Earl of Leicester . . ."

"Quite!" the dons agreed.

Gloom was general, until somebody got the bright idea of sawing off the tip and persuading the Earl that a teaspoon of ground unicorn horn was fully as efficacious as a pound. In fact, with more, complications might set in. Too much unicorn is as bad as too little or none.

The sample of horn seems to have satisfied the Earl; perhaps the emergency died down without recourse to an antidote.

The footnote to this story comes from a spoilsport zoologist in the nineteenth century. He looked at the horn and said, "Bah! that's no unicorn, it's a narwhal horn." There the matter stood, in all the guidebooks. I looked narwhal up in Webster's: it is an Arctic whale; female narwhals go around unadorned, but the male has a "long, twisted, ivory tusk." So somebody palmed off whale horn on William Port. Or did they? One wonders if the unicorn horn was a present; or did New College pay cash or favors in kind? Is it possible this William Port regarded the fellows of New College as credulous, unworldly, academic types—suckers? Did William Port sell New College a pup? An ugly thought!

We must abandon frivolous speculation and push on to the chapel, a Victorian restoration with enough early *Perpendicular* remaining to interest visitors. The great screen at the east end is an 1894 reconstruction of the original. Below Sir Joshua Reynolds' painted glass window (now faded) is Epstein's "powerful" statue of the "Risen Lazarus." "Powerful" is one of those useful critic words, which translate out to "Well—if you like that sort of thing." I happen to find "Risen Lazarus" impressive, although not very cheery, I must admit. Incidentally, Sir Joshua's window replaced the original—most beautiful—medieval stained glass. The college sold it to the glazier for

£30, a good sum in 1785, but nothing like what the glazier got for it from York Minster, where it shines today, in all its glory, just as it did for almost four centuries in New College. There must be a moral to this story, but I find it escapes me.

The great feature of New College, after the cloisters, is the Garden Court, and the gardens. The old walls of Oxford stand in New College Park, and you can sit down comfortably, amid the greenery, and peer at fourteenth-century battlements. Very pleasant.

New College is Number One on our list. Strenuous characters might walk up the block to High Street, and along the avenue everyone agrees is the "finest in the kingdom." Weaker tourists can hang out the taxi window as they progress along to Magdalen Bridge. Have the driver let you down on the far side of the bridge so that you can walk back across the Cherwell, and see Magdalen Tower, pronounced Maudlin, as in the girl's name plus the first syllable of linen: Maud-lin. The river is pronounced Char-well. I do not usually insist on tricky English pronunciations, but these two are fundamental, because otherwise people do not know what you are talking about. After thoroughly touring "Maud-lin," I examined my Oxford map, and asked, "Aren't we going to see this Mag-da-len College? It's supposed to be important."

Forward to "Maud-lin," which many critics consider the most beautiful of Oxford colleges. I put in this "many critics" to save myself outraged battle cries from partisans of other foundations. Magdalen is fairly well organized for the tourist trade, and appears to be on the main sightseeing bus route from London. "Hour's stopover at Beautiful Oxford, then on to———." If you run afoul of the megaphone crowd, detour to the park, and come back twenty minutes later for the Muniment Tower.

The history of Magdalen always intrigues me. It was founded in 1458 by William of Waynflete, but it was Cardinal Wolsey who developed a passion for the college. He was senior bursar in 1500, in charge of the building program. He appears to have been as whole-hearted about education as he afterwards turned out to be about politics, Henry VIII, and Hampton Court. Various snide critics of Wolsey argue that as a college fund raiser he was overenthusiastic. He used to tour up-country monasteries collecting "donations" for Magdalen and afterward for Christ Church. Abbots groaned when the Cardinal began to talk about the benefits of a college education, and it is evident even to the tourist eye that Magdalen Tower, the Chapel, Founder's Tower, Muniment Tower, and so on, probably did not come cheap. I must say I admire Wolsey. He may not have designed the tower single-handed, but he bossed the contractors, supervised the details, and raised the hard cash for the project. Even if the contributions were not exactly voluntary, it must be remembered that the sixteenth century was not a sentimental age. Many Yorkshire abbots had no taste for higher learning. Since Wolsey was in charge of "regulating" monasteries (preferably out of existence), historians have used the vulgar word "bribe" to describe the contributions that the richer brethren were constrained to give. If true, this was naughty of Wolsey.

The bribes were spent in a good cause: Magdalen Tower is one of the most beautiful monuments in England. The entrance to the college is a masterpiece of grace, and the cloisters are enchanting. In fact, after a good look at the courtyards, the state banqueting room and the Founder's Tower, I have added Wolsey to that select list of English heroes entitled, in my diary, "People I Approve of," which includes St. Augustine, Thomas Becket *and* Henry II, William the Conqueror (not Harold— I am fed up with him), Margaret of Anjou, Henry VII, Christopher Wren, Queen Elizabeth, and several more. I have Henry VIII in a special department, "Abhorrent But Tremendous," because of the vile way he treated Thomas More, Anne Boleyn, and Kate Howard. I hesitated about Wolsey, but after Magdalen the Cardinal was promoted. I approve of him. I think you will, too, when you go through the cloisters and see the Bell Tower.

Besides its superb quadrangles, Magdalen has a hundred acres of park—its own private island in the Cherwell, reached by an iron bridge. On a hot summer's day, the Water Walks, which Addison loved, are delightful. The paths, overhung by old trees, the cool vistas of water and lawn with ancient graceful stone in the background, are refreshing. All visitors to Oxford arrive eventually at a paraphrase of George Bernard Shaw's remark about youth: "Too good to waste on children."

The Water Walks will persuade you that Oxford is much too beautiful for college boys.

Christ Church (a good distance from Magdalen) is the third on our list of sights. If you are spacing out your university visit to two (or more) days, leave Christ Church until the morning after Magdalen, and spend your extra time strolling through the Botanic Gardens, along Merton Fields to the river, and into Christ Church Meadow, a lovely walk. But, if you must press on, take a taxi to "Tom Tower." This is the entrance to Christ Church (which for esoteric reasons, is not called a college, but is referred to as "The House").

Tom Tower is officially titled the Great Gate; over its archway is a statue of Cardinal Wolsey, the founder (1525). The famous bell in the Great Gate and the Belfry were added by Wren in 1682. The guides will tell you how much Great Tom weighs (18,000 pounds) and add that every night in term at 9:05 P.M. it tolls a curfew of 101 strokes for the 101 original college students. At the last stroke the college gates are closed, after which the students use the smaller door.

Historians debate the question of whether Wolsey did, or did not, design Magdalen Tower. There is no quibbling about the Great Quadrangle at Christ Church. By 1525 Wolsey had tried his hand as architect at Hampton Court, and he personally laid out this largest and noblest of Oxford courtyards. Building operations were delayed by Wolsey's sudden end, and the north side was not finished until 1668. Still, the design is the Cardinal's, one of his greatest triumphs.

Beyond the Great Quadrangle is the Cathedral Church of Christ, a fascinating building in history, décor, tombs, and general detail. It is the smallest cathedral in England.

Originally, Christ Church was the property of St. Frideswide's Priory. In 1522 came the Dissolution, engineered of course by Henry VIII and his chief aide-de-camp Wolsey, who had long had his eye on Christ Church. Apparently he was not satisfied to be a fund raiser for somebody else's foundation; he decided to found a college himself. You have only to walk through Wolsey's nobly proportioned Quadrangle to realize that Wolsey was an architect who knew his own mind. He took down the nave of Christ Church to make room for his idea of a courtyard. The fat revenues of St. Frideswide's Priory were settled by Wolsey (who got them from Henry VIII, naturally) on his new institution of higher learning.

This brings us to 1529. Henry VIII, that ingrate, had Wolsey attainted, and the Cardinal died in the nick of time—thus cheating his old friend of a big state execution. One of the advantages of attainting for Henry VIII was that he not only got rid of an inconvenient critic, but also legally took over the victim's property. Henry was a stickler for legal detail; he liked everything to be shipshape, signed and sealed, deeds registered at the Temple. Wolsey had already "given" Hampton Court to the King; on the occasion of Wolsey's attainder, Henry acquired Christ Church.

You will remember that, when Wolsey took up architecture at Hampton Court, Henry was struck with a blueprint fever himself. Now Henry turned his beady stare on the ex-Cardinal's efforts at Christ Church. Should it be said that Wolsey, the traitor, founded a college, and the King founded nothing? No, this should not be said. As a beginning, he rechristened the college Wolsey had started: King Henry VIII's College. Turning to the college chapel (truncated without the nave)—who was going to inhabit the *King's* church? Henry created a cathedral where the chapel had been and moved in a bishop. To this day students of Christ Church worship in the Cathedral of the Oxford diocese. Wolsey and Henry VIII, in modern times, double in brass as founders of Christ Church, although, in evening prayers, the students recite a special "use" for their royal founder.

The Cathedral style is *English*: exquisite *Perpendicular* fan vaulting rises gracefully from *Norman* pillars; the Lady Chapel is *Early English* and the guides will show you Saxon foundations.

After the Cathedral, you will want to see the Chapter House, and the Hall, which, after Westminster Hall in London, is the greatest in England. It is left over from the Priory, but a good deal of its best history is Tudor or post-Tudor. Henry VIII turned up here in 1533 for a state banquet; Elizabeth and James I came for plays, some of which may have been written by that popular dramatist William Shakespeare. Charles I used the Hall for more tragic business: in 1644 he held a meeting of

Parliament here for those M.P.'s who were faithful to his declining cause. It must have been grim when they called the roll and found almost everybody missing.

The Great Quadrangle (called Tom Quad) leads through a famous archway to Peckwater Quadrangle. Here is the statue of Dean Fell—"I do not like thee, Doctor Fell, the reason why I cannot tell . . ."

Peckwater Quad is eighteenth century, a contrast to the earlier Tom Quad; Peckwater leads into the small Canterbury Quad, and beyond to Merton Street.

I have skipped dizzily through acres of history, and blocks of architecture. I hope I have given you some idea of the full-scale project even one Oxford college can be. That is why we arbitrarily end up our Oxford tour with St. John's College, a small but venerable foundation. Some of the buildings are medieval; the lower parts of the original quadrangle are fourteenth century; the second courtyard is Renaissance, perhaps designed by Inigo Jones, and, in any case, graceful and elegant. St. John's College has strong royalist overtones, boasting portraits of Charles I, and relics of Archbishop Laud, including the skull cap he wore when he was executed, his walking stick, diaries, and so on. There is a martyr for whom I cannot scare up the least sympathy. I am opposed to martyring people, and I do not condone the Archbishop's execution; but I do not condone his life and policies. Perhaps we should not be too hard on Laud. His relentless persecution of Puritans caused the mass emigration to New England around 1630. Who knows, if it had not been for Laud, the history of the United States might have been different, and not nearly so glorious. But I am afraid the emigrants as they left their homes for exile in a strange, distant wilderness muttered in Archbishop Laud's direction: "Thanks for nothing."

We choose St. John's College for our fourth visit not alone for the charming buildings, but especially for the gardens behind the second quadrangle. These five acres have been cultivated for centuries; and the background of graceful Renaissance with artful arrangement of lawn, shrubs, and flowers makes a sensuous scene especially welcome after a long day of sightseeing.

There is a footnote to our Oxford schedule. As you enter the city, or before you leave, take a bus or taxi to the outskirts for a look at the famous *Norman* church of Iffley. Although it is surrounded by Oxford suburbs and housing projects, the village itself remains intact, and the church is delightful.

If you have another morning, or even an hour or two, at Oxford, the treasures at the university's Ashmolean Museum bring students, and admiring laymen, from half the civilized world to see.

This ends the tour of Oxford; we cannot apologize for its brevity, because that is its theory and virtue. If you fell seriously in love with Oxford (a good idea that would be), cancel the rest of your English tour, settle down and spend a week or ten days investigating every one of the colleges. If you must go on, after such a brief look, the four colleges, plus the view from the Sheldonian, will give you some small idea of England's great university.

If you plan on hiring a car for a few days of your English journey, the Cotswolds would richly repay the extra cost. If you are young and have the time and energy, the Shakespeare country is hallowed ground for bicycle or walking tours. The main items on our Cotswolds list are served by buses and trains, but half the charm, and all of the adventure, in exploring this lovely region of England are lost by bouncing from one crowded tourist center to another. If your budget cracks beneath the strain of a U-Drive-It, and your spirit is willing but your flesh too far gone to push a bicycle uphill and down (mostly up), do not despair. Take a bus from Oxford to Stratford, but after that avoid the main roads, and ride the market-town locals; the backwoods bus system in the Cotswolds is amazing. You can "discover" delightful, unhurried, sleepy villages from Stratford or Evesham or Tewkesbury; if you travel light, you will be free to stop overnight where you choose, and to explore the peaceful and untroubled "vales" as pleasantly as though you were zooming about in a Rolls-Royce—well, almost.

For example, Minster Lovell is a small village, twelves miles from Oxford. If you are driving it makes a fine overnight stop: first-class ruins,and a single street which is Cotswold at its best. But Minster Lovell is on an Oxford bus line; you can leave Oxford after tea and arrive in plenty of time to see the sunset over the ruins.

Let me divide up the Cotswold region. You will want to see the main sights of the area: Stratford-on-Avon, Warwick, Kenilworth and Tewkesbury Abbey. If you have more time, you will want to include Worcester and Hereford cathedrals and Pershore Abbey. Besides these historic places, you must see at least one or two of the beautiful Cotswold villages: they are famous for their soft golden-gray stone, their graceful architecture, for thatched roofs and peaceful dignity. Broadway is infested by sightseeing buses and, although a handsome village, is so jammed and commercial that I doubt if you will enjoy it. In any case, Chipping Campden is handsomer, not much farther, and infinitely more rewarding.

Another suggestion, leaving Oxford for Stratford, is to drive, or take the bus, to Stow-on-the-Wold. This is a charming Cotswold market town, at the center of a cluster of villages on the banks of the river Windrush—wonderful name, no wonder Shakespeare had a good ear. And there are Upper Slaughter, Lower Slaughter, Upper Swell and Lower Swell, Bourton-on-the-Waters, Northleach, Withingdon, and Bibury, the names of Cotswold villages, some within walking distance of Stow-on-the-Wold, all within a half an hour or so by car or bus.

Incidentally, I was taken aback by the Slaughters. The Cotswolds grew rich on sheep. I thought they were *sheared*, not butchered. Inquiries did not answer this teasing little puzzle. So far as the people who live in Upper and Lower go, Slaughter is a perfectly good name for a place; why should foreigners (even American cousins) come asking questions of an invidious nature.

"I didn't mean to—forgive me, I was just curious—that is, I thought it *unusual*. Don't you?"

"No," the lady behind the bar said.

"Ah!"

But aside from this small brush with local pride, the Cotswolds are welcoming, especially in fall, winter, and spring. Summer can be trying. There are too many people touring the "Shakespeare Country." But even if you come in August, do not miss the Cotswold villages.

. . .

Stratford-on-Avon is the home of what many Englishmen scornfully call the "Shakespeare Industry." There is no doubt that the Bard has been thoroughly organized; but he was an astute showman himself, and I wonder whether he would have been as distressed by the box-office takings at Stratford as modern aesthetes make out. It is one thing to deplore the maddening tourist crowds at Glastonbury or Broadway—Glastonbury is supposed to be romantic, but romance is diminished by the sharp click of the turnstiles and the souvenir industry; Broadway is billed as a "sleepy Cotswold village," although not even a cat could sneak a quick doze around Broadway at the top of the summer season. But Stratford—! How can it be supposed that the birthplace and beloved last home of William Shakespeare could be kept a peaceful backwater? The Stratford boom was inevitable; what is surprising is not the Shakespeare Industry, but its dignity. I was flabbergasted, not by the crowds and the queues, the megaphones and the souvenir stalls, but by the devotion to principle, the emphasis on fact rather than stupid legend, on good taste rather than vulgarity, and above all, by the attempt made to inspire the milling mob of tourists, not merely to take their money. I think England can be proud of its Shakespeare Industry; certainly Stratford is organized, but it is exciting and instructive. It is also rather touching.

Snobs in tourist clothing delight in telling malicious stories of the backward visitor. There is the old chestnut about the lady who was so pleased to find out that Shakespeare had written *Hamlet*; she had always wondered who the author was. Or the innocent gentleman who thought Anne Hathaway was Shakespeare's mother. These, and similar tidbits, are in my opinion downright lies, and never did or could have happened. It is obvious, after ten minutes in Stratford, that few worshipers at the shrine have counted the misprints in the first folio, or know *Venus and Adonis* by heart. During the excellent lecture at Anne Hathaway's cottage, the guide, explaining how Shakespeare went to London, quoted:

> Such wind as scatters young men through the world,
> To seek their fortunes further than at home,
> Where small experience grows . . .

A man next to me asked, "Did *he* write that?"

And some lady savant, wearing the latest in a pants suit from South Bend, Indiana, laughed.

The guide fixed a cold eye on South Bend and replied warmly and tactfully that *The Taming of the Shrew* was not one of the better-known plays. I resisted a strong impulse to kick our friend from Indiana squarely in the shins.

The crowds at Stratford do not amuse me; but they make me feel that all is not lost in this wicked and nervous world. The impulse to hero worship is deep in human experience; how many millions cheered themselves into swoons over Hitler, Mussolini, and Genghis Khan? But in England the "Sweet Swan of Avon" has become the folk hero; tourists solemnly queue up to see the tomb of Shakespeare. From earliest times, men have felt some magic virtue in walking where the Great Man walked, touching what the Hero once touched. It is a profound and impressive experience to visit Stratford and watch the crowds making the ritual obeisance not to a king, or a dictator, or even to a saint—but to William Shakespeare, poet.

The Shakespeare Industry has made the shrine intelligible and instructive for the pilgrim. Tourists may come in a vague spirit of seeking magic, but they would have to be blind, deaf, and dumb to leave Stratford without having learned something about Tudor England and the genius it produced. The birthplace, the burying ground, the cottage, and so on have been reconstructed; granted that the oaken rafters are synthetic and the thatched roofs deliberately quaint. But the reconstruction is accurate. If Stratford is a stage set, it is a good one. Surely Shakespeare would not complain that his museum is dramatized? No other tourist center in England is so meticulous in its desire to teach rather than to tickle the curiosity. The guide, as he shows you around the birthplace says, "This may have been . . . some authorities hazard the opinion that . . . the furniture in this room is Elizabethan, of a kind which would have been used by a reasonably prosperous small merchant of the period. It is, of course, not the actual furniture used by Shakespeare's parents."

Perhaps you will think this is quibbling, but I admire the

honest spirit which, in spite of the enormous pressure arising from mass worship, holds firmly to fact. The coin of truth is easily debased. There is something heart-warming in the guide's "may-have-been" or (at the cottage) the lecturer's: "There is a tradition that this was the actual bed Shakespeare willed to his wife, but of course we cannot be sure. In any case, it would have been a bed not dissimilar."

At the birthplace they have made a virtue (and a splendid exhibit) of the reconstruction. The most interesting thing in Stratford, to my mind, aside from the fact of the crowd itself, is the series of old pictures and documents telling how Shakespeare's birthplace fell into decay, was used as a shop, and finally was rescued by the forerunners of the present Shakespeare Industry. You can trace, in these yellowed pages from old magazines, the first slow trickle of interest, the gradual growth of Stratford as a place of pilgrimage, and the final, twentieth-century upsurge of curiosity and awe.

I have taken for granted a day spent making the standard Stratford tour: birthplace in Henley Street; Quiney House, home of Shakespeare's daughter; Harvard House, the home of John Harvard's mother; the New Place Museum; the Grammar School; the Church of the Holy Trinity, where Shakespeare is buried; and Anne Hathaway's cottage. Finally, there is the Shakespeare Memorial Theatre overlooking the Avon.

After such a wholehearted bow to the Shakespeare Industry in general, I may be allowed one small reservation. The décor of the Stratford Memorial Theatre is (or used to be) widely esteemed; the auditorium is comfortable, the stage well lighted and large, the dining terraces practical. But the style is 1930 "functional." Why is the theatre so aggressively *moderne* in a town so passionately quaint? Whatever gets into architects? A theatre need not be fake Tudor, or sport a thatched roof, but why something straight out of the Futurama for Shakespeare's birthplace?

Warwick usually comes after Stratford on the sightseer's schedule. Warwick again is major tourist country; but I have seen a lot of castles in England, and not a few on the Continent, and Warwick is the best all-round castle in my experience. It is satisfactory, in every sense worth the price of admission, which is no pittance.

The history of Warwick Castle is a saga of blood and woe (including a prime chapter from our Wars of the Roses), starting with Alfred the Great's daughter, and featuring troubles all along the line. Few inhabitants of the castle had much luck. One Earl of Warwick, whose given name, unfortunately for him, was Edward Plantagenet, was arrested at the age of eight by his loving uncle Richard III, who made a practice of incarcerating small nephews. In this case Richard III did not have time to give the small earl the full benefit of his affectionate attention, and Henry VII inherited the tender prisoner in the Tower. Henry VII thought the matter over for fourteen years, and then, I am sorry to record, had the Earl unchained and beheaded. Historians call the earl's execution a "blot" on Henry's record. "Blot" seems a pale word for what happened to the Earl of Warwick, aged eight to twenty-five.

Edward Plantagenet's life and times were more miserable than those of the usual run of Warwicks, but the title was not a lucky one through the centuries. Every dramatic chapter of English history has an Earl of Warwick getting himself attainted, or beheaded, or murdered, or falling on the field of battle. Remember our Earl of Warwick the Kingmaker, dying under the Red instead of the White Rose? Lady Jane Grey's father-in-law was the Duke of Northumberland and also the Earl of Warwick. His successor was Ambrose Dudley, who, it is true, died in bed, but he was married three times and never had issue that survived. His son was the "Noble Impe" buried in the family chapel at Warwick's beautiful Church of St. Mary. The present Warwick clan acquired the title in 1759. So far they have had reasonably smooth sailing. I suppose the old curse on the muzzled bear is washed up. Yet the history of Warwick Castle makes the blood run cold; such a collection of bad guessers, reckless plotters, wretched children, and all-round hard times needs to be read in detail to be believed. (The Earl's minions will be glad to sell you a pamphlet on the castle history, along with your ticket.)

One odd fact about all Warwicks is told in the stones of the castle. No sooner did a man get the muzzled bear painted on his coat-of-arms than he was seized by an acute attack of building fever. Few Earls of Warwick, no matter how short their tenure, how sudden their demise, did not find time between plots and uproars to add something to the old home. The castle is a glorious mixture of Norman, medieval, Tudor, Jacobean, Renaissance, Georgian, and Regency; the state apartments are as grand as any French palace, more elegant than Windsor. There is hardly a castle in Europe with a situation so picturesque, battlements so authentic, towers so frowning, an art gallery so full of treasures, and so much wallpaper of red satin, so many handsome fireplaces by Adam.

The town of Warwick is interesting; the one thing you will not want to miss is the Church of St. Mary's, and especially the choir tomb and Beauchamp Chapel. This last is one of the most elaborate *Perpendicular* buildings in England, with a collection of magnificent tombs, the best in the kingdom, outside Westminster and Tewkesbury Abbey. The guide for St. Mary's is crammed with fact, highly recommended. It is written by W. H. Elliott, Chaplain to the Queen, and is another triumph of popular and instructive writing. I like the Reverend Elliott's forthright stand on the personalities buried in the church. He minces no words: "It is no use to pretend that this Robert of Leicester was anything but an unscrupulous rogue," the Reverend Elliott remarks of one of the famous characters buried in the Beauchamp Chapel. Armed with the Elliott guide, you can have a wonderful two hours in the Warwick Church, after which most people push on to Kenilworth.

Kenilworth is notorious in our family. Richard and I, trailing two children, started off dutifully after a day at Warwick Castle and the Beauchamp Chapel. It was 4:26 P.M. when we reached Kenilworth, bought our tickets, passed the porter's gate, and arrived in the grassy courtyard. Above, on the hilltop, were a large number of ruins. I regarded the ruins. I said, in what Richard calls my long-suffering voice, "Look, dear, why don't you and the children go up and . . . look around? I can see it splendidly from here." I sat down on the nearest park bench.

My husband broke into offensive laughter.

I was furious. "My feet are down to the stumps."

Richard thought it was funny. It seems that in 1927 his mother, his sister, his cousin and himself had "done" Warwick Castle and St. Mary's Church, after which—on to Kenilworth! They arrived about 4:30; his mother passed the porter's gate, looked up the hill at Sir Walter Scott's copyrighted castle, and according to her son, my poor mother-in-law then said (in her long-suffering voice), "Now, why don't you children go up and see the castle? I can see it splendidly from here." She sat down on the same park bench I occupied twenty-two years later.

This story points a moral. On the whole it would seem a mistake to try to "fit in" Kenilworth and Warwick in the same day.

As for Kenilworth itself, it is a fine, romantic ruin—from a park bench at the foot of the hill.

Tewkesbury Abbey is the great church of the region. Farther on are Worcester and Hereford cathedrals, both important, both handsome and curious; but neither compares with Tewkesbury, and if your time is limited, an afternoon at the Abbey will be more rewarding than spreading the hours too thin in a vain attempt to see everything at once. Tewkesbury Abbey is—speaking personally—one of the places I found most interesting. Its beauty is moving, its history is tragic.

Tewkesbury Abbey is *Norman* in feeling. As you cross the lawn and go into the nave, you are aware of what a *Norman* church was like in the ancient days. The massive columns, the heavy shadows, the weight and quality of mystery are a shock, after the frivolities of the Beauchamp Chapel. This was a religious style; silence and time hang heavily over Tewkesbury, and even the lovely *Decorated* choir does not lighten the somber effect.

The House of Lancaster died at the Battle of Tewkesbury, and the Abbey's silences are touched by the memory of that bitter day, May 4, 1471, when Margaret of Anjou was brought to this place by her captors, led up the dark, heavy nave past the massive stone columns to the altar, where lay the body of her murdered son, Edward.

The fatal battle was in a field next to the Abbey; it is called "the bloody meadow." When the Lancastrian army broke, the wretched knights, tearing off their armor, throwing away their swords, fled into the dark nave. In the choir, Abbot Strensham was singing mass at the high altar. The Lancastrian soldiers, terrified, streaming blood from their wounds, threw themselves on their knees. But the great doors were flung open, and the three Yorkist brothers, Edward IV, Richard Crookback, and George, Duke of Clarence, flushed with triumph, crazed with battle joy, came into the sacred house of God brandishing their dripping swords, their men after them. The bell had rung for the elevation of the Host when the slaughter began; the screams of the dying echoed against the timeless gray stones.

The monks, appalled at the sacrilege, cowered in the stalls. But the Abbot seized the great cross from the bearer and, alone, walked down the aisle from the choir.

A brave man cheated the King of England and his brothers of the last of their victims—for a few hours. But the Yorkists did not long stay in awe of the Abbot's cross. They dragged their captives out of the church, and executed them in the town outside. The young Prince they reserved for a more special fate. A brass plaque beneath the great Norman tower marks where the last hope of the Red Roses was hastily buried.

The Wars of the Roses were an episode in the long history of Tewkesbury, one of the richest monasteries in England. When the Abbey was surrendered to Henry VIII, the King (as was his way) took everything portable—an immense store of silver altar vessels, even the gold embossing on the tombs. The many monastery buildings were razed, and the church itself was condemned. But before it went the way of Fountains, the people of Tewkesbury, who had long used the nave for their parish church, chipped in and bought the whole Abbey for £453, the estimated value of the lead on its roofs. The Crown kept the right to appoint the vicar of Tewkesbury, which privilege Queen Elizabeth II still holds.

Tewkesbury Abbey is full-circle, after Oxford. The university has enlightenment, charm, and Renaissance architecture; the Cotswolds scenery, the golden-gray villages, Stratford, and Warwick are smiling England at its loveliest. Tewkesbury,

dark, massive, mysterious, and beautiful, is the other side of
the coin, the medieval beginnings, and before. The traveler
needs an hour or two on the bus to cross centuries. With the
memory of Wolsey's lovely Magdalen Tower fresh in his mind,
the visitor stands surrounded by the tragic silence of *Norman*
Tewkesbury. England is wonderful; especially the Cotswolds.

WHAT TO SEE IN OXFORD, THE COTSWOLDS,
STRATFORD-ON-AVON, WARWICK,
KENILWORTH, AND TEWKESBURY

- ★★★ *Oxford*. See text.
  - ★ *Iffley*. Norman parish church in the suburbs of Oxford.
  - ★ *Minster Lovell*. A charming stone village outside Oxford. Decorative ruin.
  - ★ *Burford*. Delightful old town, in the characteristic lemon-gray Cotswold stone. The church here is first-class.
    Fairford. Another charming town in the Cotswolds.
    Bibury. A village five miles from Fairford—enchanting.
  - ★ *Stow-on-the-Wold*, on the banks of the Windrush, and nearby, *Upper Slaughter, Lower Slaughter, Upper Swell, Lower Swell, Bourton-on-the-Waters, Northleach,* and *Withingdon,* lovely Cotswold villages. See text.
  - ★ *Cirencester*. Has a superb church, Roman remains, and the park of the Earl of Bathurst.
  - ★ *Chedworth*. The best Roman villa in England. First-class.
  - ★ *Cheltenham*. A "spa" with fine Regency buildings, and good musical festivals.
    Broadway. See text.
  - ★★ *Chipping Campden*. The best of the Cotswold towns. Try to visit Compton Wynyates, fine Tudor house. From Chipping Campden, go on to:
  - ★★ *Chipping Norton*. A pleasant town, with the nearby Rollright Stones, prehistoric relics.
- ★★★ *Stratford-on-Avon*. See text.
- ★★★ *Warwick Castle*. See text.
  - ★ *Kenilworth*. So-so.
- ★★★ *Tewkesbury Abbey*. Magnificent.

Nottingham, the Midlands, Chatsworth, Haddon Hall, Chester, and the Lakes

THERE is a widespread feeling, in tourist circles, that, once outside of London, England turns "quaint." The villages are thought to be populated with wise old codgers, on the alert to greet kindly Americans with four-leaf clovers.

The trouble is, England is not quaint. If you look closely at Mr. Lancaster's comment on tourist romance, you will observe the codger has a copy of *The Racing Times* in his pocket, while his friends at the public bar cheer on his efforts to raise half-a-crown from the visiting innocents.

"THIS IS FOR YOU, MA'AM!"

And, once outside of London, great sections of England are mining and industrial areas. Birmingham, Liverpool, Man-chester, and Nottingham—these are English versions of Detroit, Cleveland, Youngstown, and Pittsburgh.

We spent more than a week threading our way through the Midlands, and most of what we saw would hardly profit the tourist with a limited time in Britain. Yet it is out of focus to leave England without matching cathedrals with at least a few coal mines and steel factories. England, for all its Cotswold villages and the splendor of Wells, is an industrial nation.

So we suggest a fast express train from London to Nottingham, and renting a car at Nottingham for your journey through the Midlands. The local bus service is excellent, too, but somewhat complicated for visitors.

The suburbs around Nottingham are the scene of some of D. H. Lawrence's novels. The queer and tragic landscapes of *Sons and Lovers*, the soft green hills, crowned by the slag heaps, the ancient villages blackened with modern industrial smoke, make the region oddly evocative.

Nottingham spreads, mile after mile, across the landscape until it melts into Sheffield, Chesterfield, Leeds, Mansfield, Derby, or Leicester. The whole region is closely built; factories, pitheads, slag heaps sprawl across the rolling hills, with every few miles a good-sized town punctuated by rows of brick houses.

Nine miles from the heart of Nottingham, by bus via Hucknall, past several large coal mines, and around the corner from a factory, are the gates to Newstead Abbey.

The effect is amazing. Here you are, studying an industrial landscape; the bus is crowded with miners; the conductor bawls: "Newstead Abbey." You get off at a large oak tree, pay your admission, and are inside a vast municipal park, which, for its wilderness of forest and heath, its formal gardens, its medieval ruins and Tudor architecture, its famous Georgian interiors, its ancient history (the monastery was founded in 1163), and, above all, for its literary associations (this was Byron's home), is in many respects unrivaled in England—and totally unexpected. Two miles from a coal mine are gardens which equal, if they do not surpass, Hampton Court's.

I love Hampton Court, but its gardens are a series of different landscape styles. Newstead Abbey is a unified composition in the great eighteenth- and nineteenth-century manner. The gardens are approached by heaths and forests; next comes the ruin of the Abbey, manicured, and lovingly set in lawns. This is a ruin of the romantic revival—scenic, "Gothick" in the Walpole manner. Next to the ruin is the Tudor and Jacobean and. Georgian manor house built around the cloisters of the Abbey. The manor house looks out over the work of art called the gardens.

The gardens of Newstead Abbey have been designed for water vistas. There are two sizable lakes, one of them ornamented by a pretty fake Gothic fort, used for sham naval battles, featuring Japanese lanterns, singing boatmen, and champagne. There are many ponds, some large, square, edged with thick green turf, and used as reflecting mirrors for formal gardens; some small, carefully irregular in shape, overhung by willows trailing scented vines, or covered with bright, rare water lilies. Finally, there are waterfalls, brooks, rivers flowing through superb sweeping lawns, or swift streams winding in and out of dwarf Japanese foliage. All these waterworks are artificial, designed by a sucession of landscape gardeners. Byron inherited a bankrupt estate, owing to the mad passion of his immediate ancestor for digging lakes and deflecting rivers to make babbling brooks through Japanese gardens.

The City of Nottingham owns Newstead Abbey today, which is obviously just as well. Only the grandest lord could afford to keep these gardens in their original splendor. Incidentally, I have never seen a municipal park so intelligently arranged for public use. The coal miners and the factory hands of Nottingham stroll through the perfumed rose gardens on a Sunday afternoon, gravely pace the "Gothick" avenues, examine with a pleased and expert eye the Japanese dwarf water gardens. Newstead Abbey is one place where the people of England have inherited the past they made with their sweat. The great-great-grandchildren of the peasants whom the "Bad Lord Byron" drove to dig his lakes sit arm and arm with their girls, or their beaux, in the Grecian summerhouse, sighing over the ravishing romantic vista of water and lawn and profusion of rich-colored flowers.

I was impressed by Newstead Abbey, quite apart from its beauty. I knew Lord Byron was a noble lord, of title and family. But somehow I had the idea he was a little seedy, like Shelley, not quite first-class, a bit run down. It does not seem natural that a bona fide poet should have been a great gentleman. Noble lords are usually gifted amateurs, not professionals—patrons, not creators, of art. I had no notion that Byron was so grand. Fancy a real poet living in a Tudor manor house and presiding over artificial waterworks! It still seems peculiar to me; how did he escape being paralyzed by snobbery? Of course Byron did go bankrupt afterward, but he was brought to Newstead Abbey at the age of ten, and presumably he soaked up the grandiose local atmosphere. There are many references in his poems to scenes at Newstead Abbey, and when, in his Italian exile, he thought of home and England, it was these lakes and gardens he remembered.

Newstead Abbey was something of a mecca during the nineteenth century. Both Nathaniel Hawthorne and Washington Irving came here. One wonders what these two made of Boatswain's monument? This last is a piece of youthful "Byronic" impudence, which still causes the gravest concern among many of the staider visitors to Newstead Abbey. Richard and I saw a whole party of workingmen, in their Sunday suits, standing before this naughty stone whim of Nottingham's officially adopted poet and shaking their heads. The young Lord Byron went to a good deal of trouble to locate the exact spot of the high altar in the ruined monastery church. (Scholars say he was wrong by a few feet.) In any case, Byron thought he had picked on sacred ground to put up an octagonal stone monument, topped by a Grecian urn, to commemorate his dog, Boatswain. Furthermore, Byron announced that he and his servant were also scheduled to share Boatswain's last resting place. Byron, however, was buried in Hucknall Church, and his servant, Joe Murrey, also declined to share Boatswain's honored earth. So the poet's dog is the sole occupant of the Abbey tomb, for which Byron wrote the poem which ends up, in a burst of, shall we say, doggerel:

> To mark a Friend's remains these stones arise;
> I never knew but one, and here he lies.

The solid citizens of Nottingham are not amused.

It is unjust to harp on Boatswain (I think Byron was about twenty when he had his dog buried on the altar). Byron later wrote:

> Before the mansion lay a lucid lake,
> Broad as transparent, deep, and freshly fed
> By a river. . . .
> The woods sloped downwards to its brink and stood
> With their green faces fixed upon the flood.

Haddon Hall and Chatsworth, two of the most interesting stately homes in England, are about seven miles apart in the Derbyshire valley of the Wye River. This green corner of England is a sort of Heaven's half-acre. Surrounded on all sides by industry and coal mines, this narrow strip is probably the most alluring twenty by ten miles in the kingdom. Every turning in the winding road is a fresh delight; every field is a garden; every clump of trees has been artfully designed to punctuate a "view." Even the cottages have been lovingly restored, or built as masterpieces in a "model" village.

The word "ducal" is the key to the Derbyshire Wye. The Dukes of Rutland and Devonshire own this enchanted valley. This came as a surprise to Richard and me. In contemporary Britain dukes appear (to the casual tourist) to be hard-pressed waifs, orphans of the cruel historical storm. Jokes about bankrupt peers are rife in current literature. Somehow, the traveler acquires the notion that dukes are colorful leftovers from the stately past, refugees from the Wars of the Roses, symbolic, like the wigs Old Bailey judges wear. All of a sudden you come across the Dukes of Rutland and Devonshire, beneficiaries of privilege and the loot of centuries, whose real-estate holdings are impressive. There is nothing synthetic about Chatsworth; Haddon Hall is not the property of the National Trust.

But now, having remarked on their grandeur, I must hastily explain that you may trot through the Rutland or Devonshire properties, the only restrictions being a request not to throw around sardine cans, and a thumping admission fee. Haddon

Hall and Chatsworth are open to the public from Easter to October, but not every day in the week. If it is possible, begin with Haddon Hall, the great Tudor and Jacobean palace, and go on to Chatsworth, the eighteenth-century masterpiece.

I do not know how you feel about stately homes; our position is on-again, off-again. We got caught in a Bank Holiday mob at Blenheim, and conceived a lasting distaste for what many people think is England's entry in the Versailles stakes. Knole, on the other hand, is wonderful.

Chatsworth—

A short pause while the author fumbles for words. Tourists are shown through in parties of fifty; several thousand visitors turn up each week during the summer season, and the guides lead the customers at a fast clip up and down stairs, through marble halls, and past the frescoes. Eyes right. Eyes left. "The paintings of Julius Caesar on the wall above are by Laguerre; kindly follow me; the room on your left is the Grotto; the statue, considered by critics a very fine example of early seventeenth-century sculpture, is called 'Diana's Fountain.' Please notice the Stars of the Garter carved in the stone; the Stars of the Garter were bestowed on His Grace, the first Duke of Devonshire, in 1694. We will now proceed to the chapel corridor. Take note of the barge given to His Grace, the sixth Duke of Devonshire, by the Sultan of Turkey. If you will now follow me into the chapel . . ."

After about fifteen minutes of this a large, aggressively hatted lady turned to her husband, and said in a severe voice, "If you ask me, Chatsworth is *very* unique."

It is, too. I am aware that the stuffy old Oxford Dictionary frowns on modifying an absolute like unique, but that's where the Oxford Dictionary is wrong. Its editors have never tramped the red carpets at Chatsworth, or gazed on the lawn where until 1755 there was a large, thriving village called Edensor. In 1755 the fourth Duke decided to shift things around. Why have the front door facing a hill? The entrance to Chatsworth ought to be overlooking the river. But there was the village, full of thatched roofs, unwashed babies, pigs, and other unscenic elements. What to do? The fourth Duke thought the matter over for about two minutes: he had the village razed, the pigs and babies moved bodily across the road and up a mile, and grass seed planted. This sort of thing was a mere nothing for the fourth Duke. He was the one who had the hills overlooking Chatsworth planted to lawn, and dotted here and there with picturesque, carefully sculptured clumps of trees. In the course of these landscape-gardening operations any number of barns, farmers' houses, churches, sheepfolds, and the like were knocked down, carried off around the corner, and put up again. It must have been a dizzy period for oldsters in the neighborhood. Landmarks famous for generations disappeared one day and reappeared a week later in an altogether different location. Imagine what a shock prodigal sons must have suffered, coming home for the fatted calf and finding nothing but grass and a view.

Catherine the Great's Potemkin villages were picayune compared to the grandeur of this English lord's. The Russian exhibits were cardboard, but His Grace the fourth Duke of Devonshire did not trifle with stage sets. The village he had so rudely removed from what he decided was his front yard he had reconstructed in solid stone, and included what were then all modern improvements.

The fourth Duke was strictly in the family tradition. The first Duke inherited a grand Elizabethan pile. In 1686 he decided to rebuild the south façade; then he thought he had better remodel the east front. He is reported to have said that he found building so "delightful" he could not stop. By 1707, when the first Duke died, Chatsworth was completely reformed, no longer Elizabethan, but a masterpiece of severe classic style. The next two dukes saved up the family cash. Duke Number Four went in for the major operations on the local village. Number Five rested. But in 1818 the sixth Duke inherited; and he spent a lifetime putting together the various parts of his ancestor's designs, adding a whole wing, doing a final brushup on remnants of the village, collecting barges from the Sultan of Turkey, etc. An energetic family.

In between hauling marble around and designing Palladian façades, the various dukes collected a library, exhibits for their art gallery, furniture, sculpture, jewelry, and other genuine and in some cases beautiful *objets d'art* to dwarf the loot of kings. Chatsworth makes Windsor and Buckingham Palace look middle class. Hampton Court is regal, but nobody has inhabited the place since George III. The Duke of Devonshire lives with his Memling, not to mention the Great Greek Apollo, which one director of the British Museum after another has considered so interesting a Devonshire possession. Quite a few curators of art galleries would not mind having the original cartoon which Holbein drew for his painting of Henry VIII.

Chatsworth is—how shall I say it?—Something. The Duke has his own private theatre (handsome); his own private art gallery (terrific); his own private gallery for sculpture (not so good, mainly big Victorian pieces); an immense lot of state apartments, Sabine rooms, chapels, gold drawing rooms, oak drawing rooms, retiring rooms, large library, small library, state music room, ordinary music room, and so on.

I will now make a heretical remark. Chatsworth is one of the true wonders of England. It is not in the least vulgar; its magnificence is authentic. But Richard and I did not like it; we were interested, but we came away oddly annoyed. Somehow the atmosphere of conspicuous waste hangs heavily over Chatsworth; the great classic façade, looking eyelessly, blindly, arrogantly out over the empty lawns, has an unpleasant, barren quality. It is beautiful, but not sympathetic. You feel your gorge rise when you look over the marble balconies and see grass where once stood a village. Personally, I do not know of any place in England where I felt so aggressively republican (not party, but nation) as at Chatsworth. Dukes! Moving around villages! "Let's see," I muttered at Richard, "about 1760. I suppose he helped cook up the Stamp Act."

Yet Richard and I fell dreamily in love with Haddon Hall, so I fear we are not logical. Haddon Hall had the virtue of a real function. Chatsworth was a display of arbitrary grandeur, built for no other purpose than to demonstrate the magnificence of a Restoration peer. Haddon Hall was first the castle of a medieval baron, who put up a fortress to fight off the neighbors; when the Tudors brought peace to the Midlands, the castle developed into a hall for the sprawling household of a rich

THE FAMILY TRADITION

country squire. Rooms were added on, and more cellars to store the meat and beer. A ballroom (with a lovely Jacobean ceiling) went into a new wing; the squire had daughters—ballrooms were the fashion. Meanwhile the gardens were walled in with Tudor brick, roses and fruit trees set out to make the terraced hillside bloom. I do not mean to suggest that Haddon Hall is homely or cozy; but its grandeur is not empty. It has no endless procession of state apartments, gilded and cold. When the heiress of Haddon Hall, Dorothy Vernon (whose father was called the King of the Peak), married the son of the Earl of Rutland, the graceful Tudor mansion was for two hundred years left empty. The Dukes of Rutland, disdaining to remodel the old-fashioned Hall, went farther afield to build their own particular version of Chatsworth. Caretakers inhabited the great courts of Haddon Hall, until, at the turn of this century, the then Duke of Rutland lovingly, patiently, accurately, restored Haddon Hall to its Tudor beauty.

The gardens of Haddon Hall are among its chief glories. I know that thousands of people go every summer to Chatsworth to see the giant fountains, and the endless cascades of waters through the formal plantings (like Versailles). But Richard and I liked the Elizabethan roses at Haddon Hall better than the acres and acres of manicured formalities at Chatsworth. Indeed, we had a delightful day at Haddon Hall. We poked around in the courtyards (the atmosphere at the Hall is unharried and unhurried) and admired the old frescoes in the chapel; we went out into the gardens and sat in the sunshine, amazed by the perfume of the massed roses. The eighteenth-century garden style of sweeping lawns and "natural" plantings is handsome. But there was much to be said for Elizabethan walled terraces; the sunshine falls softly against the mellowed bricks, and the perfume of the flowers scents the air.

Chester is west of Rowsley, Haddon Hall, and Chatsworth; in between there is nothing spectacular to see.

The center of modern Chester is a medieval town, enclosed in its original walls. No other city in England has kept so much of its Gothic character. York and Lincoln have preserved whole medieval streets. York has much of its wall. But Chester is astonishing. It suggests how the English walled towns of Edward III, the Black Prince, and Richard II really looked; when Chaucer said "towne" this is the image that rose in his mind's eye. The Guildhall of the City of London once stood in streets like Chester's; the towers of Canterbury Cathedral rose over roofs like those you will see from your hotel window. History will come to life for you in Chester. The ancient race course, where we saw a splendid military tattoo, was used long ago for medieval races like those of Siena. Wars were bitterly fought in these streets, and knights-at-arms went shopping for new armor in the Rows where you will walk.

Chester has a big quota of sights, including a handsome cathedral, but they are fun to "do." Standard practice is to begin by a brisk trot all the way round the walls. The Rows you will not need any prodding of conscience to investigate; the shops are marvelous, full of antiques, Georgian silver, jewelry.

Question at this point: What is a Row?

The Rows are two-story arcades, built under roofs. Their origin is debated, but probably they developed because Chester was an important Roman town, and when the Normans arrived and began to put up houses over the ruins, they simply added second stories to the foundations of Roman stone.

Chester, incidentally, is rich in Roman remains. The Grosvenor Museum has, among other treasures, a set of Roman false teeth, which, on the whole, are not inferior to the famous ones worn by George Washington. There is also a set of nineteenth-century dental instruments calculated to strike sheer terror into the hearts of all but the toothy brave.

Besides the Rows, the Cathedral (with its fine convent buildings), and the Walls, the chief occupation in Chester is tracking down the various famous timbered houses. (If you should happen to be motoring in this area, Moreton Old Hall, some twenty miles outside Chester, is a fantastic and delightful example of sixteenth-century half-timber work.) Chester's best and most beautiful houses are fifteenth- and even fourteenth-century. Richard and I had fun hunting the three-star mansions down in their various medieval back streets; we had a map of

Chester and put in one sunny afternoon, wandering about, locating half-timbers.

You will not need to be the serious tourist in Chester. You can relax, and feel gay, and go walking, and let the medieval history of the city seep into your bones.

You will like Chester.

The Lake District is something else again.

I flinch in advance, turning in a negative report on scenery hallowed by Wordsworth and generations of shrine-seekers. However, this is a personal book, not a Baedeker. Richard and I are not neutral about Canterbury; I may as well tell the truth about Keswick. Frankly, Richard and I thought the Lake District dull. I am sure it is lovely holiday country for Englishmen who like walking tours and mild scenery. Americans have enough scenery in the homeland to do for three lifetimes. Borrowdale, Derwentwater, Rosthwaite, Seatoller, and the other scenic wonders look pale compared to the Grand Canyon, the Rocky Mountains, or the Sierra Nevadas. They have good mountains in Switzerland, too. Why spend a fortune crossing the Atlantic, and wind up by a waterfall eleven feet high? I like scenery (fairly well), but if you are going in for scenery, it might as well be first-class. For instance, the trip up to the saddle of the Jungfrau is scenery.

The Lake District is hallowed and all that. Tourists file in by the left-hand queue and exit (amid the pushing and shoving of the Youth Hostel set) by the right, through Wordsworth's vine-covered cottage. Shelley brought one of the Mrs. Shelleys here on their wedding trip—X marks the spot. One warning: The Lakes are crowded in the top of the summer season. Probably you can find a hotel, if you should arrive unheralded, but most tourists are booked for the Lakes through travel agencies. Travel bureaus are apt to lay on heavily when describing the glories of Borrowdale. Food in the Lake District is strictly tourist grade, with plenty of that good old Windsor cooking.

What a Scrooge I sound! And the Lake District is quaint, too! You will do better to concentrate on Newstead Abbey, and the Derbyshire valley of the Wye—for this is England, industrial and glorious.

WHAT TO SEE IN NOTTINGHAM, THE
MIDLANDS, CHATSWORTH, HADDON HALL,
CHESTER, AND THE LAKE DISTRICT

Nottingham. An industrial town typical of the English Midlands. The suburbs were the scene of early D. H. Lawrence novels.

*** *Newstead Abbey.* Nine miles outside Nottingham, Byron's home. Superb gardens.

 ** *Hardwick Hall.* Near Pleasley, an Elizabethan mansion. A stately home of England.

 ** *Bolsover Castle.* Now a ruin, has a famous keep.

The Peak District. Near Derby, moderately good scenery.

Wingfield Manor. Near Ambergate, a handsome ruin, once the prison of Mary, Queen of Scots.

Rowsley. In the valley of the "infant" Wye, lies between:

*** *Chatsworth* and

*** *Haddon Hall.* (See text.) Chatsworth and Haddon Hall are two of the most interesting showplaces in England.

Buxton. A spa in the hills above Rowsley.

The High Peak District. West of Buxton, higher than the Peak District. Also has caves.

 * *Castleton.* A good castle, celebrated by Scott.

 * *Prestbury.* Three miles north, a nice old church.

 * *Gawsworth.* Four miles south, many old black-and-white "magpie" houses.

Knutsford. The original of Mrs. Gaskell's *Cranford.*

*** *Chester.* A wonderful old town, with walls, gates, cathedral, and the Rows.

 * *Nantwich.* More "magpie" houses and a good church.

Congleton. Old inns. Four miles south is:

 ** *Moreton Old Hall.* The finest black-and-white manor house in the country. It was built between 1559 and 1680, and is a crazy but somehow poetic old mansion. After Moreton Old Hall, the usual route is on to:

Ashbourne. A market town with a good church, and thus to:

Dovedale. Owned by the National Trust and renowned for

its beauty. You go through a stile, and trot along a river, sparkling-brook category, and thus back, round trip. I thought it a crashing bore; the rustic greensward was liberally covered with apple cores, cigar butts and the like. For maddened scenery lovers, Dovedale is probably England's most famous rural brook.

** *Lichfield.* This quiet town has a small and beautiful cathedral. Dr. Johnson was born here and his statue is in the market place. Lichfield is dreamy, highly recommended.

THE LAKE DISTRICT

The Lake District is called "The Playground of England." In general, it is an open, rugged area of small lakes, set in moderately grand hills. "Paradise for walkers and amblers," the guidebooks call this region. Lakeland covers more than six hundred square miles, and includes the largest English lake, Windermere, and the highest English mountain, Scafell Pike. Nearly every square foot of this region is celebrated for views, choice scenic delights. The atmosphere will remind Americans of the White Mountains. If you are an Ambler, you will need a detailed map and guide of the assorted waterspouts, peaks, pikes, lakes, rocks, lookouts. The tourist, if he invades the Lake District, should not miss:

Windermere, Ambleside, Hawkshead, Rydal (where Wordsworth died), *Grasmere* (four miles from Ambleside, Wordsworth's famous cottage), and *Keswick.*

Cambridge, Ely, and East Anglia

CAMBRIDGE is a gateway to East Anglia, and this has a certain spiritual, as well as geographical, significance. It would not be accurate to underline what is only a vague connection; yet the relation of the great university on the banks of the Cam to its hinterland always interests me.

East Anglia is flat, queer country, strangely like the Flemish lowlands. As early as the fourteenth century its seaports were busy with the wool trade, and a new, rising merchant middle class disputed for local power with the barons. Gothic England died first in East Anglia. In the fifteen hundreds, thousands of Dutch and Flemish refugees from Spanish tyranny crossed the Channel, settled in these fens so like their sea-walled native plains, and gave to their adopted land a tradition of struggle. A century later, Oliver Cromwell and his Roundhead armies rose up out of this merchant, middle-class, fighting England. The Restoration made determined Nonconformists in East Anglia; Tom Paine was born in eighteenth-century Thetford, the most gifted and famous of many a local egalitarian. A hundred years more, and East Anglia stood strong for the Chartist movement; when it went down to defeat, a wave of furious emigration to the Americas and Australia came out of these ancient seaports and flat, fertile fields. East Anglia is the cradle of uncompromising, revolutionary England.

Now Oxford and Cambridge are compared in this way: Oxford is said to be Royalist, reactionary, and mystical, while Cambridge is called Roundhead, radical, and materialistic. I do not think this balance sheet can be drawn too fine. Oxford was the headquarters of Charles I, and the stamping ground of the Archbishop Laud, but Shelley was a student there until he was "sent down" for "atheism." It is true, Cambridge was building laboratories for experimental science, debating Huxley and Darwin, while Oxford rocked with controversy about Cardinal Newman. But such neat comparisons can be pressed too far; for every mystic in modern Oxford there is a student of atomic physics, and for every radical thinker at twentieth-century Cambridge there is a defender of the *status quo*.

After these reservations, there remains some basis in fact for calling Cambridge the university of embattled East Anglia. Erasmus was a teacher of Greek at Queens' College, and although the great philosopher was not exactly lion-hearted, or "embattled," as a thinker, he was bold and original. Some people sneer at Erasmus—call him cautious, more nervous than heroic. But they burned people alive (slowly) in Erasmus's day for taking the wrong side of a debate on theology, and personally, I can understand Erasmus very well. What shall it profit a man to be burned alive over some small point in a religious controversy? Erasmus was always coming boldly up to the brink of heresy, at which point he developed a sort of philosophical stutter or twitch. Considering the chances he took, I think it is a triumph that he managed to die in bed; furthermore, I admire him. His career was an assertion that life (not only heaven) was sweet, and this in itself was an attack on the medieval appetite for immortality.

Oliver Cromwell and John Milton, both Cambridge men, were neither of them nervous or cautious. John Harvard and a whole group of Massachusetts clergymen came from Emmanuel College; this accounts for the name of the town where John Harvard founded America's first university. It also explains, in part, Bunker Hill and that shot at Lexington heard not only around the world but more specifically by George III. Our American nation owes a great debt to the Cambridge Milton knew.

The spirit of determined, bold, even reckless inquiry has often burned fiercely at Cambridge. Both Newton and Bacon, who, however much a personal villain, had intellectual daring, were Cambridge men; so was Harvey. Two hundred years later Darwin followed in Milton's footsteps at Christ's College.

Literary rebels as well as Dissenters and scientists have made the Cambridge tradition. Before Milton, Spenser and Ben Jonson were trained in these beautiful colleges along the Cam. Nowadays, when Spenser is embalmed in examination questions, and Ben Jonson's best-known work is "Drink to Me Only with Thine Eyes," we forget that these two men helped shape the new literary world which was the glory of the Elizabethan Age. Like so many other Cambridge men, Marlowe and even Fletcher, they were innovators, experimenters, pioneers, original minds.

Thomas Gray was hardly a rebel, yet his emphasis on the poor and humble, his insistence that ploughmen and youths "to Fortune and to Fame unknown" had a place in poetry was a fresh note in the eighteenth century.

The case of Wordsworth, that famous member of St. John's College, requires a footnote. Wordsworth was for so many years the good, gray, respectable, and long-winded sage of Grasmere, it is hard to remember he wrote almost all of his great poetry as a flaming revolutionary, a passionate, furious young Cambridge graduate. He did not learn to be respectable and dull at St. John's College. The Cambridge Wordsworth rushed off to France, fell wildly and most "unsuitably" in love, fought for the Rights of Man, made Thomas Jefferson his hero, defied George III—and wrote some of the most beautiful poetry in English. The Cambridge Wordsworth lasted about ten years; then he suffered a collapse of character and genius (in my opinion!). When he had thoroughly lived down his Cambridge past, he was dubbed Poet Laureate, with the usual small cash tribute. Robert Browning wrote some of the most bitter lines in English poetry to mark the laurel wreath Wordsworth wore on his reformed brow:

> Just for a handful of silver he left us,
>> Just for a riband to stick in his coat—
> Found the one gift of which fortune bereft us,
>> Lost all the others she lets us devote;
> They, with the gold to give, doled him out silver,
>> So much was theirs who so little allowed;
> How all our copper had gone for his service!
>> Rags—were they purple, his heart had been proud!
> We that had loved him so, followed him, honoured him,
>> Lived in his mild and magnificent eye,
> Learned his great language, caught his clear accents,
>> Made him our pattern to live and to die!
> Shakespeare was of us, Milton was for us,
>> Burns, Shelley, were with us,—they watch from their graves!
> He alone breaks from the van and the freemen,
>> —He alone sinks to the rear and the slaves!

(Sound of cheering off stage—the author of this book. There is nothing like first-class invective to enliven a foggy London morning.)

Where were we? Oh, yes, Wordsworth the Cambridge man.

> For I have learned
> To look on nature, not as in the hour

> Of thoughtless youth; but hearing oftentimes
> The still, sad music of humanity,
> Nor harsh, nor grating, though of ample power
> To chasten and subdue.

Or:

> The world is too much with us; late and soon,
> Getting and spending, we lay waste our powers.

The young Wordsworth of St. John's College was seconded by the young Byron of Trinity. Boatswain's monument, at Newstead Abbey, was, I am afraid, an example of a university lark, but Byron learned to love freedom at Cambridge, and he never sold out for any riband to put in his coat. His personal life may have been sadly confused, but Byron stuck to his radical guns for his whole life, and died in revolutionary Greece. Trinity College library has the statue of Byron which was roundly refused by the authorities at Westminster Abbey. Blake is not the only English writer who did not end up in Poets' Corner. In death, as in life, Byron remains the child of the university which gave Milton to England.

Now that I have made such a case for Cambridge, the cradle of a fighting, passionate Britain, I must repeat in a still, small, somewhat sheepish voice that perhaps this theory, this Oxford-Cambridge contrast, can be pressed too far. Macaulay and Tennyson were also Cambridge men, so were Thackeray and, earlier, Herrick. I am a great admirer of Thackeray and a mild one of Tennyson and Herrick (not of Macaulay, that Whiggish old bore), but there is no possible way of fitting the facts of their lives into any Miltonic mold. You might say *Vanity Fair* is a ruthless dissection of nineteenth-century fashionable society; you might say it, but it is not a convincing argument. Dickens did the dissecting for the Victorian period, and he studied in a debtors' prison, not at Cambridge. Thackeray, let us face it, was a self-admitted snob, and Tennyson was always respectable; Macaulay was positively driveling on the subject of Great Men. Palmerston, Lord Balfour, Baldwin, and Austen Chamberlain—Cambridge men all—do not add much to the atmosphere of Oliver Cromwell's alma mater.

Cambridge, I admit, is a pretty vague, fuzzy-edged gateway

to East Anglia, if it is a gateway at all. It is pleasant, if not accurate, to imagine that a sharp, salty, fertilizing wind blows across the university from the fens of flinty Nonconformist, Chartist, intransigent East Anglia. I can see Cromwell and Milton and Harvey and Darwin, in my mind's eye, flying vigorously back and forth in the clouds above their university, sounding loud chords on their golden lyres, urging on current undergraduates to sterner, bolder efforts. I must admit that Cambridge looks so lush and beautiful, it does seem odd to talk about Roundheads and materialism, evolution and dissent against a scenic backdrop of glorious *Perpendicular* chapels and Wren courtyards. How can Cambridge men bend an ear to Milton's heroic, heavenly chords when they spend the afternoons in summer term punting on the Cam?

(This last observation is strictly Puritan, an inheritance, like so much almost unconscious American thought, from John Harvard and his colleagues who trotted out of Emmanuel College to spread not only the doctrines that led to Bunker Hill, but also more repulsive notions, such as the idea that beauty is sinful, or at least enervating.)

You have acquired a certain experience with the English universities at Oxford; I hope you will recall the A.A. Tested University Method, and the reasons for it. Cambridge, even more than Oxford, can lead to nervous and physical collapse if you are not careful and wily. Besides, at Cambridge, you must allow enough time, however brief your visit, to go punting. Otherwise, you have not lived—not at Cambridge, anyway.

For the tourist, Cambridge is like and unlike Oxford. Cambridge has escaped the dreary Oxford suburbs, and the gimcrack, neon-sign atmosphere of new building in the city of Oxford: Cambridge colleges have the same pattern as Oxford foundations—walls, gates, chapels, common rooms and dining halls, quadrangles, and gardens. Oxford is mostly built in silvery-gray stone, Cambridge is largely soft, mellowed, reddish-pink brick. There is no great High Street at Cambridge, but, unlike Oxford, some of the college gardens make a continuous park along the river.

There is one item both universities share for the sightseer: a profusion of riches. It is shocking to pick only five (it has to be five at Cambridge) of the colleges. However, what can we do? Either the A.A. Method—or disaster. If you will arm yourself with a street map, and keep in mind the point about taking taxis or buses and stopping for frequent infusions of morning coffee or afternoon tea, we will start off with King's College.

King's College was (brace yourself!) founded, like Eton, and about the same time (1440), by our poor dismal Henry VI. It is odd to reflect that two of the most famous educational institutions in England were established by the House of Lancaster's unfortunate mental case. The Eton College official guide said tactfully: "Despite all his many other cares, perhaps Henry's greatest interests lay in his Colleges of Eton and King's College, Cambridge." Since his many other cares included losing the Hundred Years' War with France, the Wars of the Roses at home, a long jail sentence, followed by the strangler's noose, it would seem the significant word in the sentence quoted is the little one "perhaps." The Eton guide tried to put a brave front on the delicate question of the Founder's career.

DONS

Henry once wrote a letter to the Pope (or somebody wrote it for him?) stating that he "held learning in good reverence." This led the Eton authorities to conclude that Henry was "serious and studious." That is one way of looking at Henry. In this Eton version the wretched last crowned head of the Lancasters was so wrapped up in education that he could not bring himself to tackle more mundane matters, such as what the York crowd was up to, or how not to get captured in battle. It was all right for the little woman, Queen Margaret of Anjou, to busy herself with homely practical affairs (woman's work), but serious, studious Henry had King's College to think about.

I feel this theory will not wash. I hate to sound crass, but the evidence indicates that Henry, when he was not downright insane (pretty seldom), was not exactly quick-witted. It is all very well to be studious and serious, but it was do or die for a man in Henry's position, and he died. I fear Henry's colleges were established by those anonymous characters labeled "advisors" in the school books. However, give the unhappy Red Rose king the benefit of the doubt, and agree that he took pleasure, when he could get his mind off his troubles, in having his name hung over a great public school and a famous Cambridge college.

The chief building in the quadrangle at King's College is eighteenth century, charming; and there is a superb thick lawn which sweeps all the way down to the banks of the Cam. The chief glory of King's College, and the most renowned sight at Cambridge itself, is the Chapel.

Architects agree that the King's College Chapel is a *Perpendicular* masterpiece, perhaps the finest in this style in the whole Kingdom. It is usually compared with the Henry VII and St. George's chapels (at Westminster and Windsor); I prefer it to either of these two, because the great windows at King's College Chapel have (except the west one) their original sixteenth-century glass. I do not know how it is with most tourists, but I found *Perpendicular* a difficult style to understand. I liked *Norman*; I liked *Early English*; I had a fanaticism for Wren. But all I felt was, "H'mmmm," at the Henry VII Chapel, and "Very interesting," for the Windsor *Perpendicular*. The first time I saw the King's College Chapel it was, as I have remarked, hot. But then our Aunt Adele sent us back to Cambridge one weekend, and I trotted along, reluctantly, to the King's College Chapel. On the way I informed Richard that *Perpendicular* was over-ornate, lifeless, and decadent, which opinions caused him to fly into a dreadful rage and denounce me as backward.

By the time we got to the Chapel, I was sullen, and in no mood to make any concessions to public opinion. *"Perpendicular!"* I snarled; and I promised Pat to climb to the roof of the Chapel for the view. Richard could moon over the fan vaulting downstairs.

How curious is the experience described by Keats in "On First Looking Into Chapman's Homer." In his case, it was a poem, but it can be Titian or Beethoven or King's College Chapel:

> Then I felt like some watcher of the skies
> > When a new planet swims into his ken;
> Or like stout Cortez, when with eagle eyes
> > He star'd at the Pacific—and all his men
> Look'd at each other with a wild surmise—
> > Silent, upon a peak in Darien.

Queens' College is next on our list after King's, which sounds neat, and more than neat, when I add that our heroine Margaret of Anjou, founded Queens' in 1448. Alas, regard the position of the fatal apostrophe! The tragedy at Tewkesbury concluded, the Yorkists held poor Margaret for ransom, and the French, after haggling over the price for years, bought her off, brought her home to Anjou and allowed her to drag out her old age in penury and heartbreak. No sooner was Margaret down and out than Elizabeth Woodville, Edward IV's *nouveau riche* Queen, refounded Margaret's Cambridge college, which seems pretty low and small. Those White Roses could not allow Margaret to keep a college, let alone a kingdom, a husband, and a son. Later on, after the Tudors united the Roses, Cambridge made the college of the two queens plural.

The first court of Queens' College is fifteenth-century red brick; the whole college is wonderful, especially the Cloister Court, the President's Lodge, Pump Court, and Walnut Tree

Court. I like these lovely courts as well as anything at Cambridge; and from the Cloister Courts a wooden bridge crosses the River Cam to the enchanting college gardens. I keep saying lovely and enchanting, but Queens' College is really magic; it makes a sort of spell. You will feel detached from this nervous world at Queens'.

Battle the impulse to sit around the gardens indefinitely. Forward to Christ's College. This foundation was established by another famous lady, another Margaret, last name Tudor, *née* Beaufort—the mother, in fact, of Henry VII. You will remember Margaret as a strong-minded character who saved her son Henry from the Yorkists. Milton was a fellow of Christ's. The second courtyard, built in 1640, is beautiful, but we have chosen Christ's for our selected tour because its gardens are ravishing, voted by the experts among the most glorious at Cambridge.

Lady Margaret really must have been a serious, studious character. She founded the next college on our list, too: St. John's. The chapel at St. John's is a creation by Gilbert Scott, our mid-Victorian friend, but the quadrangles of the college are melting, sensuous compositions in pink brick and stately sixteenth- and seventeenth-century design.

St. John's gives you another opportunity to cross and recross the River Cam. The "Bridge of Sighs" leads from the third college court across the stream to New Court and the gardens. There is another bridge to return: "Old Bridge."

How cold words sound! To see the Cam from "Old Bridge" on a day in June is an experience you will remember always. In memory it takes on a faintly incredible air, as though the scene of your aftervision came from a painting, not life. For grass was never so green, or a little river so sunlit-silver, or pink bricks so mellow; surely you did not actually see this museum canvas of stately Renaissance, colored rich pink, framed in lawn, and punctuated by the gently flowing Cam?

You did, or will. Cambridge is true. You can walk through it and look at it. Happy fact.

Trinity College is the biggest foundation at either Oxford or Cambridge. The Great Gate, with the statue of the founder, leads to Great Court, which is larger than Tom Quad at Christ

Church, Oxford. If you will think back and remember that Wolsey designed Tom Quad, you will not be surprised to recognize the statue over the Great Gate as Henry VIII himself, going one better than the Cardinal.

Trinity College is handsome, but the item I like best is Wren's library. Unfortunately, it's not open to the public nowadays. However, if you write ahead to the librarian you can get a pass. It is worth the trouble.

On to Magdalene College, pronounced as at Oxford. The college itself is charming, and the seventeenth-century building which houses the Pepys treasures is a masterpiece. The most exciting thing at Magdalene is the shorthand manuscript of the diary itself. Richard and I dropped in for a look and emerged two hours later, gabbling to each other about Pepys. Richard thinks he was a disagreeable, vulgar, grasping, mean man. I guess that is true, but I admire monumental busybodies. Curiosity, in my opinion, makes the world go round—the original itch, more important than sin.

The final entry on our Cambridge list is the Round Church on Bridge Street. The Cambridge Round Church has not been bombed; on the other hand, it has been what they call "drastically" restored. Vandalism, nineteenth-century. It is an interesting, and in some ways a beautiful, relic of strange Norman design.

Now to the boathouses! Punts are rented by the hour, complete with poles. Punting is simple; the Cam is shallow, the pole is long. All you have to do is to seat your wife, mother, affianced, or in lieu of female acquaintance, best friend, in the middle of the punt; you stand in the back on a platform, just the right size. Take the pole, and push off from the bank. Excellent! Nothing to it. Now you are in the middle of the Cam. How historic! You will tell your children you went punting at Cambridge. And what makes people say punting is hard? All you have to do is dig that pole into the river bottom, and push. *Voilà!* The punt slides down the river. How silvery the water! See the beautiful buildings, left and right! Observe the lush gardens. What a charming way of spending a summer afternoon: green grass, Renaissance brick, pretty girls (or handsome

PUNTING ON THE CAM

young men) in other punts, waving and smiling; people sitting along the Cam, lolling on the sunlit turf.

"Why, this is heavenly!" you say.

At this point, if not sooner, your pole gets stuck in the mud, you give a healthy push, and the platform of the punt glides from under you. For a fraction of a second you are suspended in space, clinging desperately, feverishly, with an expression of wild dismay and surprise, to the pole. Before your beloved in the punt has had time to rise and cry indignantly, "George! What are you doing?" you have descended abruptly into the drink. You can walk out. No danger. Good, clean fun for your large audience on the riverbanks.

I admit that people falling on banana peels are tragic, not funny, but I confess that one of the most entertaining after-noons I spent was sitting on the grass along the Cam, watching tourists go pu-u-u-unting along.

After so much hilarity, it seems abrupt, but—back to cathe-drals!

Ely is sixteen miles from Cambridge, and though you are not going on to Peterborough and the rest of East Anglia, you should certainly take the extra morning or afternoon to go by bus from Cambridge to the great Cathedral of the Fens.

You have seen a good many churches at this point, and I would not urge Ely on you, except that it is superb. No matter if you go reluctantly rather than with burning anticipation, once you get to Ely you will be overwhelmed.

Every great cathedral should be studied from a distance,

but Ely has a special relation to space. I wish you could manage to be in the little cathedral town around noon: buy yourself a bottle of cheap wine, a sausage, some bread and fruit, and walk around to the park behind the Cathedral. One of the best picnics Richard and I ever had was at Ely. We sat on the sunny grass, drank chianti, and stared at the Octagon Tower. It was quiet, a few cows browsing in the pasture at the foot of the hill, and an old man asleep under an oak tree.

If you do not have time for a picnic, walk a quarter of a mile or so out of the town, in any direction, turn back, and look at the Cathedral of the Fens.

In the year 673 the fenlands around Ely were marsh and bog. St. Etheldreda, hoping to find peace and safety, led a little band of nuns across the dangerous swamps to the "Isle"—the oasis of slightly raised, dry land. On the ground where stands the cathedral, the Saxon saint built a nunnery; and this was the beginning.

The nunnery disappeared; next came canons, as at Wells; finally, with the Normans, Benedictine monks. In 1109 the abbot of the Ely monastery became a bishop, and the church of his foundation acquired the dignity of the title "cathedral."

Across these centuries from 673, and especially after the energetic Normans arrived, the fens were gradually drained; what were once man-killing bogs had been transformed by 1109 into rich and fertile fields. The Isle of Ely grew from the monastery walls to the whole of northern Cambridgeshire; and the bishop was the secular as well as the religious lord of the fenlands. This is important to remember, when you look at Ely Cathedral. The bishop was the baron, the duke, of these flat, lonely plains.

Durham Cathedral is a fortress built on a rock; Ely is a castle standing black and dramatic above the fenlands. The great Cathedral towers can be seen for twenty miles and more across the sunken, treeless plains. The proud bishops deliberately designed Ely to dominate the whole of their rich Isle. Whoever passed into the lands of the Bishop of Ely, whether he came north or south, east or west, should see the distant stone walls of the Castle of God. For the space of four hundred years Ely Cathedral towered above the fenlands, a massive stone witness, grim and beautiful, to the wealth and absolute power of the Bishop of the Isle.

Cows graze in a rough and stony pasture behind the Cathedral; the grass covers the rubble left by the Dissolution. Henry VIII did not care to have absolute power around, except his own; and the Benedictine monastery at Ely was thoroughly razed. The Cathedral stands to remind you, as you prowl around it from a distance, of medieval England.

Richard and I lolled happily in the Cathedral park. We took off our shoes, ate sausage, drank wine, and regarded Ely Cathedral. I felt a thought coming: "You know, it's a good thing they have those cows. Otherwise, it would be sinister. Chilling."

Richard considered this observation. He said politely (he was in a good mood): "No doubt you know what you mean by that. Cows!"

"What if you were some poor medieval serf? All that stone hovering above you. Scare you to death. No quarter. No democracy. One false move, and the bishop would have you burned alive, or stick you inside a dungeon."

"H'mmmm."

"But now the cows show this is modern England. Habeas corpus and all that. Free speech."

My husband assumed a sardonic expression. "Henry the Eighth! Just the sort of thing he encouraged—free speech. People were always taking out habeas corpus writs against the Tudors."

"Oh, well, I mean it was the beginning, that's all. The cows are symbolic."

"Cows are symbolic?" Richard said, in a slow, wondering way. We wrapped up our debris, and carefully stowed it in a trash basket provided for the purpose. I put this in because I despise people who litter up parks. It is a low trick to leave wine bottles or waxpaper where, before the picnic, there was a stretch of grass. I think leaving debris around in a place totally remote is antisocial and swinish; people who throw sardine cans into babbling brooks or leave paper bags under oak trees ought to be shot. Once Richard and I walked two miles uphill on a lonely Yorkshire moor; when we got to the top of the hill, all we could see was heather and horizon—plus two empty beer bottles, profusely decorated with cheese rinds and cupcake papers. Shame!

Having cleaned up the crumbs, Richard and I abandoned the Ely cows and marched down to inspect the interior of the Cathedral.

Close up, Ely is not sinister, although it exudes a strong atmosphere of power. This may be because the *Norman* nave and transepts seem especially massive, heavy, chilling. The *Norman* style had drama.

Ely is more *Island Gothic* than any other large church in England. Its three major styles (the *Norman*, plus *Early English*, and *Decorated*) are not blended together; they make three distinct, separate blocks of building. The choir is *Early English* at its far end, the Lady Chapel, Tower, and west end of the choir are *Decorated.*

This Octagon Tower, over the crossing, is Ely's most famous and beautiful feature. I mentioned before the sad fate of the original square stone central tower; it fell down, in 1322, and wrecked most of the choir. The monks beat their hair-shirted chests. Things were in a bad way—most of the choir gone, no central tower, and a great, gaping hole over the crossing. Woe! What to do?

The sacrist, Alan of Walsingham (afterward he was promoted to prior), was one day watching the crew of villeins cart away the debris; the shape of the ruinous hole above the crossing was roughly octagonal. An idea flickered in Alan's mind; and a day or two later, he drew up the blueprints for England's first eight-sided church tower. Alan thought the transept piers would take the weight of the octagonal church tower, because the stresses would be more evenly and widely distributed. (He was right, as you can see today.) But an octagonal tower, even if it did hold up, was a daring project in 1322. Nobody in Ely (Alan included) knew how to span a roof as wide as the eight-sided lantern Alan proposed. This was a knotty problem; it was all very well to put up an eight-sided tower—nice it would look from the outside. But what were you going to have inside the cathedral? A big hole? Alan brooded, and the monks argued back and forth; finally the sacrist hit on an ingenious solution; which, as you study it, will remind you of the double dome at

St. Paul's. For Alan was forced by the limitations of Gothic building to an idea which Wren deliberately and skillfully designed in Renaissance curves.

At St. Paul's a huge outer dome dominates London, and a smaller, lower dome unites the interior space.

At Ely the magnificent stone octagon rises dramatically above the fenlands, and inside a steep wooden steeple roofs the transept crossing. Alan hunted for twelve years, over England, to find beams long and strong enough for his pyramidal roof. The stone octagon was finished first; eight arches over the transept piers made it solid and secure. The huge wooden beams were fitted into place; they rested on the transept arches, and sloped steeply into the tower, until they met in a collar of timber.

When the Octagon Tower of Ely was finished, in 1345, it was the envy of every other monastery and cathedral chapter in England. It still is. Architects call it "one of the most original and poetic conceptions of the Middle Ages."

But it is not the Octagon which makes Ely Cathedral so gripping. It is the sum of frowning nave and graceful Lady Chapel, lovely choir and Galilee porch; above all the dramatic exterior mass, which gives the Cathedral of the Fens a special, tremendous glory. The combination of styles at Ely is sometimes awkward. Not everyone likes this Cathedral—but no one ever forgets it.

After Ely, Peterborough Cathedral is an anticlimax. Many architects admire the curious west façade at Peterborough (an *Early English* screen across a *Norman* front), and the painted ceiling over the nave is usually called the "finest in Europe." Two queens were buried at Peterborough: poor Catherine of Aragon, and Mary, Queen of Scots. These monumentally unhappy ladies originally had elegant tombs in the choir. However, James I took his mother's remains to Westminster, where he installed them, as you will recall, across the aisles from Elizabeth's elaborate marble coffin. Since James I had not set eyes on his mother from the age of one year, this macabre gesture seems more defiance than sentiment. That left only one queen at Peterborough, and her tomb went with the stained glass, during the Cromwell reformation. In the 1920's a collection was taken up among English Catherines and Marys, and a neat modern tomb now marks Catherine's sad bones, while a plaque points out Mary's interim resting place.

There are many interesting items about Peterborough; it is one of the major English Gothic cathedrals, and if you have developed a passion for medieval architecture, you will want to see Peterborough by all means.

East Anglia is like the Cotswolds; you can profitably hire a car at Cambridge and make a wide circle north and west and return. Or you can take local buses and see the towns and curious scenery. A pleasant way of exploring at least some of England's Angry Land would be to go from Cambridge to Ely; then northwest to Wisbech, and from Wisbech over to King's Lynn. This can be a daytime journey. You will want to stay at least two days at King's Lynn, making it your headquarters for the Seven Churches of the (nearby) Marshland. (That is their official title.) From King's Lynn you can go across the flat lands to Norwich, down the dramatic coast to Aldeburgh, and back to Cambridge (or London) via Harwich, Ipswich, and Bury St. Edmunds. If you have an extra day or two, you can see Thetford and the prehistoric flint mines in the forest.

Does this sound a formidable program? Distances are short in England, and a journey through East Anglia can be made in three or four days if you are squandering your money on a car, five if you depend on buses.

East Anglia is relatively unknown to American travelers. You will see your countrymen everywhere in Kent and in the Cotswolds, but only a few tourists have so far stumbled across the strange, beautiful Norfolk fens and the harsh but exciting Suffolk coast. Englishmen have long since "discovered" East Anglia. But holiday makers do not penetrate inland to Thetford or often go north to Wisbech. You may find your journey into East Anglia an adventure in seeking out that "real, untouched" England, always a sort of traveler's grail.

Richard and I arrived at King's Lynn on a Saturday night in summer. We hit upon King's Lynn by accident—it was the nearest town after Thetford, and we hoped we could find a hotel.

King's Lynn was a complete, total, and wonderful surprise. When we came back to London, we discovered (sheepishly) that Lynn, as they call it for short, has for years been famous among English intellectuals, scholars, architects, poets, painters, novelists, and sophisticates in general.

"King's Lynn?" one man said at a cocktail party.

"Yes, we were—"

Alas, my eager chatter was drowned out. "By far the most beautiful and interesting town in Europe," this gentleman remarked, in a loud, angry voice.

"Yes, that's what I—"

"Remarkable. The Saturday Market Place is probably as good an example of—"

A third party horned in on the conversation. "Oh Lynn! There's absolutely nothing in England like St. Nicholas' Church. R-r-r-ravishing, and the Customs House!"

I hope I shall not spoil your pleasure if I tell you in advance that King's Lynn is a remarkable and beautiful town. It looks and feels like no other town in England; the Flemish influence appears in the church brasses, in the shape of the great town squares (called "market places"), in the proud merchants' houses along the handsome streets. Yet it is English, not Continental. The flintwork, characteristic of East Anglia (and in other towns heavy, somber, awkward) is used here with a light, graceful touch. The Georgian doorways are charming; the Tudor half-timbered houses lean against eighteenth-century bricks, mellowed by time and sun.

King's Lynn has the melancholy romantic charm of a town that has died. From the beginning of the wool trade in the fourteenth century, until about 1850, King's Lynn was one of the great seaports. The system of rivers and canals, first dug by the Romans, connected Lynn and the ocean with a great system of inland waterways. But in the middle of the nineteenth century railroads killed Lynn overnight. The merchants moved away; or they stayed, each year a little poorer, barricaded in their beautiful, decaying houses. Yet there remains, oddly, the feeling of a seaport, gay, reckless, proud.

The sharp, salty breeze blows through these medieval stone alleys. The pubs are packed on a Saturday evening; and, stand-

TUESDAY MARKET PLACE, KING'S LYNN

ing in the middle of the huge Tuesday Market Place, you can hear, late at night, people singing, and the sound of distant laughter.

The churches of Lynn stand witness to the great days of the proud seaport. St Margaret's is a rich profusion of English styles, but St. Nicholas, decaying now, has a breath-taking splendor. You may remember how Wren wanted to make halls of his nave and transepts; and how the Chapter of St. Paul's shuddered at such an innovation. But the wool merchants of Lynn, a hundred and fifty years before Wren, built St. Nicholas with one great roof spanning the whole of the magnificent interior. St. Nicholas was probably the first church in England to use this daring new design. More: the *Perpendicular* style at St. Nicholas is developed beyond the Gothic. The whole east and west walls of the Lynn church are glass; the interior is radiant with light.

The crumbling splendors of St. Nicholas are a good introduction to the Seven Churches of the Marshland.

Imagine a sunken plain, a green and straw-colored sea. A haystack is a black mountain against the wide pale skies; a man riding a bicycle moves slowly across the infinite horizon. The Sunday bus is a ship, rocking across waves of dull yellow grain.

From this strange earthy ocean, sharp in the monotone distance, rise the towers of seven ancient churches.

The Marshland of Lynn is melancholy, and the medieval merchants must have felt this sadness. The Seven Churches are a defiance, a human boast against the timeless wide skies, the empty, eternal plains.

Today the wool trade is dead. One or two of the Seven Churches have been repaired, and the bells ring from some of the towers, sounding sweetly across the Sunday stillness. But most of the proud spires are slowly falling into ruin. The Seven Churches of the Marshland are beautiful; they display a profusion of Gothic style of rich ornamentation and imaginative, original detail. But they will inescapably remind the traveler of Ozymandias.

South of King's Lynn, and throughout much of inland East Anglia, other stone disappears, and every house, every barn, every church, even every pub and wayside inn, is built of flint. This grim, gray-black stone, set in walls of cement, gives a melancholy cast to the whole of England's Angry Land. Thetford is not so much ugly as sad and oppressive. Smiling England, the Kentish thatched cottage set in its rose garden, the golden-gray villages of the Cotswold hills, this is a whole world distant from the bleak streets of Thetford. It is easy to imagine the Roundheads marching out of these flinty Norfolk towns. The man who wrote bitterly of "summer soldiers" and said, "These are the times that try men's souls," learned endurance in a Thetford house. You can see it today; there is a plaque against the flint wall, but although the inscription is fulsome, there is no word of the Norfolk squire who beat Tom Paine, aged twelve, until his naked back ran blood. The squire meant to teach young Paine respect for his betters; but the lesson the boy learned was called *The Rights of Man.* The squire should have known better; it has never been wise to treat a free-born Norfolk man as though he were some mean slave. Flint is not a beautiful stone; but it is hard.

Norwich is an industrial town, smaller, but not unlike Youngstown or Toledo. However, at its center is "The Old Town," of interest and beauty. Steep, narrow winding streets lead to a Norman castle; medieval houses, a flint Guildhall, Tudor half-timbering, two or three fine parish churches, cluster around the great fame and glory of its Cathedral.

Norman is an ancient style, near our Western beginnings. Caen, its prototype, was tragically destroyed in World War II; and now the two greatest pre-Gothic cathedrals are in England, the first at Norwich, the other at Durham. The great fortress church of the North has perhaps the more dramatic situation, high on its black rock, but architects consider Norwich the most perfect and beautiful large *Norman* church left today. From Norwich Castle you can look down on the square *Norman* tower, with its glorious spire; but the most exciting moment is when you first walk from the nave into the transept and choir, and feel the impact, the shock of *Norman* at its best—pure, tremendous, overwhelming.

Centuries are hard to keep straight. So much history is telescoped into a single town, even a single square, that the tourist begins to leap dizzily, like a careless goat, from 1520 to 1311 to 1617; everything seems long ago, and in the general haze, *Norman* fades into Gothic. But you need to get a grip on time at Norwich Cathedral. This shadowed, massive nave, these tremendous stone transepts, these heavy round piers in the choir were standing, as you see them today, in the year 1119. The cornerstone for the Cathedral of East Anglia was laid in the year 1096; the base of the present tower and a lower spire were completed in 1145.

I put these dates down because otherwise Norwich has no meaning. The Octagon Tower at Ely was built in 1322, two hundred years after Norwich. Two hundred years is a long time—especially for Americans.

Norwich—1119.

Henry VIII—1509.

The cornerstone at Norwich was laid thirty years after William the Conqueror landed at Pevensey. These round arches in the transepts are more than eight hundred years old. Eight hundred years makes me feel queer; four hundred years is all right; I can take that sort of history in my stride. But 1096 is eerie.

Norwich Cathedral is pure *Norman*, except for the top of the choir (a little trouble with part of the tower falling down, as usual), the beautiful fifteenth-century vaulted and bossed roof, and the outlying monastery buildings. These last, the handsome gate leading to the close, the library, and so on, are *Early English* and *Decorated*, which is interesting, in my opinion. The reason for these pointed arches and handsome *Decorated* windows was a local riot. It appears that England's Angry Land was angry as early as 1272. You can read history, in East Anglia, backward from the Chartists, or forward from the infuriated citizens of Norwich, who, resenting the monks' taxes and the bishop's courts, came charging across the monastery walls to protest. Tom Paine's ancestors made a thorough job of the monastery, and the same with not a few of the monks; fortunately for twentieth-century tourists, stone does not burn, although there are smoke stains on the ancient arches, and the earliest piece of wood in the Cathedral is dated 1273. Everything else went up in flames. The riot was presently quelled, or the citizens of Norfolk went home, carrying everything portable they could put their hands on; and after "order" was restored, the bishop taxed the town guilds to rebuild the monastery gates. Down at Bury St. Edmunds, another East Anglian town, the abbot really exasperated the forefathers of the Roundheads; there is nothing left of Bury St. Edmunds except rubble. At Norwich the bishops appear to have drawn conclusions from the riot of 1272; perhaps it would be best not to irritate the people of East Anglia. A Bishop of Norwich could not be too careful.

The Norfolk Broads, near Norwich, are a vast and dismal system of rivers spreading over mud flats; channels run drearily through reeds and waterfowl nests and gnats, down at long, long last to the sea.

My authority for these dispiriting statements is my cousin Margaret. There are some people who think sailing the Norfolk Broads is delightful and exciting. Margaret went on a cruise in the Norfolk Broads; they were becalmed on gnatty mud flats for roughly eight days, or 192 hours; the other two days they spent furiously tacking back and forth up a stale and shallow inlet to the grocery store.

The Norfolk Broads are not recommended. Family solidarity.

The Suffolk coast is wonderful, all the way from Southwold, Walberswick, Blythburgh, Leiston, and Dunwich to Aldeburgh. The towns are dramatic, set on the edge of sand dunes; sea-weed dries against the stones of handsome *Perpendicular* churches. Dunwich especially is beautiful and mysterious.

Why mysterious?

I feel battered as I address myself to the problem of Dunwich and Aldeburgh, too. One of the difficulties of touring about with children is that they ask direct, penetrating questions, and expect direct, penetrating answers. All the guidebooks say that Dunwich and Aldeburgh, during the Middle Ages, were big prosperous seaports, flourishing with the wool trade. Then, the "sea rose" and covered all of Dunwich except a single street, ending now in the lonely dunes; at Aldeburgh, the old Guild-hall stands on the sandy beach, and more than half the medi-eval town is buried under the ocean waters.

Richard explained these fascinating items to our daughter, Eileen, then aged six. She blinked.

"Just think, dear," Daddy said, carried away by the romance of it all, "under those waves is a whole town, churches, and houses and streets and—"

"Why?" Eileen said.

Three days later, Daddy was trying to explain that one; we had been rather thoroughly over junior geography, dynamics, tides, ocean beds, the possibility of little girls in London being abruptly drowned in their beds when they were not paying attention (remote), the reasons why medieval wood traders built their cities in such precarious spots (sheer carelessness, no doubt), the outlook for Paris, Brussels, New York, and Los Angeles, staying above water in the immediate future (good), and related topics. Among the more difficult related topics was the one about Winchelsea, a port until the sea went away, leaving it (unlike Aldeburgh and Dunwich) high and dry.

"Why, Daddy?"

"For the last time," Daddy said, in a clipped, desperate tone, "I do not know why the sea went away from Winchelsea; I do not even know why it rose at Aldeburgh, and in conclusion, I do not care, and the next person in this automobile who mentions the sea rising or not rising is not going to get his sweets. Do I make myself clear?"

Silence.

Patrick, aged twelve: "Yes, but Daddy . . ."

For tourists without young inquiring minds to ask "Why?" the Suffolk coast ought to be charming.

On the way back from Aldeburgh to Cambridge or London, stop at Hadleigh. The wool church is magnificent, and the Deanery Tower fine Tudor brick; across a grassy courtyard is the great Guildhall. Hadleigh is a quiet Suffolk town today, half empty in a peaceful sun. But its great three-sided square, church, tower, and Guildhall is the history of East Anglia; these proud merchants challenged Gothic England, marched in Cromwell's armies, and sent their sons to Cambridge to learn liberty. Bury St. Edmunds, rich and beautiful, seems the other side of the flinty Thetford coin; but the vast ruins, today enclosed in gardens, and the martyrs' memorial will remind the traveler that East Anglia, and the great university at its gateway, have for many centuries been the special home of English liberty.

From this soil, we Americans inherited John Harvard and Tom Paine.

Rhetoric is a poor summary for a journey in England as various, as beautiful, and (especially punting on the Cam!) as thoroughly entertaining as Cambridge and East Anglia.

WHAT TO SEE IN EAST ANGLIA

*** *Cambridge.* See text.
*** *Ely.* See text.
  * *Huntingdon.* Oliver Cromwell was born here and represented Huntingdon in Parliament for twelve fateful years.
 ** *Peterborough.* One of the most celebrated cathedrals in England. Not far away are the interesting old towns and villages of:
  * *Oundle, Warmington, Fotheringhay, Wansford,* and *Castor.* Noted for their splendid churches. Oundle is a delightful stone town. Farther on, past Oundle, are:
  * *Stanwick* and *Higham Ferrers.* Lovely towns, famous in this countryside of "Springs, Spires, and Squires." Of all these towns, our favorites were Higham Ferrers and Stanwick, although we spent a happy morning poking about the Castor church, which is Norman. In the other direction from Peterborough (northwest) is the town of:
 ** *Stamford.* Our candidate for England's most beautiful small town. It has six superb churches, one of them with a great broach spire. Its houses are Elizabethan and Jacobean, built of the silvery Barnack or Ketton stone. We came for an hour to Stamford and stayed for the weekend, with an excursion to the nearby (eleven miles) smaller town of:
 ** *Oakham.* Oakham is enchanting; its market place sleeps in the sun, its church is delightful, and there is a relic of the local castle, a banqueting hall hung with horseshoes. These horseshoes are collected according to the "immemorial right" of the lord of the manor to demand a souvenir

of passersby, kings and the like. The sightseer may be a little surprised that most of the horseshoes are dated after 1880 (about the period they revived the Lord Mayor's procession in London, and other "immemorial" traditions) but it is wrong to carp— the horseshoes are most amusing.

EAST ANGLIA (arranged by routes from Cambridge).

East Anglia is "painters' country," the region of Constable, Gainsborough, and the Norwich School, high points of English art.

** *Wisbech.* A curious wool town not unlike Bruges, in Flanders, even down to the canal and stately merchants' homes.

*** *King's Lynn.* See text.

*** *The Seven Churches of the Marshland,* between Wisbech and King's Lynn. See text.

The northern seacoast of East Anglia is strange and beautiful; good bathing and summer resorts. From King's Lynn the most interesting journey is inland to:

** *Thetford.* A bleak, grim flint town, where Tom Paine was born. In the outskirts of Thetford is a stretch of curious heath and warren, called the Breckland, and prehistoric flint mines, abandoned and hypnotic in feeling. Thetford is a detour from King's Lynn to:

*** *Norwich.* See text. From Norwich, do not go to Great Yarmouth, a noisy seaside resort, but head south to the East Anglian coast for:

* *Lowestoft, Wrentham, Southwold, Blythburgh, Leiston, Dunwich,* and *Aldeburgh.* All fascinating towns and villages of this curious sunken land. Then inland to:

* *Ipswich.* A dullish industrial town with one superb Elizabethan and Jacobean block of buildings in the center of town, Nearby is:

** *Hadleigh.* An old wool town with a fascinating church and guildhall. From Hadleigh, you may include some or all of the following sights, depending on whether you are returning to London or heading north or west.

* *Sudbury.* Another wool town, its old buildings defaced by modern store fronts. But the skull of Simon of Sudbury is

in St. Gregory's church. (He was beheaded by Wat Tyler, who did not care for this particular Archbishop of Canterbury.)

** *Bury St. Edmunds.* Famous monastery ruins. See text.

* *Saffron Walden.* A pretty town, has a good church and castle ruins.

* *Little Maplestead.* Not far away, has one of the four round Norman churches, but alas, also "restored."

Colchester sounds better than it is in actual fact. The Roman relics, the most extensive in England, are not impressive, not up to St. Albans.

Lincoln, York, Yorkshire, Durham, Hexham, and the Border Country

THE most exciting journey in England (Richard and I think) is north from York, across the moors to Durham, Hexham, and the Border Country.

I hope this statement does not exasperate you. I realize that we have been blithely calling everything (well, almost everything) glorious, tremendous, wonderful, and enchanting. I feel hangdog about the adjectives in this book, but what can I do? Every "glorious" is true. There is nothing so enchanting as Haddon Hall, unless it is Bodiam Castle, Chipping Campden, Winchelsea, or Newstead Abbey; nor anything so wonderful as Oxford, except Cambridge, Wells, Chester, Tewkesbury Abbey, and Norwich Cathedral; and what is more tremendous than Canterbury? St. Paul's? Hampton Court? The Tower of London?

Against this background of superlatives, after I hate to think how many allurings, fascinatings, lovelies, superbs, and ravishings, it is shameful to wind up this book with categorical statements about the Border Country. But I must mutter (in a small voice), that Richard and I liked Durham, Blanchland, and Hexham best out of our wanderings. I see the heather yet, blooming on the lonely Northumbrian moors; I shall always remember standing on the ancient stones of the Roman Wall, looking across the windswept, timeless hills into Scotland.

I despise snobs, and I deny the theory that a beautiful place can be "spoiled" by a queue of tourists. But it is true that in summer Stratford and the Cotswolds are overcrowded, and the wild horses in New Forest are hard to see for the traffic. North of York, as in East Anglia, not many Americans go; if your trip to England is made at the top of the July-August season, you might find more adventure, more sense of freedom, space, and ease in the Border Country than on the south coast.

We must be practical, however. It is a four- or five-hour train journey from London to York; and after York distances are greater than in the tightly populated south of England. Bodiam Castle, in Sussex, is on a main bus line, service every half hour; our beloved Blanchland, in Northumberland, has a local bus into Hexham, which leaves the market square in a leisurely way every morning, and returns around suppertime, with the mail and the milk. The traveler can see many marvels, and "do" a whole catalogue of sights in a single weekend spent in Kent, or Oxford, or Bath. But a week is short time for the Border Country; without a car, you will need ten days to see a little of the strange landscape, the lonely ruins, the beautiful villages folded into the empty moors.

Time is everything for the American traveler. Sometimes, I know, Europeans make fun of our intensity. The tourist from Indiana, gallantly tackling Stratford, Warwick, Tewkesbury Abbey, and Bath in a single weekend flabbergasts the Englishman, and dismays the leisurely Belgian tripper. But when shall we Americans come this way again? How many times can we cross the Atlantic? It is all very well for the Frenchman to turn up his nose at the determined American, marching through cathedrals, guidebook clutched to his bosom, and a wild fixed look in his eye. But the Frenchman has only to go around the corner to see Chartres, or cross the Channel to explore Canterbury; for Americans, England is do, or die without it. The first is usually our last time; when we get back to the airport, it is, for most of us, *And So We Say Farewell to Beautiful England.*

That is why we take seriously the question of a trip north to the Border. All along in this book we have said, and we repeat it again with emphasis, do not try to overcrowd your English schedule; see less and enjoy it; be selective, not exhausted. Do not come to York and Durham unless you have more than a month in England; the south and Midlands are easier for a brief journey and it would be silly to see Hexham and not Canterbury, Rievaulx and not Cambridge.

But now that we have been plain and practical, and hoisted the proper warnings, we should be allowed to say that, if you do have the time and money, the Border Country is glorious. Tremendous. And all those other adjectives.

There is a last point. The population explosion has long been explicit to scientists. But Americans have only begun to understand it. Suddenly everything in our homeland is too crowded, too dirty, too *public.* Holidays turn into a struggle to find an empty place, silent, and alone.

If you are sensitive to crowds (and not everyone is) then the journey to Durham is worth—well, not Canterbury, but, at the top of the summer season, almost everything else outside of London.

This is a place silent, beautiful, and alone.

If you are coming north to the Border, the logical journey is London to Cambridge, Ely, King's Lynn, perhaps Boston, perhaps Lincoln, and then to York. (Boston and Lincoln are stopovers on the express train routes.)

At York you will want to spend a whole day, or two, exploring the Minster, the walls, the museums.

From York, if you can possibly afford it, squander the family cash on renting a car; perhaps you can find two or three fellow travelers to share expenses. A car is a great advantage in the Border Country.

If you are driving, make a wide circle, west and north, for

Haworth, the ruined abbeys and the western Yorkshire moors; then north to Durham, Blanchland, Hexham, and Housesteads; now due east to Bamburgh and the wild and lovely Northumbrian coast; south (skirting Newcastle and the big industrial area of the Tyne) to Whitby, Goathland, across the Yorkshire moors again to Pickering, Rievaulx, and return to York, express train back to London.

If your budget does not allow even a motorcycle, be brave; maybe you will see more of the north country than your millionaire fellow Americans. The British Railways run an excellent circular tour from York across some of the moors, a side trip to Haworth, to Fountains and Bolton Abbey, and return to York. The local English trains fascinate me. We went part of the way on one of these circular tours; we had a good time, and saw a lot of moors, a lot of ruins, and a lot of Englishmen. It was fun.

Back in York from the circular tour, take the express north to Durham. I am afraid you will have to skip Blanchland, unless you have an extra day to wait for the bus connections to Hexham. From Hexham you can get a bus to Housesteads and the Roman Wall and return. If your time has run out, the London express goes from Newcastle-upon-Tyne; or you can bounce along over the hills to Bamburgh, and take local buses straight south down the seacoast to Whitby, and over to Goathland, the moors and heather; here also are direct connections with the London express, from the moors to Piccadilly Circus.

In a way it would be more of an adventure to make the northern trip via local buses and branch-line trains. It is exciting to end up for the night in some unknown town; Northumberland is remote (for England). Of course market buses take much more time than speeding along in a rented car, and I underline the fact that the Border Country is not Kent. Bus connections twice a day are about as much as you can expect. Another dismal point. Newcastle-upon-Tyne is a sprawling northern Pittsburgh. All buses and all roads (motorists will have to look alert on their maps) lead, in the Border Country, to Newcastle. You will have to plan your bus trip carefully after

Durham; otherwise you will spend half your time jouncing along beside a coal mine, trying to make connections for Bamburgh.

So much for practical details.

In 1630, John Winthrop and a large company of embattled Nonconformists, some of them from Boston, Lincolnshire, settled in the harsh new world of Massachusetts; after some hesitation, they called their new village *Boston,* which no doubt encouraged the Vicar of Boston, Lincolnshire (a certain gentleman named John Cotton), to follow the first boatload of emigrants, in 1633.

It is a queer feeling to go walking in the salty old seaport of Boston, Lincolnshire, and stand in the beautiful church of St. Botolph's, to see what John Cotton and his comrades left behind forever on the long voyage to freedom. I wonder if the Reverend Cotton dreamed of St. Botolph's great tower, or regretted the pink brick houses and fine streets of his homeland? Maybe part of the hard, cold streak in the New England mind was a protective wall around a longing for the old home, the dear places so familiar? I never knew what John Cotton had lost until I saw the tower of St. Botolph's.

Lincoln is difficult for a book of this general nature. The Cathedral is most beautiful. Indeed, it is labeled in all the books "the flower of English Gothic," and its "Angel" choir is called the most perfect example in the kingdom of *Early English* merging into the *Decorated* style. The great Cathedral stands high on a cone-shaped hill; from a distance its towers float magically in space, a view of breathtaking, incredible drama.

But Lincoln Cathedral and the castle sit squarely on top of a big, dull, modern industrial city, about as charming as Newark, New Jersey. For miles in every direction from Lincoln there is nothing but flat factory lands, and little to see but toolsheds. If you can make train connections for an afternoon in Lincoln, and on that night to York, the Cathedral will reward you with its magnificence. If not, you cannot use up too many of the hours, that are now becoming pearls of great price, in a visit to Lincoln.

I suppose, if I were logical, I would repeat the same dreary warning about Beverley; it is thirty miles off the beaten track from York, either going or coming. But Beverly Minster is one of the most ancient and beautiful churches in England; we like it better (to be truthful) than either Lincoln or York. It has a shadowed, still glory on a late afternoon. At York the sightseers are marched through in parties of fifty, but at Beverley the verger will spend the whole afternoon showing you the ancient Saxon Fridstol, the wonderful Percy Shrine, the old staircase to the destroyed Chapter House. There is a point of diminishing returns for cathedral *tourisme*. The crowds at York, the megaphones, and the queues are distracting.

But Beverley is silent, its beautiful *Decorated* nave is empty; at evensong, a few townspeople come into the choir, and the music sounds sweetly through the ancient Gothic church.

York Minster is a sister church of Beverley, but more famous. It is the proudest Cathedral of the North, and it has more ancient stained glass than any other church in England.

We have been rather thoroughly into the question of Gothic architecture, so I shall not make many comments about York Minster, except to say that it is often considered, after Canterbury, the most beautiful of English medieval churches. It is characteristically *Island Gothic*—the nave and west front *Decorated*, the choir and towers *Perpendicular,* the transepts *Early English*. The great east window is said to be the largest expanse of medieval glass in existence, and has all its original glazing, dated 1405–1408.

As I write about one after another of England's Gothic masterpieces, I come to the end of my adjectives. Either one must say everything or nothing about a stone monument of such size and grandeur, beauty and antiquity as York Minster. This northern Cathedral has great pomp, with the famous east window, a fabulous history (King Edwin of Northumbria was baptized here in 627), and all sorts of curious treasure, including Saxon relics with a definitely Byzantine cast.

But by this time you have found out for yourself whether Gothic architecture moves you deeply, or some, or not at all: after so many churches, you have acquired a practiced eye, and a steely glance. "H'mmmm, yes, *Decorated*," you say, and bend only an indifferent ear toward the verger as he clears his throat, gives a clerical chuckle, and addressing a large party of Boy Scouts, begins, "Legend tells us . . ."

If you have developed taste and passion for Gothic, both York and Beverley minsters will be experiences of the first magnitude; if churches have begun to weigh a little, the glass at York will be interesting, and the story of the ancient Cathedral will fit into the pattern of the medieval and Tudor history you have acquired down south in London.

Warning: avoid the guided York Minster tours. They are geared for the Youth Hostel set.

The next item in York after the Minster is a trot around the handsome (but heavily restored) medieval walls. Richard and I made the circuit one pleasant evening in early September; you climb stairs at one of the gates, and stroll along on what seems like elevated sidewalks. The view is charming—the lawns of the Minster Yard, the towers of the Minster, fruit trees heavy with pears in the Dean's Tudor-walled garden.

"But they certainly didn't have much luck with these walls," I remarked to my long-suffering husband. I like to tell him the history I have just read; it makes me feel profound and learned.

"Oh?" Richard said, peering at a wonderful clump of lupin. "I wonder how they get lupin to flower this late? Mine used to go by July."

"Cut them back. Anyway, every time—but every time—they had a war up here, York lost. Somebody was constantly besieging the town, and then right away they would surrender. Lionhearted, ha, ha! Either they'd surrender, or the other side would scale these walls and make havoc. As fortifications they certainly—"

"Eeeeeek!" Richard and I said (or some similar noise of dismay and shock).

Because, at our feet, four towheads, four pairs of shiny blue eyes, four broad grins, and four snubbed freckled noses had appeared as a kind of frieze or border along the medieval walls of York.

"Hey," I said feebly.

The four little boys, judging the coast clear (obviously tourists did not count), shinned up the branches of the Dean's forbidden fruit trees, and, blouses bulging with looted pears, jumped down over the barbed-wire barricade as lightly as goats, or army sappers.

"Well, hello," Richard remarked.

The four bandits of York gave us only the briefest glance. Laden with booty, they scrambled down the ramparts of the medieval walls. Richard and I rushed to the iron spikes (sharp) and looked down on a twenty-five-foot sheer drop to a ditch below.

"Don't!" I bawled. "Richard! Do something!" The youngest and blondest pear robber was not a day over seven, and the captain of this bold band of marauders was rising ten, perhaps.

My fears were wasted. The children of York are obviously descended from a long line of wall climbers. The medieval stones looked smooth, naked, sinister and forbidding to our appalled alien glance; but the boys went down the fourteenth-century fortifications of York, following some secret avenue, no doubt inherited from papa and grandpapa.

We watched from the giddy ramparts as the army unloaded its booty in the ditch; the bandits swung themselves up on an old oak tree, and from this vantage point jumped at the medieval walls for their first toehold. Apparently this was a difficult feat. The seven-year-old fell off twice; he was far behind his comrades as he appeared, scratched, but grinning, above the iron spikes. Richard, carried away by such dash and gallantry, gave him a boost over the Dean's barbed wire.

"Aiding and abetting," I pointed out. "You can see why they never won any wars up here. Some fortifications. I suppose they have been running up and down these walls since 1350."

York is an interesting town, not only walls and Minster, but medieval streets and museums, as well. The Museum Gardens feature outdoor and indoor ruins, Roman, Saxon, and Henry VIII, all first-class. The Railway Museum has old engines, Victorian iron horse carriages and the like, amusing. The most remarkable museum in York, and the best of its kind I have seen anywhere, is across from Clifford's Tower, in the eighteenth-century "model" prison. It is titled the York Castle Museum of Bygones. The "Bygones" include everything from valentines, 1811, to corsets, 1765 and 1891, fire engines, nineteenth-century, the first milking machine, the first alarm clock to hit Yorkshire, false teeth from the reign of Charles II, and the fans ladies carried into Victorian balls. Some of the exhibits—old newspapers, repeater watches, butter molds—are cleverly arranged in cases or against the walls, but the most evocative displays are a series of rooms describing life in the north of England from 1500 to 1900. You look in, from an open doorway, on how life was for a Jacobean squire, or Yorkshire farmer, 1810. There are the fireplace where the wife cooked, the bread pans she used, the baby's cradle, the candle snuffers, the bootjack, the oaken table. Across the corridor is a Yorkshire gentleman's parlor, 1870: red plush, wax flowers under glass, picture of the Queen on the wall, jet bead fringe on the velvet throw across the claw-footed horsehair sofa. The museum tour ends in a nineteenth-century street, so convincing you forget the glass overhead. You walk on cobblestones, look in at the chemist's windows, inspect the stagecoach, peer at the children's toys, read the newspaper posted at the bookseller's and look, shuddering, at the town jail. Fascinating!

Bolton Abbey is a Bygone, too, but in a different and grander style. Yorkshire has the most famous of England's monastery ruins; every summer thousands of visitors come to peer at these broken, antique stones. Aside from the scenery itself, strange and beautiful, the ruins are the chief sights in the Yorkshire dales. I am not sure how many of these ancient abbeys you will have time to see, or in what order, so I shall make a general report.

You will remember that we went into the theory and practice of monastery ruins back in London at St. Bartholomew's. In Yorkshire, Henry VIII dissolved the opposition thoroughly. This was probably the monks' and abbots' own fault. Instead of cheerily applauding a fine, forward-looking piece of social reform, the backward brothers and their local supporters held an uprising on the subject. It was called the Pilgrimage of Grace. That sort of thing was deeply resented by Tudors in general, and Henry VIII in particular. The Pilgrimage of Grace ended in ignominious defeat.

Everyone who was anyone in the affair was hanged, and Henry ordered "such dreadful execution to be done upon a good number of the inhabitants in every town, village and hamlet . . . as they may be a fearful spectacle to others hereafter that would practice in like manner."

That was the winter of 1536. Henry, having attended to rebels, gave his attention to the great stone fortresses in the Yorkshire dales. Down south, Henry usually sold what was left of the monasteries to Tudor real-estate operators, who built manor houses over the ancient crypts, or remodeled cloisters and dormitories into palaces. But Henry was taking no chances up north. A place like Fountains Abbey, in 1536, was what a modern general would call a "strong point." Even the church was a castle, and the frowning walls, the great gates, the commodious storehouses, the acres of dormitories, hostels and the like, the good supply of fresh water—these details made Fountains Abbey an ideal rallying ground for a fresh revolt. Henry was greedy, but not so greedy that he cared to sell or give Fountains Abbey to any Yorkshire nobleman. The place was razed. When Henry got through, the rubble at Fountains would never again afford shelter to so much as a goat, let alone an army. Indeed, Fountains and the other Yorkshire abbeys became stone quarries for years, until the Romantic Revival, when carting away wagonloads of *Norman* arches, *Early English* gargoyles, and the like was abruptly forbidden, and tourists arrived to admire the view. At Fountains there is a handsome Jacobean manor house, built right on the monastery grounds; every stone came from what was the cloister.

I think ruins are fairly interesting. There are many places in England where you can see chapter houses, cloisters, abbey churches and the like in good working order, so the Yorkshire ruins are more romantic than instructive. A picturesque ruin, surrounded by thick lawn, and nestled in a beautiful valley, has its points.

Fountains Abbey, near Ripon, is the largest and most renowned of the relics; it is on all the sightseeing tours, and gets a tremendous summer trade. Everybody files through the ruined kitchens, peers at the hospital built across the river (it must have been a little damp), and admires the *Perpendicular* tower.

Kirkstall Abbey, sixteen miles from Harrogate, is grand, but it has the misfortune to stand in a suburb of Leeds, and the romantic effect is dingy. The ruins are covered by coal smoke.

Bolton Abbey, near Ilkley in Wharfedale, is very beautiful indeed. It lies in a hollow of such ravishing green that the Duke of Devonshire has a "shooting box" across the lawn. This holiday hideaway, called Bolton Abbey as well, seems to be a small affair of some thirty rooms, a mere nothing after Chatsworth.

There is a set walk up Wharfedale, along the river from the Abbey, which features a phenomenon called the Strid. A Yorkshire strid is a narrow point in a river, gorge we would call it, and the usual strid is overlaid with a rich Indian-maiden-type folklore. Every respectable-sized rock in the United States has an Indian legend attached. I lived on a rock called "Lover's Leap." In Yorkshire, Legend Hath It that people fell into strids and were drowned; brothers pushed each other, maidens tossed themselves into the drink, or sporting youths bet a foaming beaker of mead they could leap the dangerous gorge, and were never, never seen again. Not even their bodies. I must say anybody who could not get across the Bolton Abbey Strid must have been trying it in a wheel chair, or wrapped in a sack. However, let us not be cynical; think of all the Indian maidens back home.

Byland Abbey is near Coxwold. For some reason, Byland is deserted; nobody pays much attention to it; the ruin stands in the middle of a field, carelessly fenced in; no guides, no admission fee, and no scenery.

Finally, there is Rievaulx (pronounced *Reevo* or *Rivvez*, take your choice), which is my favorite. It is three miles from Helmsley, down a steep hill, set in a lonely valley. The ruins are thick in rich lawn, framed by beautiful trees. A little river runs swiftly past the ancient stones, and the afternoon we were there we had the place to ourselves, except for the young caretaker who was mowing the grass. We could see his cottage beyond the Abbey gates, and presently, in the quiet air, we heard a door opening, and a woman's voice laughing tenderly. We moved away from the caretaker, idly inspecting the stones and reading the signs: SITE OF CLOISTERS, MONKS' WARMING ROOM. When we turned back, the caretaker was moving his lawn mower up and down the ruined nave and two little girls, twins, not quite three years old, were gravely trotting along behind

Daddy. They were blonde little girls with beginning pigtails tied in red ribbons; they were barefoot, and we could see them curling their toes in the lovely feel of the new-mown grass. As Daddy turned a transept corner, the children began to play at hide and seek. I still remember the two blonde little girls, running (a little unsteadily) down the nave at Rievaulx Abbey, to hide behind an *Early English* pillar. Very good ruin, Rievaulx.

From ruins to Haworth, the home of the Brontës, is a considerable leap, not so much in space, as in spirit. The Brontës are a little over the peak of their cult, just now. Writers go through periods, ups and downs of fashion. Dickens, after lying fallow for several decades, is working his way back up. The Brontës had a major boom, 1950–60, but Haworth is not quite the literary shrine today it was in, say, 1965.

I do not mean to sound snide. One of the reasons Richard and I wanted to go to Yorkshire was for Haworth. For that matter, we enjoyed our morning at Haworth as much as anything in the north; it was a success, although queer.

Haworth is out of tourist bounds. The scenic moors, the picturesque towns, the romantic ruins, change abruptly into a dreary industrial area. Coming from Skipton, there are mile after mile of black stone factories, rows of smoke-blackened workers' houses. The sign says, finally: HAWORTH. Nothing could look less like a literary shrine. At the foot of a steep hill is a textile factory, next to it a dismal pub, across the way a modern housing development, rather bare, under a misty, smoky sky. The street climbs steeply up what was once a moor, and makes a sharp turn. Another small factory; more rows of houses; another dreary pub. Then, over a crowded shop, displaying tin bathtubs, clotheslines, and egg beaters, there was a sign: HEATHCLIFF IRONMONGERS.

"Brontë country!" I cried, much excited.

Two shops later, a large placard over a tobacco and stationery store pleaded, "Stop here for your Brontë Postcards! Large Selection! Cheap! Also Complete Stocks of Books."

The signs of the Brontë Industry multiplied. The lady proprietor of a grocery store advertised: AUTHENTIC BRONTE RELICS!"

We passed the Charlotte Tea-Shoppe, and parked behind the Brontë Undertaking and Furniture Parlours; the Heathcliff (he seems to be a favorite) Coal and Wood Supply solicited the favor of our patronage, and the Brontë Arms promised to supply Guinness Stout.

Haworth was touching. In the middle of this harsh factory world, surrounded by coal smoke and council houses, the Brontë Industry valiantly flourishes, a gallant tribute to the three daughters of the local parson. How odd it would have seemed to the Brontë girls to have an undertaking parlor named after them! For that matter, if their ghosts hover over their parsonage (and it is not difficult to imagine the Brontës haunting on a stormy winter's night) what a shock these early Victorian wraiths must get at the museum kindly admirers have made of their old home. Charlotte's stockings, boldly displayed in public under a glass case! Emily's underbodice! What next!

As a matter of fact, it is a fascinating little museum. Richard was particularly bemused by Papa Brontë's study; one can imagine this turbulent, harassed Reverend sitting at his desk, writing inferior poetry, while upstairs, downstairs, in the kitchen and under the staircase his son Branwell and his three daughters busily produced juvenile literature on a mass scale. Some of the novels, poems, illustrated dramas and the like which the Brontë children turned out are preserved, although the gun the Reverend used to fire from his study window is missing.

The tragedy of the Brontës is vivid in the parsonage. These intense, gifted children grew up to live so briefly; the genius of their imagination flowered; for a few years they poured out poems and books which hold readers with their hypnotic spell; then they died. Branwell, the most tormented and troubled of the children, died, in September, 1848, at the age of thirty-one years; Emily died in December of that same year. She was thirty. The following May, Anne died. She was twenty-eight. Charlotte lived until March, 1855; she was thirty-eight and a few months married, when she too died.

This terrible recitation of dates and facts makes the Haworth museum heavy with remembered sorrow. The Reverend Brontë lived for six years after Charlotte—alone. What must it be like to be the father of children so vivid, so intense, so strong with life; and to watch them one by one pass away, until there is only silence in the house once so vibrant with youth?

There is another literary shrine in Yorkshire. We drove into Coxwold one morning, and were instantly enchanted by the delightful village: a broad street, lined with eighteenth-century silvery stone houses, a splendid old church and a handsome square. But where was Shandy Hall? We drove up and down and around. No signs. No pilgrims. No nothing. Silence drowsed over Coxwold. We felt vulgar, making a chug-chug sound with our rented car. At the pub, the proprietor gave us a baffled look when we asked for the home of Laurence Sterne.

"Sterne?"

I peered at the map. Obviously, we had the wrong village.

Richard said thank you, and we were backing out the door when the solitary customer in the bar parlor called out, "The old parsonage, that's what they want. Fellow here yesterday asking about it."

"Oh!" The proprietor regarded us with a mild interest; it was clear we were a bit touched, but then, who is not? He came out on the porch and pointed. "First house past the church; you can't miss it."

Shandy Hall is an eighteenth-century brick farmhouse; a small, home-made, neatly lettered sign is tacked up above the doorbell: HOME OF LAURENCE STERNE, 1760–1768.

"Somebody lives here now," I said nervously. "It's not a museum."

The lady of the house appeared. She was getting lunch for her husband and sons—the family owned a farm outside the village—but she was so pleased to see us that we rather reluctantly accepted her invitation to come in. I do not know when I have enjoyed a literary shrine more. We saw the study where Sterne wrote the last part of *Tristram Shandy* and all of *A Sentimental Journey*. We peered at his bathing arrangements, admired his old furniture, and inspected the good first editions of our hostess.

"Are you a National Trust Museum?" we inquired respectfully; we took our new friend for an extremely competent professional. But she blushed with a modest and engaging delight when we called her a "guide."

"Oh, I just do this for the church. All we ladies are working for new altar fittings, and this is how I raise my share of the money. Instead of baking cakes."

Our hostess smiled. "Poetic justice," she said. (Sterne despised this church, and made no secret of his furious distaste for everything rural, especially Coxwold.)

"The ladies are going to be mighty surprised," the present owner of Shandy Hall remarked as we signed the visitors' book. "Nobody around here, makes anything of Sterne. They never heard of him. I tried to get the council to put up a sign, but they said, 'What for?' "

We wrote down New York City, U.S.A., and our hostess read the signature with satisfaction. "That makes two New Yorks and one Indiana already this week. And there was a young man on a bicycle. He was an Oxford student, and he said they thought highly of Sterne at the university."

So Richard added an enthusiastic testimonial to the visitors' book. However, when we tried to spread propaganda for Coxwold's world-famous author at the pub, we met a total defeat. "Oh, yes, writing fellow," the proprietor said politely. "We had a writer staying right here at the pub last summer. He used to go for long walks. He wrote with a typewriter."

More than Sterne did, I gathered. But perhaps it is as well there is no Sterne Industry. We stayed for lunch at the pub, and the waitress told us shyly there was only "plain farm cooking, if you want that. Yorkshire ham, and garden beans, and missus just baked a fresh apple tart." It makes me hungry yet to remember that lunch. When I think of what would happen to the farm cooking if tourists started coming in gross lots, perhaps it is better the council did not put up the sign.

Besides literary shrines, ruins, castles, Yorkshire has scenery, grand and dramatic. Wharfedale and Swaledale are the most picturesque of the famous dales, but our favorite stretch of Yorkshire was at Goathland, which has heather-covered moors. Goathland is within striking distance of Whitby, and other Yorkshire fishing villages, all of them most beautiful. Furthermore, unlike Cornwall, you can take a bus down to the fishing nets, and back up again—an important point!

Durham!

Durham is the most dramatic vision of the past in all England. The great *Norman* church, for centuries a fortress and holy shrine, stands, a massive black mountain of stone, high above a shadowed river valley. I am not sure if it is beautiful; it is not beautiful after the manner of Canterbury or Salisbury, let alone St. Paul's. It is crude and heavy; dark with time. It weighs on the heart. A primitive people, a few centuries away from a heathen, murdering past, raised these stones as a monument to a mysterious and terrifying God, made this fortress against an implacable and ferocious enemy. No Chaucer wrote poetry about Durham; no gaudy, cheerful pilgrims crowded up this steep hill to gossip, and pray a little, and buy souvenirs and admire the elegance of nave or choir. The pageantry of the medieval world disappears at Durham. It is easy to remember, looking across the river at those heavy towers, that the medieval world believed in death, not life.

The origins of the Cathedral are terrifying. There is a smiling, gentle quality about St. Augustine laying the first stones of the Saxon church at Canterbury. The old pictures show the King and his Christian Queen receiving the nervous saint under a spreading oak tree. Flowers bloom in the background; it is springtime in Kent, the sun shines fair on the Queen's long yellow tresses. The Canterbury legend begins with April.

But at Durham the beginning of the story is a black-cowled procession of monks, shown in the ancient tapestries, struggling up the bleak, naked rocks, backs bent low under the weight of a great coffin. At the summit, the monks put down their burden to warm their hands, frozen in the cruel wind of a Northumbrian winter. When they stoop once more to lift the long-dead body of their holy saint, a miracle has happened. The coffin has taken root. St. Cuthbert has come home; Durham must be his shrine.

So Durham begins with a cult of death. Some historians write with admiration of St. Cuthbert's posthumous migrations. But I think it is a horrible story of harsh mysticism; it has a childlike quality, an awful innocence. I use the word "childlike" exactly. Who has not heard little boys playing at war? "Zzzzzzzz— BOOM! All the people are dead and bloody! O.K.! Get out the next stick of atom bombs! We're coming in for the second run! ZZZZZZZZ—BANG! More people dead. All over! Everything blown up!"

Years will pass before the little boy who plays at atom bombs acquires his first true feeling of compassion. Patient teaching, endless words repeated endlessly by mother and father and schoolteacher, a thousand printed pages from Shakespeare, Dickens, Lincoln, the Bible, music heard, pictures seen, the climate of an adult culture, will (perhaps) transform the savage child into a civilized man. Wholly innocent of pity and mercy, unconscious of the meaning and sweetness of life, the little boy is fascinated by the drama of death.

In this sense, the story of St. Cuthbert's posthumous adventures is childlike; innocent and primitive.

St. Cuthbert himself was a mystic; monk and bishop both, he lived the last years of his life as a hermit. He died in 687 on the island of Lindisfarne, off the Northumbrian coast. In those early days saints appeared casually, abruptly. The moment Bishop Cuthbert was dead, the monks at the Lindisfarne monastery unanimously voted him a saint, and installed his body in a shrine. For some two hundred years pilgrims from the mainland rowed across the channel, or walked across the sands at low tide, to Lindisfarne, the Holy Isle. St. Cuthbert's saintly reputation grew apace. Miracles happened frequently during the pilgrimage season. Lindisfarne, like Mont St. Michel, grew rich. St. Cuthbert's shrine glittered with jewels, and his coffin was decorated with solid gold.

Prosperity was a misfortune. So much honey drew the marauders: the Danes came down out of the cold north seas. Lindisfarne was a rich prize, and Thor would surely applaud the attack on the big magic of the enemy Christians.

The first wave of Danes was beaten off, but the monks realized that Lindisfarne was untenable—too far from the mainland to allow an emergency retreat. The monks dug up St. Cuthbert's body and bore it across the sands to the Northumbrian shore. That was 875. For the next 120 years St. Cuthbert was carried up and down Northumbria; the monks were perpetually one foot ahead of the Danes, who plundered, looted, burned, and pursued the saintly shrine. At each fresh halt the brothers opened St. Cuthbert's coffin and solemnly examined the body, after which they pronounced it "incorruptible" and "sweetly smelling." The emphasis put on the condition of the saint's remains is macabre in the old chronicles. Fingernails were constantly being measured, and so on. With all this miracle mongering, the cult of St. Cuthbert had its downs as well as its ups. At one point during the 120 years, the body was dragged about Northumbria by a handful of mystics who were not even monks. The monastery system fell to pieces under the constant attacks of the Danes; in Northumbria, as in the rest of England, the Normans later refounded the monasteries which had been all but wiped out in the last uncertain years of Saxon rule.

In 995 an energetic Saxon bishop named Adhun took over St. Cuthbert's body, and migrated with it from Chester-le-Street to Durham, where it was announced that St. Cuthbert had come to stay. The first cathedral at Durham was consecrated in 999; in 1006, the Scots attacked. For the next 597 years, Durham Cathedral held Northumbria against the northern enemy.

The Cathedral has been much changed, restored, altered, rebuilt; yet its primitive, magic character remains. You do not so much see the immense, colored, carved *Norman* piers in the Durham nave as feel them. The *Norman* in the south of England is not like this; Durham is cruder, older, almost barbaric. To walk from the bustling modern city of Durham, to climb from the local Woolworth's up the hill to the rock, across the lawn, and into the nave of the cathedral is a shock. If you once see this dark stone monument to the past, you will remember it always.

Blanchland has the same haunting quality; Richard and I have seen scores of pretty English villages, but I remember every house in the square at Blanchland. I see the hills yet, rising behind the gray stone gates.

Blanchland was once a rich monastery. It was partly de-

stroyed by the Scots. At the Dissolution, the monastery buildings were bought by a local squire, and today the little village
is still the shape of the original cloisters; the post office occupies
the monastery gates, the villagers live in the monks' quarters,
the parish church occupies the choir of the minster ruins, and
a hotel does business in the abbot's house.

If you are driving around, you can make Blanchland your
headquarters, both for Durham, and, in the opposite direction,
for Hexham and Housesteads.

Hexham is a lonely little town in the Northumberland hills;
time has moved slowly across the market place and ancient
abbey.

All the same, I do not suppose Richard and I would have
lingered long in Hexham; we were on our way to the Roman
Wall. We had seen a good many churches, and after Durham,
we thought Hexham Abbey would be an anticlimax. However,
at the market place traffic light, our rented car had a physical
collapse—something mysterious and dreadful, we feared. The
Hexham garage spent all morning repairing it. We loitered
around the market square for a few minutes, and having nothing else to do, looked in on Hexham Abbey.

The nave was modern, a good reproduction of *Early English*,
but after all—!

At the transept crossing, we stood still and blinked. Nobody
had told us that Hexham Abbey was extraordinarily beautiful.
When we got back to London, we discovered that, like King's
Lynn, it was famous; everybody knew about it, and either had
been, or was going to see it.

But, for us, Hexham Abbey was a moment of delight. After
Durham, it was a revelation of the poetry of the human spirit.
For Durham is impressive, but forbidding. Hexham Abbey, on
a much smaller scale, has the lyrical warmth of Canterbury.
It is English Gothic at its most graceful and fanciful. It is a
whole world away from the death cult of Durham; it is the
medieval mind, learning, reaching out, experimenting, throwing up dizzy arches, making ornamented lace out of stone.

At Hexham Abbey was Mr. W. T. Taylor, clerk and verger,
archaeologist and scholar, impassioned guide, and the man who

let Richard help wind up the Hexham clock. Among other items.

Mr. Taylor was winding the clock (the weights are worked on pulleys, it is a complicated and athletic operation) when the cleaning woman bawled up the church tower that two tourists wanted to buy the guide. We could hear Mr. Taylor growl-tourists, when he was winding the clock!

"Never mind!" we yelled up the tower. We were embarrassed to make the verger come all the way down the winding steps to sell us a guide.

Mr. Taylor abandoned his weights and arrived in the transept in what we correctly diagnosed as an irritable mood. Richard winced, apologized profusely. "So terribly sorry...."

"Humph!" Mr. Taylor said.

I felt a little nervous. "Uh ... the cleaning lady says you have the key to the crypt. We ... uh ... wondered if we could see the Saxon foundations?"

The expression on Mr. Taylor's face changed. "You are interested in architecture?"

We said we were tourists, but surely Hexham Abbey was a most beautiful *Transitional* and *Early English* church? It reminded us in many ways of Canterbury....

"Ah," Mr. Taylor said. "Of course Canterbury is beautiful, but personally, I like our Abbey better. I may be prejudiced, but ..."

We had, I think, the happiest morning in our English travels with Mr. Taylor. He was that most perfect of guides, a scholar who took the trouble and time to explain details and fundamentals to the layman. He knew the history of every Abbey stone; he loved this beautiful church with a passion that he caused us to share. He began at the beginning, with the Saxon foundations, showed us the Roman markings on the stones that the ancient Northumbrians had dug out of the ruins. About ten-thirty he remembered the clock, so we all went up to the tower, and helped wind it. Then we came back down the giddy spiral stairs and inspected an early Saxon saint Mr. Taylor had helped dig up from the stones under the medieval choir. This saint was buried beyond the Saxon church walls; he was excommunicated when he died, but later he started to do miracles, so it was thought there must have been some mistake. The reason he was excommunicated was shocking: he was so eager to make Hexham Abbey the most beautiful church in the north that he sold the bones of the local Hexham saint— to the Scots.

Mr. Taylor shook his head. "That was going too far."

Everything in Hexham Abbey is exciting, but perhaps the most touching treasure is a Roman gravestone. The ancient slab shows a Roman warrior charging into battle on his horse. Crouching under the horse's forelegs is a savage Briton—he looks like a Fuzzy-Wuzzy, or an Australian Bushman, and the sculptor carved him in the moment of piercing horse and rider with a primitive spear. The words carved beneath this long-ago tragedy are: "To the Gods, the shades, Flavinus of the Cavalry Regiment of Petriana, a standard bearer of the White Troop, aged 25, and of seven years service, is here buried."

The Roman Wall runs across all the north of England. At Housesteads, a Roman outpost has been excavated, and you may see the ruined storehouse, the little shops, the governor's house, the soldiers' barracks; finally, there is a plank across the broken stones, and you walk onto the Wall itself.

The dark hills stretch over the horizon; the wide sky is blurred bluey-gray where England ends.

Flavinus saw these hills from this wall as he stood guard against the barbarians; and there he died, defending a civilization which seemed all in all to him, but which perished, and was lost and forgotten, and was followed by another world, another flowering of the human spirit.

In the autumn sunlight under the Northumbrian sky, Richard and I looked out over the hills to Scotland. Flavinus stood here before us; we were reminded that others would come here after us.

England is an old land, and immortal. Its spell is strong, its magic enduring. We came here after Flavinus, and others will stand in our place, thinking of

> This royal throne of kings, this scepter'd isle,
> This earth of majesty, this seat of Mars,
> This other Eden, demi-paradise,

This fortress built by Nature for herself
Against infection and the hand of war,
This happy breed of men, this little world,
This precious stone set in the silver sea,
Which serves it in the office of a wall,
Or as a moat defensive to a house,
Against the envy of less happier lands,
This blessed plot, this earth, this realm, this England. . . .

These are the words of William Shakespeare, an Englishman. We Americans have inherited his language, as we have learned, however brief our journey, to love his homeland.

WHAT TO SEE IN THE NORTH

GOING NORTH TO YORK:
* ** *Boston.* See text.
* *** *Lincoln.* See text.
* ** *Selby.* Fourteen miles south of York, has a magnificent abbey church.
* ** *Beverley.* East of York. We liked the lovely Minster as well as any great church in England.
* *** *York.* See text.

YORKSHIRE (arranged in a circular tour from York):
* *Bridlington.* A dismal seaside resort, but the old town is pleasant, and has a fine priory church. From Bridlington north to and far past Whitby is one of the most striking sections of the whole English seacoast. For scenery, we preferred this to Cornwall and almost as much as Northumberland. On the way up the coast is:
* ** *Robin Hood's Bay.* A picturesque fishing village. You can buy fresh lobster after the catch comes in at noon. Cooked in pots by the fishermen. Very good.
* ** *Whitby.* A gay, colorful seaport with ruins on a cliff and sailboats at the docks.
* ** *Runswick Bay* and *Staithes.* North of Whitby, enchanting Yorkshire villages on the sea. We became hardened to "quaint" fishing resorts, but these two we recommend. From Whitby to our beloved:
* *** *Goathland.* See text. After you tear yourself away from the

moors at Goathland, onward to Helmsley, and three miles more for:

★★★ *Rievaulx Abbey.* Our favorite ruin. See text. From Rievaulx, buses run to:

Oswaldkirk. Very nice.

Ampleforth. Pleasant.

★ *Byland Abbey.* Ruins.

★★ *Coxwold.* A wonderful Yorkshire village of stone, with a remarkable church, pub, and Laurence Sterne's Shandy Hall. See text. Now on to:

Ripon. Which has a good cathedral and many tourists. The wakeman blows a horn every night in Ripon at nine o'clock. Quaint, or perhaps edifying is more accurate. From Ripon it is four miles to:

★★★ *Fountains Abbey.* The stars are a bow to public opinion; frankly we feel like ★★½ for Fountains because of the tremendous crowds. After Fountains, you go from Ripon to:

Harrogate. A modern spa, and four miles more for:

Knaresborough. A synthetic, tourist-made, fourteenth-century town, complete with castle and "Dropping Well." This well drops limestone water on objects such as a gentleman's comic hat or a baby's chair, and petrifies them. It sounds a silly thing to see, and it is, but we liked it anyway. A change from ruins and grandeur. From Harrogate, you may go sixteen miles toward Leeds to:

Kirkstall Abbey. Considered "fine" but unfortunately is surrounded by factories and coal smoke. Probably from Harrogate the best plan is to go via:

★ *Blubberhouses.* Which we liked very much, wonderful name, good moors, to:

★★★ *Bolton Abbey.* As a confirmed non-admirer of ruined abbeys, I admit this is wonderful. The scenery is lovely. The nearby Strid is not recommended. See text. Now from Bolton Abbey to:

★ *Skipton.* Which has a good castle, and sixteen miles more to:

★ *Haworth.* Home of the Brontës. See text. After Haworth, you can either return to York, or go on through Giggleswick (wonderful), Clapham, and Ingleton (some of the best scenery in Yorkshire), to Hawes. At Hawes you are in:

** *Wensleydale.* Which we thought the most spectacular of the Yorkshire dales.

* *Swaledale.* Also beautiful, and remote.

* *Richmond.* A charming town with a fine castle. From Richmond you could return to York, or go straight north to:

*** *Durham.* See text. West of Durham is Teesdale and the town of Barnard Castle, both interesting, and northwest are:

*** *Blanchland.* See text.

** *Hexham.* See text. From Hexham, you visit the Roman Wall at:

*** *Housesteads.* Near *Chollerford.* Then on to:

* *Alnwick.* A bleak old town with fine churches and a splendid castle. From Alnwick, head up the Northumberland seacoast, black and dark and wild, and dotted with craggy castles, especially at:

* *Bamburgh.* Where the Norman keep frowns over the whole barren seacoast. Still farther north is:

** *Lindisfarne.* The Holy Isle. This is two and a half miles off the coast, reached at low tide by walking or driving over the sands. I thought it was romantic, but the actual ruins on Lindisfarne are small potatoes compared to the glories of the mainland. Do not expect a second Mont St. Michel.

* *Berwick-on-Tweed.* The capital of the Border Wars, and its Elizabethan walls command a historic view. The bridges across the Tweed are famous. Going down the Tweed from Berwick, you come to:

* *Norham.* Another fine castle. Nearby is:

** *Flodden Field.* The scene of the tragic battle in 1513. Farther on is:

* *Chillingham Castle.* In the beautiful Cheviot hills. The Castle has a herd of wild white cattle, the last in England.

PART III: SIGHTSEERS' HANDY KEY TO
HISTORY AND ARCHITECTURE

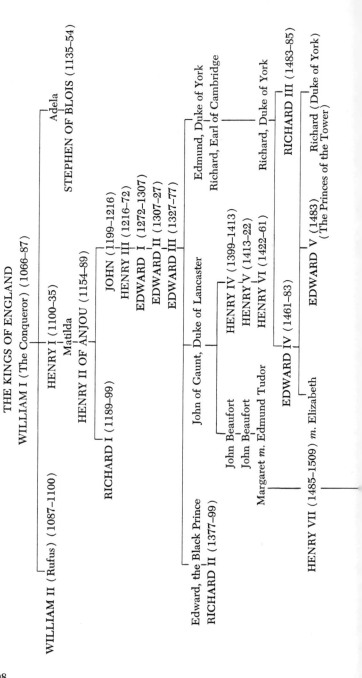

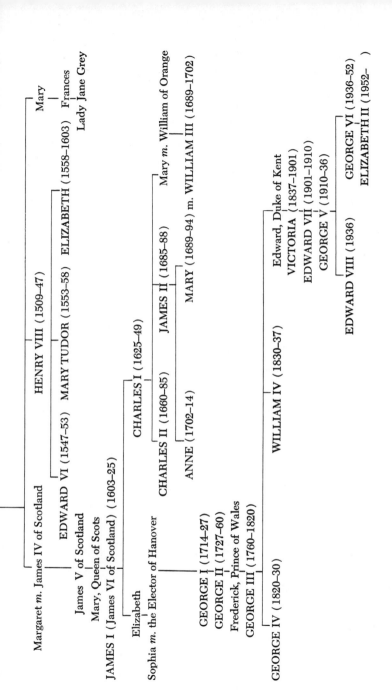

MASTER CHART OF ENGLISH HISTORY

ANGLO-SAXON KINGS	NOTABLE DATES IN ENGLISH ARCHITECTURE AND LITERATURE	CONTEMPORARY RULERS AND EVENTS
Reign *Married*		
ALFRED THE GREAT 871- 899 Alfred saved Anglo-Saxon civilization from the Danes. Thereafter, he turned to raising the standards of religion and culture among his people.	Alfred's Translation of *The History* by the Venerable Bede.	936-73—Otto the Great, founder of the Holy Roman Empire.
EDWARD THE ELDER 899- 925 AETHELSTAN 925- 939 EDMUND 939- 946 EDRED 946- 955 EDWY 955- 959 EDGAR THE PEACEABLE 959- 975 EDWARD THE MARTYR 975- 979 ETHELRED THE UNREADY 979-1016 In 980 the Danes again invaded England and imposed heavy tribute, which was transferred to the people in the form of a burdensome tax known as the *Danegeld*.	*Anglo-Saxon Chronicle*.	1000—Leif Ericsson of Iceland sailed with Norsemen, discovered the North American continent (Vinland).
EDMUND 1016 CANUTE THE DANE 1016-1035 HAROLD HAREFOOT 1035-1040 HARDICANUTE 1040-1042 EDWARD THE CONFESSOR 1042-1066 Edward was half Norman, the son of the Unready. He was neither as weak nor as wise as he is sometimes pictured. His passion was the building of Westminster Abbey.	1050—Early Norman Architecture. 1052—Westminster Abbey begun.	1056-1106—Emperor Henry IV.
HAROLD 1066 Harold was defeated at Hastings by William the Bastard, Duke of Normandy. For two centuries thereafter, England was ruled by foreign kings.		

NORMAN KINGS

WILLIAM THE CONQUEROR 1066-1087 Matilda of Flanders. William crushed the Saxon rebels and broke up the English earldoms, building the power of the King.

WILLIAM II (Rufus) 1087-1100
The Conqueror's son had no principles at all. Immoral and blasphemous, his chief interest was to collect funds for his private dissipation. Rufus was killed while hunting in the New Forest—his death is a mystery: was he murdered by William Tyrell?

HENRY I (Beauclerc) 1100-1135 Matilda of Scotland
Younger brother of Rufus, he crushed a revolt of the barons at Tinchebrai (1106) in Normandy. His hobby was efficient government.

STEPHEN OF BLOIS 1135-1154 Matilda of Boulogne
The succession was disputed by Henry I's daughter Matilda, and Stephen, son of the Conqueror's daughter Adela. Stephen was crowned king by the nobles. Civil war ensued sporadically. A time of anarchy and uncertainty.

ANGEVIN KINGS OR PLANTAGENETS

HENRY II (of Anjou) 1154-1189 Eleanor of Aquitaine
Henry II, son of Matilda and grandson of Henry I, was vigorous, energetic, active of mind and body, married to the most accomplished lady of the Middle Ages. His reforms had an immense influence on English life and character. A blot on his reputation is the murder of Thomas Becket, Archbishop of Canterbury, with whom Henry quarreled and who was struck down at the altar by nobles who sought to ingratiate themselves with Henry.

1083-1189—Ely Cathedral built.

1100—Mature Norman architecture.
1093-1133—Durham Cathedral built.

1150—Transition to Gothic Style.

1167-68—Oxford University founded.
1174—Choir of Canterbury Cathedral built.
1176-1209—London Bridge built (stood till 1832).

1073-85—Pope Gregory VII (Hildebrand).

1096-99—The First Crusade.
1100-87—Kingdom of Jerusalem.

1106-25—Emperor Henry V.

1147-49—The Second Crusade.

1152-90—Emperor Frederick I, Barbarossa (died on the Third Crusade).

MASTER CHART OF ENGLISH HISTORY

Reign	Married	NOTABLE DATES IN ENGLISH ARCHITECTURE AND LITERATURE	CONTEMPORARY RULERS AND EVENTS
RICHARD I (Cœur de Lion) 1189-1199	Berengaria of Navarre		1180-1223—Phillip II (Augustus) of France.
Richard, Henry's son, was a brave leader of the Third Crusade, a sensitive poet, a musician, but he took almost no interest in England, and spent hardly any time in his island possession.			1189-93—The Third Crusade. 1202-04—The Fourth Crusade. 1208—Pope Innocent III places England and Wales under the Interdict, greatly increases the power of the Papacy.
JOHN (Lackland) 1199-1216	Avisa of Gloucester Isabella of Provence	1200—Early English Gothic style.	1212—The Children's Crusade.
John, Richard's brother, is considered the worst of English kings. He waged war on France, murdered his little nephew Arthur, and so aroused public opinion that he met with disastrous defeats in France. He quarreled with Pope Innocent III over the appointment of Stephen Langton as Archbishop of Canterbury, and was forced to give way. He aroused the nobles to move against him and was forced to sign an agreement with them at Runnymede (1215)—the Magna Carta, which granted freedom from taxation levied without consent of the nobles, and the right to trial by jury.		1209-1235—Nave of Lincoln Cathedral built. 1214-1235—Nave of Wells Cathedral built.	1215—Genghis Khan conquers China.
HENRY III 1216-1272	Eleanor of Provence	1250—Transition to Decorative Gothic style. 1258-60—Thomas Aquinas, *Summa Contra Gentiles*. 1284—Peterhouse, first Cambridge college, founded.	1228-29—The Fifth Crusade. 1233—Inquisition established in Spain by Pope Gregory IX. 1248-1254—The Sixth Crusade under Louis IX (St. Louis) of France.
John's nine-year-old son, Henry III, grew into a weak, devout well-meaning incompetent. His reign was plagued by revolts of the barons, particularly that faction led by Simon de Montfort, Earl of Leicester. The institution of Parliament had its beginnings at this time.			1255-69—Marco Polo's first trip to China.
EDWARD I 1272-1307	Eleanor of Castile	1300—Mature Decorative Gothic style.	
Edward, son of Henry, was the first truly English king. He wanted a united Britain, and did much to achieve this end. He conquered Wales and a part of Scotland.			

EDWARD II 1307-1327 Isabella of France
Indolent, irresponsible, Edward II was intensely unpopular. He lost Scotland to Robert Bruce. His wife, Isabella, fell in love with Mortimer, a young exiled nobleman who led an army against Edward. The King fled; later he was captured by Mortimer's forces and murdered by his order.

EDWARD III 1327-1377 Philippa of Hainault
In 1330, Edward III had his father's murderer, Mortimer, beheaded. Edward was not a great statesman, but he was a well-liked king, particularly successful during the first half of his long reign. In 1338 the Hundred Years' War commenced, with its initial great victories for the English at Crécy (1346) and Poitiers (1356), under the leadership of Edward's young son, the Black Prince. But Edward's reign also saw the horror of the Black Death.

RICHARD II 1377-1399 Anne of Luxembourg
Son of the Black Prince, Richard was vacillating and unstable. His reign saw frequent revolts of the nobles; Richard was finally deposed by his cousin, Henry Bolingbroke. Richard died in prison. The peasants revolted early in his reign, under the leadership of Wat Tyler, but were violently and cruelly suppressed.

HOUSE OF LANCASTER

HENRY IV 1399-1413 Mary Bohun
Most of the usurper's efforts were taken up with retaining the throne. To keep the support of the nobles, Henry gave them new lands and allowed them to act as they liked, thus weakening the authority of the Crown. Owen Glendower's revolt in Wales; saga of the Percys in border warfare.

HENRY V 1413-1422 Katherine of France
As Prince of Wales (Shakespeare's "Prince Hal"), Henry was a grim, stern-looking young man, intelligent and cold-hearted. To strengthen his grip on the throne, he decided

---

1320-84–John Wycliff, translator of the Bible into English.

1350–Transition to Perpendicular Gothic style.

1387-1400–Chaucer: *Canterbury Tales*.

1400–Mature Perpendicular style.

1415–Thomas à Kempis: *De Imitatione Christi*.

1260-94–Kubla Khan rules China.
1295–First regular English Parliament.
1314-21–Dante's *Divine Comedy*.

1328-50–Philip VI of France.
1348–The Black Death devastates Europe.
1348-53–Boccaccio's *Decameron*.
1360–Birth of Richard Whittington, thrice Mayor of London.

1381–Wat Tyler's Rebellion.

1415–John Huss burned at Constance by order of Pope Alexander V.

MASTER CHART OF ENGLISH HISTORY

Reign / *Married*	NOTABLE DATES IN ENGLISH ARCHITECTURE AND LITERATURE	CONTEMPORARY RULERS AND EVENTS
on war with France. At the battle of Agincourt (1415) the English showed the immense superiority of the longbow over knights in armor. By the Treaty of Troyes (1420), Henry married the daughter of Charles VI of France, and was acknowledged heir to the French throne.		
HENRY VI 1422–1461 *Margaret of Anjou* Henry VI was but a few weeks old when his father died and he became king. He never really grew up. Events in France changed: Joan of Arc inspired the French to resist the English, and by 1438 the English retained only Normandy and Guienne. The weakness of the English King, who had spells of madness, placed power in a council where the members quarreled among themselves. England was plagued by anarchy, similar to that during Stephen's time. English arms suffered; the Hundred Years' War dragged to an end, with the English holding on in Calais—all of France that remained to them.	1446–1515—King's College Chapel, Cambridge, built.	1431—Joan of Arc burned by the English at Rouen. 1453—Constantinople taken by the Turks. 1453–55—Gutenberg's *Bible*.
## HOUSE OF YORK **EDWARD IV** 1461–1483 *Elizabeth Woodville* The Wars of the Roses (between the House of York and Lancaster) was primarily a struggle between two groups of nobles for power. Edward IV, great-great-grandson of Edward III, seized power for the faction of the White Rose, locked Henry VI in the Tower, and confiscated all Lancaster properties. But Edward fell out with his most powerful supporter, Warwick, who dragged poor old Henry VI from the Tower, and placed him on the Throne	1460–83—St. George's Chapel, Windsor, built. 1476—Caxton establishes printing press at Westminster.	1461–83—̃ouis XI of France. 1469–150₄—Ferdinand and Isabella of Spain as joint rulers.

in 1471, and ruled in his name. Warwick was slain in battle; Henry VI's son also fell, and the old King was murdered in the Tower. Edward IV reigned undisturbed for the next twelve years.

RICHARD III   1483-1485   Anne Neville

Edward IV died young, leaving the Throne to his twelve-year-old son, Edward V. But his father's brother, Richard, Duke of Gloucester, took the boy and his little brother away by force, and after accusing the Princes of not being eligible for the Throne due to some irregularity in Edward IV's marriage, Richard had the two young Princes murdered in the Tower. This so shocked both factions of Lancaster and York, that they joined to support Henry Tudor, Earl of Richmond, who, with the backing of the King of France, landed in England accompanied by an army. At Bosworth, Richard III was defeated and killed—and the Wars of the Roses ended.

HOUSE OF TUDOR (York and Lancaster united)

HENRY VII   1485-1509   Elizabeth of York

The accession of Henry VII is taken as the dividing line between medieval and modern times. Henry himself was neither lovable nor noble in personality, but he was shrewd and far-sighted. He rigorously put down the remaining flickers of civil war, and kept the nobles in their place by giving greater power to the court of the Star Chamber, which had jurisdiction over the powerful landholders. In foreign policy, Henry avoided war, attempted to break the alliance between France and Scotland, and built up the wool trade with the Netherland towns of Ghent, Bruges, and Ypres.

1484—Bull by Pope Innocent VIII condemning witchcraft.

1485—Malory: *Morte d'Arthur*.
1500-60—Tudor style in Architecture.

1492—Columbus discovers the New World.
1497—Vasco da Gama rounds the Cape of Good Hope.
1498—John Cabot and son discover Canada and claim the territory for England. Savonarola burned in Florence.
1503-13—Pope Julius II.

MASTER CHART OF ENGLISH HISTORY

	Reign	*Married*	NOTABLE DATES IN ENGLISH ARCHITECTURE AND LITERATURE	CONTEMPORARY RULERS AND EVENTS
HENRY VIII	1509–1547	Catherine of Aragon (divorced) Anne Boleyn (beheaded) Jane Seymour (died in childbirth) Anne of Cleves (divorced) Catherine Howarl (beheaded) Catherine Parr (survived)	1515–Hampton Court built. 1516–Thomas More's *Utopia.* 1525–Tyndale's translation of the New Testament. 1525–Wolsey founds Christ Church (re-endowed–1546). 1535–First English Bible translated and published by Miles Coverdale.	1513–Balboa discovers the Pacific; Ponce de Leon lands in Florida. 1515–47–Francis I of France. 1516–56–Emperor Charles V. 1519–27–Cortez in Mexico. 1520–Magellan sights the strait bearing his name. 1521–Luther excommunicated by Diet of Worms. 1523–34–Pope Clement VII. 1529–Suleiman II defeated at Vienna. 1532–34–Pizarro in Peru. 1534–Society of Jesus organized by Ignatius Loyola. 1541–Calvin in Geneva. 1545–Council of Trent condemns heresies of Calvin and Luther.

"Prince Hal" inherited from his father a united England, a full treasury, and increased power for the Throne. He was tall, handsome, accomplished in sports, poetry, and musical composition. His wars against France led to no success, but he managed to prevent England's enemies, Spain and France, from uniting against his kingdom. Henry brooked no opposition—as seen by his executions of his father's extortionate ministers, Empson and Dudley, his throwing out of Cardinal Wolsey, his executions of Thomas Cromwell, Sir Thomas More, and John Fisher. In the dispute with Pope Clement VII over his divorce of Catherine of Aragon (Henry sought, among other things, a male heir), Henry was led from petitioning for a decree to a break with the Roman Church. He became head of the Church of England, uniting Church and State. In his struggles against the Pope, Henry confiscated Church lands and property, greatly augmenting the wealth and power of the Crown.

EDWARD VI 1547–1553
Henry's son by Jane Seymour was ten years old at accession. The country was ruled by Lord Protectors—Edward Seymour, Duke of Somerset, and then Warwick, Duke of Northumberland. Somerset was incompetent. He failed in his war against Scotland, and he failed to put down Kett's Rebellion. Northumberland took over by force.

MARY I 1553–1558 Philip, King of Spain
When the boy Edward VI died, Northumberland planned to hold power by crowning Lady Jane Grey as Queen. Mary was supported by the people and easily took the Throne. Daughter of Catherine of Aragon, she was a fanatic Catholic. She was able to suppress Wyatt's Rebellion, but then unleashed a reign of terror to restore Roman Catholicism that earned her the sobriquet of "Bloody Mary." Among those executed by the jealous and obsessed Queen were Lady Jane Grey, Latimer, Ridley, Cranmer, and three hundred persons, young and old, men and women. During her reign England lost its last foothold in France, and abandoned Calais.

ELIZABETH I 1558–1603
The "Virgin Queen," daughter of Anne Boleyn, faced three dangers as she opened the English high Renaissance: the claim of Mary, Queen of Scots, for the Throne; religious strife engendered by her predecessor and half-sister, Mary Tudor; and foreign invasion. In policy was one of procrastination where possible. In the end, Elizabeth beheaded her cousin Mary of Scotland; she compromised on the religious question; and she avoided war with Philip of Spain—until he sent the Spanish Armada to England. Elizabeth fomented strife among her foreign enemies, subdued Ireland (earning the everlasting resentment of the

1555–Bishops Ridley of London and Latimer of Worcester burned at Oxford.
1556–Archbishop Cranmer of Canterbury burned.
1556–98–Philip I of Spain.

1555–60–Gray's Inn Hall built Renaissance in Architecture.

1559–65–Pope Pius IV.
1560–74–Charles IX of France.
1566–72–Pope Pius V.
1572–85–Pope Gregory XIII.
1572–St. Bartholomew's Day Massacre in France.
1579–Drake goes ashore in California.
1584–Raleigh's first expedition to Virginia.
1585–90–Pope Sixtus V.
1587–Mary, Queen of Scots,

1560–1600–Elizabethan style.
1562–*Gorboduc:* First English tragedy in blank verse.
1562–72–Middle Temple Hall built.
1579–North's *Plutarch.*
1581–Sidney: *Defence of Poesy.*
1589–Marlowe: *Dr. Faustus.*
1590–96–Spenser: *The Faerie Queene.*
1593–*Venus and Adonis.*

Reign / *Married*	NOTABLE DATES IN ENGLISH ARCHITECTURE AND LITERATURE	CONTEMPORARY RULERS AND EVENTS

people of that country), and when she felt sufficiently powerful, began stamping out Catholic dissidents at home. The Queen showed steadfast courage before the great dangers to the Kingdom. England was born as a great nation.

HOUSE OF STUART

JAMES I 1603–1625 Anne of Denmark

James I of England (James VI of Scotland) was the great-great-grandson of Henry VII and the son of Mary, Queen of Scots. Pedantic and vain, he stubbornly insisted on the doctrine of divine right, which held that sovereigns received their authority from God and were therefore above criticism. Moreover, James considered himself adept at "kingcraft." During his reign, James's craft weakened the Crown in its struggle with the rising merchants and country gentlemen by attempting to ignore the power of Parliament. James won the hatred of the Puritans by his highhanded expulsion of Nonconformist clergymen from their livings, and of the Catholics by failing to live up to promises of not molesting those who remained loyal subjects—but the Catholic plot, led by Guy Fawkes, to blow up Parliament and the King did not help the Roman cause. James wooed Spain, hoping to marry his son to the Spanish Catholic Queen. The failure of his matchmaking, however, brought on war with Spain instead.

CHARLES I 1625–1649 Henrietta of France

James's son Charles was dignified and spirited, with an obstinate belief in divine right. He was also a High

NOTABLE DATES IN ENGLISH ARCHITECTURE AND LITERATURE

1597—Bacon's *Essays*.
1600–20—Jacobean style in architecture.

1603—*Hamlet*.
1607—Jonson: *Volpone*.
1611—King James (Authorized) Version of the Bible.
1612—*The Tempest*.
1617–18—Bodleian Library built.
1621—Burton: *The Anatomy of Melancholy*.
1620–60—Inigo Jones dominates English architecture.
1623—Shakespeare's first folio published.

1628—Harvey's treatise on circulation of the blood.
1633—Donne's, Herbert's and

CONTEMPORARY RULERS AND EVENTS

executed.
1588—The Spanish Armada is dispersed.
1589–1610—Henry IV of Navarre, King of France.
1602–4—Galileo's laws of motion.

1605—The Gunpowder Plot of Guy Fawkes.
1607—Jamestown, Virginia, settled.
1610–11—Henry Hudson explores Hudson Bay.
1610–43—Louis XIII of France.
1619–37—Emperor Ferdinand II.
1620—Pilgrims land at Plymouth Rock.

Churchman; most members of Parliament believed he was a Roman Catholic at heart and feared his adviser George Villiers, Duke of Buckingham. Parliament refused to grant Charles the right to collect customs duties for a longer period than a year (until then sanctioned for an entire reign). Charles dissolved Parliament. He became involved in wars with Spain and France which he was unable to prosecute for lack of funds. His attempt to raise taxes without Parliamentary sanction was disastrous. Parliament, summoned, grew increasingly critical and hostile to the King's arbitrary rule, until in 1629 Charles dismissed Parliament and decided to rule without the legislature. At the same time he appointed William Laud as Archbishop of Canterbury to cleanse the country of Puritanism (which led to the flight of Puritans to New England). Charles's one remaining chance of preventing an upheaval in the nation was to win the trust of the Parliament. Instead of which, he attempted to arrest five leading members of the Commons; failing that, after a period of wrangling, Charles raised his banner at Nottingham in 1642, pledged to overthrow Parliamentary rule.

THE CIVIL WAR 1642-1646

For four years, civil war raged between Charles and his Cavalier supporters, and Parliament. At first, Charles gained the advantage. But the Scots, fearing a royal victory would mean the imposition of the Episcopal Church, offered support to Parliament, entering into the Solemn Covenant, which pledged protection to the Presbyterian Church in Scotland and the imposition of this church on England. At the same time English were reorganized by Oliver Cromwell, a Puritan gentleman farmer. The New Model Army of professionals emerged, sworn to preserve complete freedom for all

Cowley's poems published.
1635—Sir Thomas Browne: *Religio Medici.*
1637—Milton: *Lycidas.*

1646—Vaughan's and Crashaw's poems published.

1648—Herrick: *Hesperides.*

1643-1715—Louis XVI of France.

MASTER CHART OF ENGLISH HISTORY

Reign	NOTABLE DATES IN ENGLISH ARCHITECTURE AND LITERATURE	CONTEMPORARY RULERS AND EVENTS

Married

forms of Puritan worship. Within six months Cromwell and Fairfax, commander of the New Model, won the war against the King. Charles surrendered to the Scots, who handed him over to Parliament in return for money due them for support during the war. Parliament, now in the hands of a narrow Presbyterian majority, again persuaded the Scots to attack, this time against the New Model Army which was considered too tolerant in religious matters. Cromwell seized the King from Parliament: Charles made the mistake of continuing secret negotiations for his escape. Parliament condemned Charles to death. The King was executed in Whitehall in 1649.

1644–Manchu Dynasty in Peking.

1648–Treaty of Westphalia.

THE COMMONWEALTH 1649-1653

Struggling against a hesitant and increasingly fearful Parliament, Cromwell eliminated the House of Lords and purged the Commons of weak and hostile elements. After the death of the King, the Army formed a government, setting up a "Rump" Parliament, which ruled through the strength of the New Model Army. Cromwell left for Ireland, where a Catholic faction had plunged the country into anarchy; with terrible bloodshed, Cromwell conquered Ireland and imposed his rule. The Scots also revolted; Cromwell transferred the Army to Scotland, then crushed opposition at Worcester, and forced Prince Charles, son of the beheaded King, to flee to France. The Rump Parliament, resenting Army influence, attempted to call a general election, which Cromwell felt would result in a royalist victory. He dispersed Parlia-

1651–Hobbes: *Leviathan.*
1653–Walton: *The Compleat Angler.*

ment. In the only foreign war of the period, waged against Dutch maritime power and rival commerce, Cromwell won a favorable peace.

THE PROTECTORATE 1653-1660

OLIVER CROMWELL   1653-1658   Elizabeth Bourchier
The Army Council devised a system of government based on a Lord Protector and an elected House of Commons. Cromwell as Protector was able, tolerant, and farseeing, though the struggle between Army and Parliament, which Cromwell was unable to resolve, continued and the Protector was forced to rely on Army strength. His victories over Spain helped drive the Spanish from the Lowlands. He restored the House of Lords, granted wide religious freedom, and instituted other reforms.

RICHARD CROMWELL   1658-1659   Dorothy Mayor
The constitution of the Protectorate granted Cromwell the right to name his successor, and he nominated his intelligent oldest son, Richard. But the generals, afraid of a civilian, tried to limit Richard's powers, and the young man resigned office and returned to private life. There followed months of uncertainty. The country was now tired of New Model Army domination. From Scotland, General Monk led an invasion of England. The New Model Army fell apart; and a new Parliament was elected. This body sent an invitation to Prince Charles to assume the Throne, on condition that all who supported the Republican government would be pardoned, no confiscation of Republican lands would be sanctioned, religious freedom would be upheld, and the King would respect Parliament's power.

1658-1705—
Emperor Leopold I.

1659—Pepys begins his diaries.

311

THE HOUSE OF STUART	NOTABLE DATES IN ENGLISH ARCHITECTURE AND LITERATURE	CONTEMPORARY RULERS AND EVENTS

Reign   *Married*

CHARLES II   1660–1685   Catherine of Portugal
The son of Charles I was shrewd, cynical, charming. He was greeted with enthusiasm by a nation persuaded that he would bring peace and order. Much influenced by his chief adviser, the cautious Lord Clarendon, Charles hanged all who had directly participated in the beheading of his father; but he protested against Parliament's "Code of Clarendon," which persecuted religious minorities, in particular the Dissenters. Plague, the Fire of London, and defeat in the Second Dutch War forced Clarendon to resign and go abroad. The rising threat of France under Louis XIV persuaded England to reverse its policy and form the Triple Alliance with Sweden and the Dutch against French aggression in the Netherlands. But Charles still had hopes of freeing himself from Parliamentary control and of liberating the Catholics. He entered into the Dover Plot, wherein he accepted a secret subsidy from Louis XIV in return for joining Louis in an attack on the Dutch. The combined assault failed; Parliament was alarmed by the discovery of the Popish Plot; persecution of Catholics became hysterical; and there was an attempt to bar Charles's brother, heir to the Throne, from accession.

1660–1723—Sir Christopher Wren is the leading architect creating a school of followers.
1666–Dryden: *Annus Mirabilis.*
1667–Milton: *Paradise Lost.*
1678–Bunyan: *Pilgrim's Progress.*
1681–Dryden: *Absalom and Achitophel.*

1665-1700–Charles II of Spain.
1665–The Great Plague.
1666–The Great Fire of London.
1679–Habeas Corpus Act passed Parliament.

JAMES II   1685–1688   Anne Hyde
Charles's brother James was a vain and overbearing man. But on his accession, the hysteria of the past years died down, and though James was known to be a Catholic, it

1687–Isaac Newton: *Principia.*

was believed he would uphold the law. Unfortunately, James had a talent for ineptness. While he was able to repress Monmouth's Rebellion—the attempt to place a Protestant on the Throne—his reprisals during the Bloody Assizes were shocking to all factions. Since James insisted on pursuing his policy of persecuting Protestants, a group of leading men invited Mary, James's daughter and her husband, William, Prince of Orange, to invade England and take the Crown. William received enthusiastic support from most Englishmen. James and his wife fled to France.

WILLIAM III   1689–1702

MARY II   1689–1694

The new King and Queen ruled jointly as constitutional monarchs—the Sovereign was forbidden to act in defiance of Parliament. Scotland accepted the new monarchs, but William III was forced to lead troops against James II in Ireland, and only after a difficult campaign and a protracted struggle was Ireland subdued. There followed the expensive and hard-fought wars against Louis XIV of France; in 1697, by the Treaty of Ryswick, Louis recognized William as King of England and promised to give no further support to James II. In the quarrel among the European nations as to who should succeed to the Spanish throne, William challenged Louis, and was eagerly supported by his English subjects. But before the War of the Spanish Succession could be resolved, William III died.

ANNE   1702–1714   George of Denmark

William was succeeded by his sister-in-law, Anne, a weak and limited woman almost entirely under the influence of

1689–1725—Peter I, the Great, of Russia.
1692—Witchcraft hysteria at Salem, Massachusetts.
1701—Captain Kidd hanged.

1690—Locke: *Essay Concerning Human Understanding.*
1695—Congreve: *Love for Love.*

1705—Blenheim Palace built.

1702–13—War of the Spanish Succession.

MASTER CHART OF ENGLISH HISTORY

Reign *Married*	NOTABLE DATES IN ENGLISH ARCHITECTURE AND LITERATURE	CONTEMPORARY RULERS AND EVENTS
Lady Marlborough. Fortunately for England, Lord Marlborough, handsome, engaging, and ambitious, was an able man. On his deathbed, William had recommended that Marlborough command the forces of the Alliance against Louis XIV; and the General proved himself equal to this task. By his brilliant victory at Blenheim, the Allies (England, Germany, the Dutch, and the Holy Roman Empire) gained temporary ascendancy over the French. But by refusing to make peace at the height of their success, the Allies allowed Louis to regain his position. An end to the war, of which the people were heartily tired, was made at Utrecht. At home, final union was achieved between England and Scotland.	1711-12—Addison and Steele: *The Spectator.* 1712—Pope: *Rape of the Lock.*	1704—British capture Gibraltar; Battle of Blenheim. 1705-11—Emperor Joseph I. 1711-40—Emperor Charles VI. 1713—Treaty of Utrecht; Protestant succession in England, separation of France and Spain. 1713-40—Frederick William I of Prussia.
THE HOUSE OF HANOVER GEORGE I 1714-1727 Sophia of Zell Since Anne produced no living heir, the rightful succession to the English Throne was in dispute. Anne's half-brother was a Catholic and refused to conform to the Church of England; therefore Parliament passed the Act of Settlement by which the Elector of Hanover took the Throne on Anne's death. George I, great-grandson of James I, was fifty-four when he came to the Throne; he spoke almost no English and had little interest in English problems. His reign saw the defeat of James Edward, Anne's half-brother and son of James II, who as Pretender to the Throne raised an army and attempted to overthrow the Government. At Sheriffmuir he gained no clear-cut victory, and his supporters drifted away from his leadership. The Government was also faced by the fury of	1719—Defoe: *Robinson Crusoe.* 1720-1800—Georgian style in Architecture. 1721-26—St. Martin-in-the-Fields built. 1726—Swift: *Gulliver's Travels.*	1715-74—Louis XV of France. 1717—Triple Alliance of England, Holland and France against Spain.

the people over the failure of the South Sea Company—the South Sea Bubble burst in 1720 when the fantastic financial structure of the company collapsed. At this point, Sir Robert Walpole, as Chancellor, was able to cut the losses by skillful manipulation of the company's actual assets, saving the Whig party and establishing his own power. Through patronage, Walpole kept the support of Parliament; he wooed the Tory squires by lowering the land tax; and he avoided foreign wars.

GEORGE II   1727-1760   Caroline of Anspach
With the accession of George I's son, Walpole's career seemed ended. But George II was unable to dispense with Walpole's services, and through the Queen, Walpole was able to persuade the pompous, stuffy, limited monarch to follow his advice. For a decade Walpole preserved peace and allowed British commerce to expand. But by 1739, Walpole could no longer resist the popular clamor for war with Spain, and in that year "The War of Jenkins's Ear" commenced, which soon expanded in the War of the Austrian Succession. This confused series of engagements for no very precise end dragged on and sharpened conflicts with the French in America and India. Walpole was replaced by Pelham; the French supported another bid by a Stuart Pretender, repulsed in 1746; and the war ended in an indefinite truce. In England, the landed aristocracy of the Whig party came into ascendancy. It was a time of privilege for the great dukes who owned the huge estates and for the revival of religion among the people with the spread of the Wesleyan Methodist Movement. In 1756 the Seven Years' War opened, at first with disaster for England, but in the end, under the leadership of William Pitt the Elder, the Earl of Chatham, the war was concluded with great gains—Clive swept through India and

1728—Gay: *The Beggar's Opera.*
1737-49—Gibbs's Radcliffe Camera built.
1740—Richardson: *Pamela.*
1749—Fielding: *Tom Jones.*
1750—Gray's *Elegy.*
1755—Dr. Johnson's *Dictionary.*
1759—Dr. Johnson's *Rasselas.*

1740-86—Frederick II, the Great, of Prussia.
1740-80—Marie Theresa of Austria.
1752—Benjamin Franklin discovers electricity in lightning while flying a kite.
1754-63—French and Indian War in America.
1756—Black Hole of Calcutta.

MASTER CHART OF ENGLISH HISTORY

GEORGE III

Reign 1760–1820
Married Charlotte of Mecklenburgh

Wolfe defeated Montcalm at Quebec, to lay the foundations of the British Empire.

The grandson of George II was the first truly English sovereign since Queen Anne. He came to the Throne determined to end the Whig oligarchy and as "The Patriot King" to dominate the Cabinet and to restore the power of the Crown, which had been weakened by the quarrels of the Revolution and the Jacobite pretensions. The first step of the new monarch was to force Chatham out of office and to end the Seven Years' War with a favorable peace in 1763. With the appointment of George Grenville as Prime Minister, George consolidated his hold on Parliament (where he had created support by showering favors and gifts on a group who became known as the "King's Friends"). Finally making peace with Chatham, he restored the old leader to the head of the Cabinet, but Chatham was a poor peacetime politician, and was soon replaced by a succession of appointees, culminating with Lord North. The disastrous struggle with the American Colonies became more venomous; the systematic bungling of colonial affairs, the oppression of the colonies, and the stupidity of the King's insistence on taxing the Americans without granting them representation, led to war, the Declaration of Independence, and aid to the revolutionaries from France and Spain. George was forced to recognize the independence of the American Colonies, in order to prevent worse losses

NOTABLE DATES IN ENGLISH ARCHITECTURE AND LITERATURE

1760-66—Sterne: *Tristram Shandy.*
1762—Goldsmith: *Vicar of Wakefield.*
1771—Smollett: *Humphrey Clinker.*
1775—Sheridan: *The Rivals.*
1776—Adam Smith: *The Wealth of Nations.*
1776-88—Gibbon: *Decline and Fall of the Roman Empire.*
1778—Fanny Burney: *Evelina.*
1789—Blake: *Songs of Innocence.*
1791—Boswell: *Life of Johnson.*
1791-2—Thomas Paine: *The Rights of Man.*
1795-1827—Bank of England built.
1798—The *Lyrical Ballads* of Wordsworth and Coleridge.
1800-40—Regency style in architecture.
1805—Wordsworth's *Prelude.*
1813—Jane Austen: *Pride and Prejudice.*

CONTEMPORARY RULERS AND EVENTS

1762-96—Catherine II, the Great, of Russia.
1765—Stamp Act passed by Parliament.
1770—The Boston Massacre.
1771—Arkwright's first spinning mill.
1773—The Boston Tea Party.
1774—First Continental Congress of the American Colonies.
1775—Battles of Concord and Lexington.
1776—Declaration of Independence.
1778—France recognizes American independence.
1781—Cornwallis surrenders at Yorktown.
1784—Watt manufactures steam engine commercially.
1788—Warren Hastings tried by Parliament.
1789—Washington inaugurated as first President of the United States; Bastille is

in his war with the European nations. Following this *débâcle*, England hoped for peace. William Pitt the Younger, son of Chatham, emerged as Cabinet leader; the country's industry and commerce advanced; and suddenly the nation was confronted with what its privileged and reactionary rulers considered the new menace of the French Revolution. The English unsuccessfully attempted to contain the Revolution and became involved in war with France. The pressures from reaction outside, led by England, forced the French to press the Revolution drastically. Napoleon Bonaparte emerged. For a decade England fought against this military genius and in the end conquered with the help of Nelson's naval victories and Wellington's campaign of the Spanish Peninsula. Napoleon over-extended himself; his decisive defeat by the Prussians and English at Waterloo was inevitable. The end of George III's long reign saw England exhausted and in economic depression, but still the world's greatest empire and commercial power. George, old, blind, and mad, died after years of confinement, during which his son acted as Regent.

GEORGE IV   1820–1830   Caroline of Brunswick During the years of his father's madness Prince George had acted as Regent; with his father's death he assumed the Throne as George IV, an old and dissolute man, intelligent, intensely reactionary, and, like his father, stubborn. But, despite the King's opposition, his Tory Ministers, Lord Liverpool, Canning, and the Duke of Wellington, were forced to give way to the rising clamor for reform. In foreign policy England attempted to remain aloof from entanglements on the Continent, though with Russia and France (and without a declaration of war) the British fleet helped sink the Turkish fleet and to ensure the success of

1819—Scott: *Ivanhoe*; Byron: *Don Juan*.

1820—Keats: *Hyperion*; Shelley: *Prometheus Unbound*.
1821—De Quincey's *Confessions*.
1823—Lamb: *Essays of Elia*.
1825—Buckingham Palace and Marble Arch built.
1826—Disraeli: *Vivian Grey*.

stormed.
1792-1835—Emperor Francis II.
1792-99—First French Republic.
1793—Marat stabbed by Charlotte Corday; Marie Antoinette beheaded.
1795—Triple Alliance of Great Britain, Russia, Austria.
1796—Jenner discovers vaccination.
1799-1804—Napoleon Bonaparte is First Consul.
1801-25—Alexander I of Russia.
1804—Alexander Hamilton killed in duel with Aaron Burr.
1804-15—Napoleon, Emperor of France.
1805—Battle of Trafalgar.
1807—Fulton's first steamboat.
1812—Second war between U.S. and Britain; Napoleon's retreat from Moscow; Wellington drives the French from Spain.
1814-24—Louis XVIII of France.
1814—Congress of Vienna; Great Britain and U.S. sign treaty of peace.

MASTER CHART OF ENGLISH HISTORY

Reign *Married*	NOTABLE DATES IN ENGLISH ARCHITECTURE AND LITERATURE	CONTEMPORARY RULERS AND EVENTS

the Greek revolt for national independence. At home the Industrial Revolution transformed England into the most powerful industrial nation in the world. And with this came reform of the criminal laws under Robert Peel, the partial recognition of the right of workers to join trade unions, and the granting of political and religious equality to Dissenters and Roman Catholics.

WILLIAM IV   1830–1837   *Married*   Adelaide of Saxe-Meiningen

At George's death his brother William succeeded. William IV posed as a liberal; he was neither astute nor particularly intelligent, and his reign again cost the Crown prestige and strength. The Catholic Emancipation Bill was opposed by Wellington; the Government fell, and with the Duke went Tory power, which had held the reins of government for sixty years. The Whigs under Lord Grey attempted to put through electoral reform; defeated in Parliament, they called a general election. The Government won, but success in the Commons was opposed by the Lords. Grey asked William to appoint new Whig peers to overcome the adverse vote in the Lords. William refused: Wellington took over the government, but indignation was so great in the nation that William was forced to recall Grey and the Lords capitulated. Thereupon a wave of reform followed, alarming the old King, who seized on a chance defeat in Parliament to ask Peel to form a Cabinet. But Peel could not control Parliament, and gave way to Lord Melbourne. Parliament passed the Factory Act for-

NOTABLE DATES IN ENGLISH ARCHITECTURE AND LITERATURE

1830—Tennyson's first poems.
1832–38—National Gallery built.
1836—Dickens: *Pickwick Papers.*

CONTEMPORARY RULERS AND EVENTS

1815—Battle of Waterloo.
1820—The Missouri Compromise.
1823—Enunciation of Monroe Doctrine.
1824–30—Charles X of France.
1825—Stephenson's locomotive; first practical railroad.
1823—Revolution in France.
1830–48—Louis Philippe of France.
1832—Reform Bill passed by Parliament.
1833—Slavery outlawed by Parliament.

1837—Carlyle's *French Revolution*.
1840-52—Houses of Parliament built.
1840-1905—The Victorian style in architecture—Neo-Gothic.
1843—Ruskin: *Modern Painters*; Mill: *System of Logic*.
1847—Charlotte Brontë: *Jane Eyre*.
1848—Thackeray: *Vanity Fair*.
1849-61—Macaulay: *History of England*.
1850—Dickens: *David Copperfield*; Tennyson: *In Memoriam*.
1850—Construction of the Crystal Palace.
1851—Great Exhibition.
1857—Trollope: *Barchester Towers*.
1859—Darwin: *Origin of Species*; Tennyson:*Idylls of the King*; Fitzgerald: *Rubaiyat of Omar Khayyam*.
1864—Browning: *Dramatis Personae*.
1865—Matthew Arnold: *Essays in Criticism*.
1866—Lewis Carroll: *Alice's*

1837—Invention of telegraphy.
1839—Belgium's perpetual neutrality pledged by the Great Powers.
1843—First telegraph line in the U.S.
1845—Corn Laws repealed by Parliament.
1848—Revolutions in France, Hungary, Italy, Ireland, Venice, Denmark, Lombardy; Franz Josef crowned Emperor of Austria; gold is discovered in California.
1848-52—Second Republic of France.
1852-70—Napoleon III of France.
1853—Perry opens trade with Japan.
1854-55—Crimean War.
1857—Great Mutiny in India.
1859—John Brown's raid on Harper's Ferry.
1861-66—Civil War in the United States.
1863—President Lincoln decrees emancipation of slaves; Battle of Gettysburg.
1865—Lincoln assassinated.

bidding employment of children under nine and restricting hours for those under eighteen. The New Poor Law adjusted wages slightly and set up workhouses for the destitute—to all intents prisons.

VICTORIA   1837-1901

Albert of Saxe-Coburg & Gotha

William's niece, the young Victoria (granddaughter of George III), was crowned Queen, and three years later she married her German cousin, Prince Albert. Victoria had little influence on the course of government; but her husband, later to become the Prince Consort, was intelligent, earnest, humorless, and pedantic, and was able to play a small role in the promotion of education and applied science. Albert was most anxious to maintain the constitutional position of the Crown, and attempted to force the Foreign Minister Palmerston to refer questions of relations with other countries to the Queen. In this crusade Albert and Victoria came out badly. Albert was largely responsible for the Great Exhibition of 1851, dedicated to peace and commerce, and ironically serving as a prelude to the meaningless and dreary Crimean War, by which England, in conjunction with France, Prussia, and Austria, kept Russia out of the Dardanelles. Albert helped smooth down friction that developed with the United States over English aid to the Confederacy during the American Civil War. He died in 1861, and Victoria for many years retired from the public eye. The result of her protracted mourning was to clinch control by Parliament of public affairs—a trend begun as far back as the execution of Charles I, which had inevitably grown stronger throughout the years. The Sovereign had now become a figurehead. Victoria's reign embraced the years of the completion of the Industrial Revolution; of reform that repealed the crippling Corn Laws, enfranchised most

MASTER CHART OF ENGLISH HISTORY

Reign   *Married*

of the people, revised the school system, improved the prisons, the armed forces, and other institutions; and saw the growth of British imperial power and the forging of the modern Empire, which was the strongest in the world and remained so until the second decade of the twentieth century. Two great spokesmen of the Conservative and Liberal parties respectively—Disraeli and Gladstone—were the leading figures of the middle years of the Victorian Era. Peace was preserved except for the interruption of the Crimean War, the Indian Mutiny, and the constant forays to keep the natives in hand and rival nations from making inroads on the expanding Empire. The Suez Canal became a British holding, linking the Empire through the Mediterranean and the Indian Ocean. Victoria was crowned Empress of India. The century ended with Britain at war in South Africa against the Boers, an expensive war which was won painstakingly. No solution was found to the Irish problem; and Irish hatred of English oppression grew, augmented by resentment against the intransigence of the English rulers.

THE HOUSE OF SAXE-COBURG & GOTHA

EDWARD VII   1901-1910   Alexandra of Denmark

The son of Victoria came to the Throne as Britain faced isolation on the Continent and danger from the rising threat of the new German imperialism. At the turn of the century, proposals by Joseph Chamberlain for an end to free trade and the placing of duties on imports from elsewhere than the Empire caused the fall of the Unionist party. Re-

---

NOTABLE DATES IN ENGLISH ARCHITECTURE AND LITERATURE

1870—Rossetti: *Poems.*
1879—Stevenson: *Treasure Island.*
1887—Conan Doyle: *A Study in Scarlet.*
1890—Wilde: *Dorian Gray.*
1891—Hardy: *Tess of the D'Urbervilles.*

Adventures in Wonderland.

1899—Yeats: *The Wind Among the Reeds.*
1900—Joseph Conrad: *Lord Jim.*
1904—J. M. Barrie: *Peter Pan.*
1905—Shaw: *Major Barbara.*
1906—Galsworthy: *A Man of Property.*

CONTEMPORARY RULERS AND EVENTS

1870—Franco-Prussian War; Kingdom of Italy proclaimed.
1871-1939—Third French Republic.
1871-88—William I of Germany.
1876—The telephone invented.
1877—Russia declares war on Turkey.
1881—Alexander II of Russia and President Garfield of U.S. assassinated.
1882—Electric lights used domestically.
1885—"Chinese" Gordon slain; Kitchener defeats Mahdi.
1886—Haymarket Massacre at Chicago.

1888-1918—William II of Germany.
1891—The automobile invented.
1894—Dreyfus is unjustly degraded in France.
1896—Ethiopians defeat the Italians.

1898–Spanish-American War; radium discovered by the Curies; the Fashoda Affair.
1899-1902–The Boer War.

1900–King Humbert of Italy assassinated; Boxer Rebellion in China.
1901–Marconi sends wireless message across Atlantic; President McKinley of U.S. assassinated.
1903–First airplane flight by Wright brothers.
1904-05–Russo-JapaneseWar.
1911–Italo-Turkish War.
1912–*Titanic* disaster.
1914-18–First World War.
1914–U.S. sends expeditionary force to Mexico.
1917–U.S. enters First World War; Russian Revolution.
1919–Versailles Treaty.
1920–First meeting of League of Nations; women granted suffrage in U.S.; prohibition.
1922–Benito Mussolini seizes power in Italy.

1908–Arnold Bennett: *Old Wives' Tale.*

1910–H. G. Wells: *History of Mr. Polly.*
1913–D. H. Lawrence: *Sons and Lovers.*
1916–Somerset Maugham: *Of Human Bondage.*
1918–Lytton Strachey: *Eminent Victorians.*
1922–James Joyce: *Ulysses.*

form bills, such as that granting old-age pensions, were passed by Parliament. The long-standing struggle between the Commons and the Lords came to a head with a proposal to limit the power of the Lords–and the Commons succeeded in cutting down the ability of the Lords to veto and invalidate progressive legislation. England was able to conclude the Entente Cordiale with France, which was supplemented by a similar understanding with Russia. Germany retained the Triple Alliance with Austria-Hungary and Italy.

GEORGE V   THE HOUSE OF WINDSOR   1910-1936 Victoria Mary of Teck

The reign of Edward VII's son saw the outbreak of the First World War in 1914. At first the Entente was badly mauled by the advance of the Germans into France and Russia. But the positions were stabilized, and in 1917 the United States joined the conflict on the side of the Entente. This advantage was offset somewhat by the Russian Revolution. During the postwar era the price paid to survive the war plagued all Europe; the Versailles Treaty had set up the League of Nations, which the United States failed to join, and the League found itself impotent to take decisive action. Labor struggles in England led to the General Strike, which was soon followed in 1929 by economic crisis and the abandonment of the gold standard. Germany showed active signs of recovery under Hitler and his Nazis after 1933; the danger of the spread of Socialism from the new Soviet Union caused further alarm.

EDWARD VIII   1936

The brief reign of Edward VIII, son of George V, was a tense moment for the English monarchy. A crisis arose over whether Edward should be permitted to marry the

MASTER CHART OF ENGLISH HISTORY

Reign	*Married*	NOTABLE DATES IN ENGLISH ARCHITECTURE AND LITERATURE	CONTEMPORARY RULERS AND EVENTS

twice-divorced American, Mrs. Simpson. Despite pressure on Edward from the Press, the Cabinet, the Church, and the people he persisted in his desire to marry the divorcee—and in the end was forced to abdicate in favor of his younger brother.

GEORGE VI   1936–1952   Lady Elizabeth Bowes-Lyon

The world crisis deepened at the start of George VI's reign. The search for a solution led England under Prime Minister Neville Chamberlain to embrace the policy of appeasement, which meant permitting Hitler and Japan steadily to increase their power at the expense of independent nations. The sacrifice of China and Spain, followed by the Munich Agreement, the inability to come to agreement with the Soviet Union on mutual action to prevent war, led inevitably to the Second World War of 1939. The struggle was borne heroically by the English people. After the fall of France in 1940, they faced and repulsed the German onslaught alone. By 1941 both the Soviet Union and the United States had joined the vast struggle, and by 1945 the Axis powers of Germany, Italy, and Japan were crushed. Before the end of hostilities with Japan, the war leader and Prime Minister, Winston Churchill, was defeated at the polls and a Labor Government took office. The nations engaged in the war joined together to form the United Nations, an organization which was intended to prevent another war—but in five years the United Nations was unable to stop the severe worsening of inter-

1923—French occupy the Ruhr; Hitler's Beer Hall Putsch.
1925—The Locarno Treaty.
1927—Lindbergh flies the Atlantic; Sacco and Vanzetti executed.
1929—Panic on New York stock exchange inaugurates world depression.
1932—Japanese invade Manchuria.
1933—Franklin D. Roosevelt inaugurated as President of U.S.; Adolf Hitler seizes power in Germany.
1936–39—Civil War in Spain.
1938—The Four-Power Agreement of Munich.
1939–45—Second World War.
1940—Fall of France; the Battle of Britain.
1941—The Soviet Union and the U.S. enter the war.
1942—El Alamein; invasion of North Africa.
1943—Stalingrad.
1944—Invasion of France.
1945—V-E and V-J Days; ex-

plosion of atomic bomb over Hiroshima; formation of the United Nations Organization.

national relations. England, strained by the war, embraced an economic policy of austerity by which its leaders planned to restore the nation to its pre-war position.

ELIZABETH II   1952–   Philip Mountbatten Duke of Edinburgh

A popular young Queen brought added unity to the Commonwealth and ushered in what was hopefully called the "new Elizabethan era."

Brief Résumé of English Architectural Styles

NORMAN: 1050–1200
Typified by the use of the round arch with flat buttresses which do not project greatly, and barrel vaults. Norman style had its beginnings in England in advance of the Norman Conquest. Generally speaking, the buildings were heavy and solid. The towers were for the most part square, and important doorways were richly ornamented.

Examples: Iffley, Oxford; Chapel, Tower of London; parts of cathedrals at St. Albans, Ely, Peterborough, Rochester, Gloucester, Durham and Norwich; St. Bartholomew's and the Temple, London.

GOTHIC: 1150–1500

Early English: 1150–1300
The pointed arch has replaced the round; buttresses are heavy; "lancet"-headed windows appear in groups. The early thirteenth-century style became the basis of English Gothic and the beginning of a style that was uniquely English with little trace of influence from abroad. The round arch was superseded by the sharp and pointed arch; the buildings became less squat and heavy, more graceful. Pointed vaults were topped by steep roofs. The spire appeared, a new addition. The dogtooth ornament and trefoil design in carving are typical.

Examples: Salisbury (east end); parts of York, Lincoln, Ely, Worcester, Canterbury; Chapter House, Westminster Abbey.

Decorated Style: 1250–1400
The rounded arch disappeared in favor of the pointed; experience taught mastery of vaulting and in consequence the number and complexity of ribs increased. The description "decorated" meant that ornament had become a part of the construction and was not added as an afterthought, or merely for effect. Windows were wider, more ornamental, and divided into two or more sections by mullions. The upper division was intricate, delicate, and filled with tracery based on geometric forms. Spires were more frequent, sharp, elaborate; roofs were ornate, and the use of porches more frequent.

Examples: Exeter, York (nave and west window), Ely (angel choir), Wells (chapter house and lady chapel), Glastonbury (Abbot's Kitchen).

Perpendicular Style: 1350–1500
Paneling is used whenever possible, and vertical lines are accented. Arches have become flatter and broader, and vaulting evolves into the elaborate fan tracery. Buildings are less heavy, both in construction

and appearance. Domestic architecture grows in importance and is given more attention. Timber roofs are a noticeable feature in the Perpendicular.

Examples: Winchester (west front and nave); Canterbury (tower and nave); York (choir); Gloucester (tower); King's College Chapel, Cambridge; Warwick Castle.

TUDOR: 1500–1560
In this period, domestic architecture is more noteworthy than ecclesiastic. The great country dwelling and manor house are coming into their own. Many of the Perpendicular motifs continue, particularly tracery, the arch held within square frames, and fan vaulting. Plaster and brick are now more commonly used.

Examples: Henry VII Chapel, Westminster Abbey; Hampton Court; Christ Church, Oxford; Gateway to St. James's Palace, London.

RENAISSANCE: 1560–1720
Elizabethan: 1560–1600
The style is Gothic in character but includes the use of classical details still somewhat crude. Mullioned windows with square caps are typical and "strap-work" ornament appears, square blocks decorated; half-timber work; lovely paneling, usually highly modeled.

Examples: Staple Inn, Holborn; the Temple, London; Haddon Hall; tomb of Henry VII, Westminster Abbey; Hardwick Hall.

Jacobean: 1600–1620
The classical orders (Doric, Ionic, Corinthian) appear, though they are still not used accurately. The Jacobean mansions are large and magnificent, more elaborate than comparable structures before or later. The work is done by English craftsmen trained in Flanders or influenced by Flemish examples. The carving is in low relief, charming and delicate.

Examples: Hatfield House; Holland House, Kensington; Bodleian Library, Oxford; Clare College, Cambridge.

Inigo Jones: 1620–1660
The first English architect to give his name to an English style, master of the early years of the developed Renaissance. The Greek orders are used with taste and logic; design is more formal with an eye to total effect. Jones used columns and pillars in groups, after the example of the Italian Palladio. The cornice was accented and the porticoes, now important, gave the ensemble great richness.

Examples: Banqueting Hall, Whitehall, London; the Queen's House at Greenwich; Lincoln's Inn Fields.

Christopher Wren: 1660–1720
Wren developed Jones's classical style into a uniquely English expression. He favored bold masses, and brick and stone placed side by side to give a contrasting texture. Domestic architecture developed. Craftsmen were encouraged, with design drawn directly from nature, very delicate, yet at the same time weighty and bold.

> *Examples:* St. Paul's Cathedral; Chelsea Hospital; Hampton Court (in part); Trinity Library, Cambridge; the Monument, London; St. Stephen's Walbrook.

GEORGIAN: 1720–1800
Smaller houses have repose and purity, with an insistence on symmetry. Mansions are noble. Toward the middle of this period, there was an increasing tendency toward simplicity and an almost academic approach; texture of materials became less important. Interiors were graceful, delicate, and elaborate.

> *Examples:* Prior Park, Bath; Blenheim Palace; Horse Guards, London; St. Martin-in-the-Fields; Mansion House; St. Mary-le-Strand; Queen's College, Oxford; Harewood House; streets in Bath; Somerset House; Bedford Square, London; Pulteney, Bath.

REGENCY: 1800–1840
Georgian developed into the greater elegancy of the Regency style, with stucco that was often painted superimposed on plain surfaces. Ornamentation diminished.

> *Examples:* Terraces of Brighton; Cheltenham; Hastings.

VICTORIAN: 1840–1905
Gothic forms were used.

> *Examples:* Houses of Parliament; Law Courts; Royal Albert Hall; Albert Memorial.

Glossary of Architectural Terms

AISLE—Passageway between columns in a church, or between columns and outer wall.

AMBULATORY—Sheltered walk, in the gallery of a cloister, or the apse aisle of a church.

APSE—Projecting part of a church, usually east of the choir, semicircular, square, or polygonal in shape.

ARCHITRAVE—Lowest division of an entablature; that part resting immediately on a column or pillar.

BOSS—Projecting stud or knob, decorating a ceiling or window; an ornamental block at the intersection of ribs in a vault.

BUTTRESS—Masonry or brickwork built on outside wall as a support of walls or vaults. A FLYING BUTTRESS is an arched brace to support the thrust of a vault rising above the rest of the building.

CAP—Uppermost of any assemblage of principal parts, on a door, column, capital, coping, cornice, lintel, etc.

CAPITAL—Head or top of a column, pillar, or pilaster.

CHANCEL—Part of church where altar stands.

CHANTRY—A side chapel; room for chanting masses.

CHAPEL—Subordinate place of worship; in cathedrals, chapels are placed in a section of the apse or outer aisles. LADY CHAPEL is a chapel dedicated to the Virgin Mary.

CHAPTER HOUSE—Meeting place of the clergy of a cathedral.

CHOIR—Section of church where bands of singers are placed.

CLERESTORY—Upper part of nave, choir, and transepts, containing a series of windows clear of the roof of the aisles.

COLUMN—Round pillar to support or adorn a building.

COMPOSITE—An order of capitals and columns which combines the Ionic and Corinthian forms.

CORINTHIAN—A Greek order of capitals and columns; the capital is the most ornate of the classic orders, bell-shaped and decorated with acanthus leaves.

CORNICE—Highest projection or border of wall or column.

CRYPT—Subterranean cell or vault, sometimes used as a chapel or shrine.

DORIC—A Greek order of capitals and columns. The capital is the simplest of the classic orders.

DORMER—Window set vertically in the side of a roof gable.

EAST END—That part of a church where the altar is situated.

ENTABLATURE—The whole parts on top of a pillar or column, composed of architrave, frieze, and cornice.

FAN VAULT—Vaulting with fanlike ribs, typical of the Perpendicular Gothic.

FRIEZE—The middle part of the entablature between the architrave and the cornice; usually ornamented with sculpture, etc.

GABLE—Triangular end of a building; the end wall.

GROIN—Angular curve made by the intersection of two arches.

IONIC—A Greek order of capitals and columns. The capital is characterized by the volute or ram's horn scroll.

JOIST—Horizontal timber to which boards of floor or laths of ceiling are fastened.

LANTERN—Tower with windows, usually over the section where the nave of a church joins with the transept.

LANCET—A pointed window.

LEADED WINDOW—Panes of glass set in or separated by lead.

LINTEL—Horizontal top piece of a door or window.

METOPE—A square space between the triglyphs in a Doric frieze.

MULLION—An upright bar or division between the lights of windows, screens, etc., in a Gothic arch.

NAVE—Middle or body of a church, extending from the chancel to the principal west entrance.

NICHE—A recess in a wall for a statue or other decoration.

ORDER—System of constructing columns, comprising the Tuscan, Doric, Ionic, Corinthian, and Composite.

ORIEL WINDOW—A projecting window in an upper story; the Oriel itself is a large recess with a window, of polygonal plan projecting from the outer face of a building, usually from the upper story.

PEDESTAL—Base of a column, statue, etc.

PEDIMENT—The triangular ornament over the entablature of a building.

PIER—A mass of masonry supporting an arch, vault, etc.

PILASTER—A square column or pillar partly inserted in a wall.

PINNACLE—A small polygonal turret projecting above the rest of the building.

PORCH—A covered approach to a building.

PORTICO—Colonnade, roof supported by columns at regular intervals, usually attached as porch to a building.

RIB—One of the curved pieces of stone-, timber-, or ironwork which forms the framework of an arch or vault.

ROSE WINDOW—A circular window with compartments branching from the center.

SCREEN—Partition of wood, stone, or ironwork dividing a room or building (e.g., church).

SPANDREL—Triangular space between the outer curve of an arch and the rectangle formed by the moldings enclosing it.

TRACERY—Intersecting ribwork in the upper part of a Gothic window or screen.

TRANSEPT—The transverse part of a church at right angles to the nave.

TREFOIL—An ornamental foliation used in architecture, resembling three-leaved clover.

TRIFORIUM—The open gallery or arcade above the arches of a church separating the nave arches from the aisles.

TRIGLYPH—Ornament of the Doric frieze, placed directly over each column and at equal distances.

TUSCAN—A primitive order of columns which is completely without ornament.

VAULT—1. An arched roof. 2. A burial chamber below the floor of a church.

WEST END—The part of a church at the main entrance to the nave.

Index

76 77 78   10 9 8 7 6 5 4